RUSSIAN
VOCABULARY

FOR ENGLISH SPEAKERS

ENGLISH-
AN

vords
nd sharpen
ills

Russian vocabulary for English speakers - 7000 words

By Andrey Taranov

T&P Books vocabularies are intended for helping you learn, memorize and review foreign words. The dictionary is divided into themes, covering all major spheres of everyday activities, business, science, culture, etc.

The process of learning words using T&P Books' theme-based dictionaries gives you the following advantages:

- Correctly grouped source information predetermines success at subsequent stages of word memorization
- Availability of words derived from the same root allowing memorization of word units (rather than separate words)
- Small units of words facilitate the process of establishing associative links needed for consolidation of vocabulary
- Level of language knowledge can be estimated by the number of learned words

Copyright © 2019 T&P Books Publishing

All rights reserved. No part of this book may be reproduced or utilized in any form or by any means, electronic or mechanical, including photocopying, recording or by information storage and retrieval system, without permissi[...] [...] [...] [...]e publishers.

T&P Books Publishing
www.tpbooks.com

ISBN: 978-1-78071-282-6

This book is also available in E[...]
Please visit www.tpbooks.com o[...]

RUSSIAN VOCABULARY
for English speakers

T&P Books vocabularies are intended to help you learn, memorize, and review foreign words. The vocabulary contains over 7000 commonly used words arranged thematically.

- Vocabulary contains the most commonly used words
- Recommended as an addition to any language course
- Meets the needs of beginners and advanced learners of foreign languages
- Convenient for daily use, revision sessions, and self-testing activities
- Allows you to assess your vocabulary

Special features of the vocabulary

- Words are organized according to their meaning, not alphabetically
- Words are presented in three columns to facilitate the reviewing and self-testing processes
- Words in groups are divided into small blocks to facilitate the learning process
- The vocabulary offers a convenient and simple transcription of each foreign word

The vocabulary has 198 topics including:

Basic Concepts, Numbers, Colors, Months, Seasons, Units of Measurement, Clothing & Accessories, Food & Nutrition, Restaurant, Family Members, Relatives, Character, Feelings, Emotions, Diseases, City, Town, Sightseeing, Shopping, Money, House, Home, Office, Working in the Office, Import & Export, Marketing, Job Search, Sports, Education, Computer, Internet, Tools, Nature, Countries, Nationalities and more …

TABLE OF CONTENTS

Medicine 75

HUMAN HABITAT 81
City 81

Dwelling. House. Home 89

HUMAN ACTIVITIES 99
Job. Business. Part 1 99

NATURE 170
The Earth. Part 1 170

The Earth. Part 2 178

Fauna 180

Flora 190

PRONUNCIATION GUIDE

T&P phonetic alphabet	Russian example	English example

Consonants

[b]	абрикос [abrikós]	baby, book
[d]	квадрат [kvadrát]	day, doctor
[f]	реформа [refórma]	face, food
[g]	глина [glína]	game, gold
[ʒ]	массажист [masaʒīst]	forge, pleasure
[j]	пресный [présnij]	yes, New York
[h], [x]	мех, Пасха [méh], [pásxa]	home, have
[k]	кратер [krátɛr]	clock, kiss
[l]	лиловый [lilóvij]	lace, people
[m]	молоко [mɔlɔkó]	magic, milk
[n]	нут, пони [nút], [póni]	name, normal
[p]	пират [pirát]	pencil, private
[r]	ручей [ruʧéj]	rice, radio
[s]	суслик [súslik]	city, boss
[t]	тоннель [tɔnélʲ]	tourist, trip
[ʃ]	лишайник [liʃájnik]	machine, shark
[ʧ]	врач, речь [vráʧ], [réʧʲ]	church, French
[ts]	кузнец [kuznéts]	cats, tsetse fly
[ʃʲ]	мощность [móʃʲnɔstʲ]	sheep, shop
[v]	молитва [mɔlítva]	very, river
[z]	дизайнер [dizájner]	zebra, please

Other symbols used in transcription

[ʲ]	дикарь [dikárʲ]	palatalization sign
[·]	автопилот [aftɔ·pilót]	interpunct
[ˈ]	заплата [zapláta]	primary stress

T&P phonetic alphabet	Russian example	English example

Stressed vowels

[á]	платье [plátje]	shorter than in ask
[é]	лебедь [lébetʲ]	elm, medal
[ǿ]	шахтёр [ʃahtǿr]	New York
[í]	организм [ɔrganízm]	shorter than in feet
[ó]	роспись [róspisʲ]	pod, John
[ú]	инсульт [insúlʲt]	book
[ɨ]	добыча [dɔbɨ̃ʧa]	big, America
[æ]	полиэстер [pɔliǽstɛr]	candle, lamp
[ʲú], [jú]	салют, юг [salʲút], [júg]	cued, cute
[ʲá], [já]	связь, я [svʲásʲ], [já]	young, yard

Unstressed vowels

[a]	гравюра [gravʲúra]	neutral vowel, similar to the schwa [ə]
[e]	кенгуру [kengurú]	neutral vowel, similar to the schwa [ə]
[ə]	пожалуйста [pɔʒálǝsta]	driver, teacher
[i]	рисунок [risúnɔk]	shorter than in feet
[ɔ]	железо [ʒelézɔ]	neutral vowel, similar to the schwa [ə]
[u]	вирус [vírus]	book
[ɨ]	первый [pérvɨj]	big, America
[ɛ]	аэропорт [aɛrɔpórt]	man, bad
[ʲu], [ju]	брюнет [brʲunét]	cued, cute
[ɪ], [jɪ]	заяц, язык [záɪʦ], [jɪzɨ̃k]	neutral vowel, similar to the schwa [ə]
[ʲa], [ja]	няня, копия [nʲánʲa], [kópija]	young, yard

ABBREVIATIONS
used in the vocabulary

English abbreviations

ab.	-	about
adj	-	adjective
adv	-	adverb
anim.	-	animate
as adj	-	attributive noun used as adjective
e.g.	-	for example
etc.	-	et cetera
fam.	-	familiar
fem.	-	feminine
form.	-	formal
inanim.	-	inanimate
masc.	-	masculine
math	-	mathematics
mil.	-	military
n	-	noun
pl	-	plural
pron.	-	pronoun
sb	-	somebody
sing.	-	singular
sth	-	something
v aux	-	auxiliary verb
vi	-	intransitive verb
vi, vt	-	intransitive, transitive verb
vt	-	transitive verb

Russian abbreviations

возв	-	reflexive verb
ж	-	feminine noun
ж мн	-	feminine plural
м	-	masculine noun
м мн	-	masculine plural
м, ж	-	masculine, feminine
мн	-	plural

н/пх	-	intransitive, transitive verb
н/св	-	biaspectual verb
нпх	-	intransitive verb
нсв	-	imperfective aspect
пх	-	transitive verb
с	-	neuter
с мн	-	neuter plural
св	-	perfective aspect

BASIC CONCEPTS

Basic concepts. Part 1

1. Pronouns

I, me	я	[já]
you	ты	[tí]
he	он	[ón]
she	она	[ɔná]
it	оно	[ɔnó]
we	мы	[mí]
you (to a group)	вы	[ví]
they	они	[ɔní]

2. Greetings. Salutations. Farewells

Hello! (fam.)	Здравствуй!	[zdrástvuj]
Hello! (form.)	Здравствуйте!	[zdrástvujte]
Good morning!	Доброе утро!	[dóbrɔe útrɔ]
Good afternoon!	Добрый день!	[dóbrij dénʲ]
Good evening!	Добрый вечер!	[dóbrij vetʃer]
to say hello	здороваться (нсв, возв)	[zdɔróvatsa]
Hi! (hello)	Привет!	[privét]
greeting (n)	привет (м)	[privét]
to greet (vt)	приветствовать (нсв, пх)	[privétstvovatʲ]
How are you? (form.)	Как у вас дела?	[kák u vás delá?]
How are you? (fam.)	Как дела?	[kák delá?]
What's new?	Что нового?	[ʃtó nóvɔvɔ?]
Bye-Bye! Goodbye!	До свидания!	[dɔ svidánija]
See you soon!	До скорой встречи!	[dɔ skórɔj fstrétʃi]
Farewell! (to a friend)	Прощай!	[prɔʃʲáj]
Farewell! (form.)	Прощайте!	[prɔʃʲájte]
to say goodbye	прощаться (нсв, возв)	[prɔʃʲátsa]
So long!	Пока!	[pɔká]
Thank you!	Спасибо!	[spasíbɔ]
Thank you very much!	Большое спасибо!	[bɔlʲʃóe spasíbɔ]
You're welcome	Пожалуйста	[pɔʒálǝsta]

| Don't mention it! | Не стоит благодарности | [ne stóit blagodárnosti] |
| It was nothing | Не за что | [né za ʃto] |

Excuse me! (fam.)	Извини!	[izviní]
Excuse me! (form.)	Извините!	[izviníte]
to excuse (forgive)	извинять (нсв, пх)	[izvinʲátʲ]

to apologize (vi)	извиняться (нсв, возв)	[izvinʲátsa]
My apologies	Мои извинения	[moí izvinénija]
I'm sorry!	Простите!	[prostíte]
to forgive (vt)	прощать (нсв, пх)	[proʃátʲ]
It's okay! (that's all right)	Ничего страшного	[nitʃevó stráʃnovo]
please (adv)	пожалуйста	[poʒálosta]

Don't forget!	Не забудьте!	[ne zabútʲte]
Certainly!	Конечно!	[konéʃno]
Of course not!	Конечно нет!	[konéʃno nét]
Okay! (I agree)	Согласен!	[soglásen]
That's enough!	Хватит!	[hvátit]

3. Cardinal numbers. Part 1

0 zero	ноль	[nólʲ]
1 one	один	[odín]
2 two	два	[dvá]
3 three	три	[trí]
4 four	четыре	[tʃetĩre]

5 five	пять	[pʲátʲ]
6 six	шесть	[ʃæstʲ]
7 seven	семь	[sémʲ]
8 eight	восемь	[vósemʲ]
9 nine	девять	[dévɪtʲ]

10 ten	десять	[désɪtʲ]
11 eleven	одиннадцать	[odínatsatʲ]
12 twelve	двенадцать	[dvenátsatʲ]
13 thirteen	тринадцать	[trinátsatʲ]
14 fourteen	четырнадцать	[tʃetĩrnatsatʲ]

15 fifteen	пятнадцать	[pitnátsatʲ]
16 sixteen	шестнадцать	[ʃɛsnátsatʲ]
17 seventeen	семнадцать	[semnátsatʲ]
18 eighteen	восемнадцать	[vosemnátsatʲ]
19 nineteen	девятнадцать	[devitnátsatʲ]

20 twenty	двадцать	[dvátsatʲ]
21 twenty-one	двадцать один	[dvátsatʲ odín]
22 twenty-two	двадцать два	[dvátsatʲ dvá]

23 twenty-three	двадцать три	[dvátsatⁱ trí]
30 thirty	тридцать	[trítsatⁱ]
31 thirty-one	тридцать один	[trítsatⁱ ɔdín]
32 thirty-two	тридцать два	[trítsatⁱ dvá]
33 thirty-three	тридцать три	[trítsatⁱ trí]
40 forty	сорок	[sórɔk]
41 forty-one	сорок один	[sórɔk ɔdín]
42 forty-two	сорок два	[sórɔk dvá]
43 forty-three	сорок три	[sórɔk trí]
50 fifty	пятьдесят	[pɪtⁱdesⁱát]
51 fifty-one	пятьдесят один	[pɪtⁱdesⁱát ɔdín]
52 fifty-two	пятьдесят два	[pɪtⁱdesⁱát dvá]
53 fifty-three	пятьдесят три	[pɪtⁱdesⁱát trí]
60 sixty	шестьдесят	[ʃɛstⁱdesⁱát]
61 sixty-one	шестьдесят один	[ʃɛstⁱdesⁱát ɔdín]
62 sixty-two	шестьдесят два	[ʃɛstⁱdesⁱát dvá]
63 sixty-three	шестьдесят три	[ʃɛstⁱdesⁱát trí]
70 seventy	семьдесят	[sémⁱdesɪt]
71 seventy-one	семьдесят один	[sémⁱdesɪt ɔdín]
72 seventy-two	семьдесят два	[sémⁱdesɪt dvá]
73 seventy-three	семьдесят три	[sémⁱdesɪt trí]
80 eighty	восемьдесят	[vósemⁱdesɪt]
81 eighty-one	восемьдесят один	[vósemⁱdesɪt ɔdín]
82 eighty-two	восемьдесят два	[vósemⁱdesɪt dvá]
83 eighty-three	восемьдесят три	[vósemⁱdesɪt trí]
90 ninety	девяносто	[devɪnóstɔ]
91 ninety-one	девяносто один	[devɪnóstɔ ɔdín]
92 ninety-two	девяносто два	[devɪnóstɔ dvá]
93 ninety-three	девяносто три	[devɪnóstɔ trí]

4. Cardinal numbers. Part 2

100 one hundred	сто	[stó]
200 two hundred	двести	[dvésti]
300 three hundred	триста	[trísta]
400 four hundred	четыреста	[tʃetⁱresta]
500 five hundred	пятьсот	[pɪtⁱsót]
600 six hundred	шестьсот	[ʃɛstⁱsót]
700 seven hundred	семьсот	[semⁱsót]
800 eight hundred	восемьсот	[vɔsemⁱsót]
900 nine hundred	девятьсот	[devɪtⁱsót]
1000 one thousand	тысяча	[tɨsɪtʃa]
2000 two thousand	две тысячи	[dve tɨsɪtʃi]

3000 three thousand	три тысячи	[trí tɨ́sɪʧi]
10000 ten thousand	десять тысяч	[désɪtʲ tɨ́sʲatʃ]
one hundred thousand	сто тысяч	[stó tɨ́sɪʧ]
million	миллион (м)	[milión]
billion	миллиард (м)	[miliárd]

5. Numbers. Fractions

fraction	дробь (ж)	[drópʲ]
one half	одна вторая	[ɔdná ftɔrája]
one third	одна третья	[ɔdná trétja]
one quarter	одна четвёртая	[ɔdná ʧetvǿrtaja]

one eighth	одна восьмая	[ɔdná vɔsʲmája]
one tenth	одна десятая	[ɔdná desʲátaja]
two thirds	две третьих	[dve trétjih]
three quarters	три четвёртых	[trí ʧetvǿrtih]

6. Numbers. Basic operations

subtraction	вычитание (с)	[vɨʧitánie]
to subtract (vi, vt)	вычитать (нсв, пх)	[vɨʧitátʲ]
division	деление (с)	[delénie]
to divide (vt)	делить (нсв, пх)	[delítʲ]

addition	сложение (с)	[slɔʒǽnie]
to add up (vt)	сложить (св, пх)	[slɔʒɨ́tʲ]
to add (vi, vt)	прибавлять (нсв, пх)	[pribavlʲátʲ]
multiplication	умножение (с)	[umnɔʒǽnie]
to multiply (vt)	умножать (нсв, пх)	[umnɔʒátʲ]

7. Numbers. Miscellaneous

digit, figure	цифра (ж)	[tsɨ́fra]
number	число (с)	[ʧisló]
numeral	числительное (с)	[ʧislítelʲnɔe]
minus sign	минус (м)	[mínus]
plus sign	плюс (м)	[plʲús]
formula	формула (ж)	[fórmula]

calculation	вычисление (с)	[vɨʧislénie]
to count (vi, vt)	считать (нсв, пх)	[ʃʲitátʲ]
to count up	подсчитывать (нсв, пх)	[pɔtʃʲítivatʲ]
to compare (vt)	сравнивать (нсв, пх)	[srávnivatʲ]
How much?	Сколько?	[skólʲkɔ?]
sum, total	сумма (ж)	[súmma]

| result | результат (м) | [rezulʲtát] |
| remainder | остаток (м) | [ɔstátɔk] |

a few (e.g., ~ years ago)	несколько	[néskɔlʲkɔ]
little (I had ~ time)	мало	[málɔ]
the rest	остальное (c)	[ɔstalʲnóe]
one and a half	полтора	[pɔltɔrá]
dozen	дюжина (ж)	[dʲúʒina]

in half (adv)	пополам	[pɔpɔlám]
equally (evenly)	поровну	[pórɔvnu]
half	половина (ж)	[pɔlɔvína]
time (three ~s)	раз (м)	[rás]

8. The most important verbs. Part 1

to advise (vt)	советовать (нсв, пх)	[sɔvétɔvatʲ]
to agree (say yes)	соглашаться (нсв, возв)	[sɔglaʃátsa]
to answer (vi, vt)	отвечать (нсв, пх)	[ɔtvetʃátʲ]
to apologize (vi)	извиняться (нсв, возв)	[izvinʲátsa]
to arrive (vi)	приезжать (нсв, нпх)	[prieʒʒátʲ]

to ask (~ oneself)	спрашивать (нсв, пх)	[spráʃivatʲ]
to ask (~ sb to do sth)	просить (нсв, пх)	[prɔsítʲ]
to be (vi)	быть (нсв, нпх)	[bĭtʲ]

to be afraid	бояться (нсв, возв)	[bɔjátsa]
to be hungry	хотеть есть (нсв)	[hɔtétʲ éstʲ]
to be interested in …	интересоваться (нсв, возв)	[interesɔvátsa]
to be needed	требоваться (нсв, возв)	[trébɔvatsa]
to be surprised	удивляться (нсв, возв)	[udivlʲátsa]

to be thirsty	хотеть пить	[hɔtétʲ pítʲ]
to begin (vt)	начинать (нсв, пх)	[natʃinátʲ]
to belong to …	принадлежать … (нсв, нпх)	[prinadleʒátʲ …]
to boast (vi)	хвастаться (нсв, возв)	[hvástatsa]
to break (split into pieces)	ломать (нсв, пх)	[lɔmátʲ]

to call (~ for help)	звать (нсв, пх)	[zvátʲ]
can (v aux)	мочь (нсв, нпх)	[mótʃʲ]
to catch (vt)	ловить (нсв, пх)	[lɔvítʲ]
to change (vt)	изменить (св, пх)	[izmenítʲ]
to choose (select)	выбирать (нсв, пх)	[vibirátʲ]

to come down (the stairs)	спускаться (нсв, возв)	[spuskátsa]
to compare (vt)	сравнивать (нсв, пх)	[srávnivatʲ]
to complain (vi, vt)	жаловаться (нсв, возв)	[ʒálɔvatsa]
to confuse (mix up)	путать (нсв, пх)	[pútatʲ]
to continue (vt)	продолжать (нсв, пх)	[prɔdɔlʒátʲ]
to control (vt)	контролировать (нсв, пх)	[kontrɔlírɔvatʲ]

to cook (dinner)	готовить (нсв, пх)	[gotóvit^j]
to cost (vt)	стоить (нсв, пх)	[stóit^j]
to count (add up)	считать (нсв, пх)	[ʃʲitát^j]
to count on …	рассчитывать на … (нсв)	[raʃʲítivat^j na …]
to create (vt)	создать (св, пх)	[sozdát^j]
to cry (weep)	плакать (нсв, нпх)	[plákat^j]

9. The most important verbs. Part 2

to deceive (vi, vt)	обманывать (нсв, пх)	[ɔbmánivat^j]
to decorate (tree, street)	украшать (нсв, пх)	[ukraʃát^j]
to defend (a country, etc.)	защищать (нсв, пх)	[zaʃʲiʃát^j]
to demand (request firmly)	требовать (нсв, пх)	[trébovat^j]
to dig (vt)	рыть (нсв, пх)	[rĩt^j]

to discuss (vt)	обсуждать (нсв, пх)	[ɔpsuʒdát^j]
to do (vt)	делать (нсв, пх)	[délat^j]
to doubt (have doubts)	сомневаться (нсв, возв)	[sɔmnevátsa]
to drop (let fall)	ронять (нсв, пх)	[ron^ját^j]
to enter (room, house, etc.)	входить (нсв, нпх)	[fhɔdít^j]

to excuse (forgive)	извинять (нсв, пх)	[izvin^ját^j]
to exist (vi)	существовать (нсв, нпх)	[suʃestvovát^j]
to expect (foresee)	предвидеть (нсв, пх)	[predvídet^j]
to explain (vt)	объяснять (нсв, пх)	[ɔbjɪsn^ját^j]
to fall (vi)	падать (нсв, нпх)	[pádat^j]

to find (vt)	находить (нсв, пх)	[nahɔdít^j]
to finish (vt)	заканчивать (нсв, пх)	[zakántʃivat^j]
to fly (vi)	лететь (нсв, нпх)	[letét^j]
to follow … (come after)	следовать за … (нсв)	[slédovat^j za …]
to forget (vi, vt)	забывать (нсв, пх)	[zabivát^j]

to forgive (vt)	прощать (нсв, пх)	[proʃát^j]
to give (vt)	давать (нсв, пх)	[davát^j]
to give a hint	подсказать (св, пх)	[potskazát^j]
to go (on foot)	идти (нсв, нпх)	[it^jtʃí]

to go for a swim	купаться (нсв, возв)	[kupátsa]
to go out (for dinner, etc.)	выходить (нсв, нпх)	[vihɔdít^j]
to guess (the answer)	отгадать (св, пх)	[ɔdgadát^j]

to have (vt)	иметь (нсв, пх)	[imét^j]
to have breakfast	завтракать (нсв, нпх)	[záftrakat^j]
to have dinner	ужинать (нсв, нпх)	[úʒinat^j]
to have lunch	обедать (нсв, нпх)	[ɔbédat^j]
to hear (vt)	слышать (нсв, пх)	[slĩʃat^j]
to help (vt)	помогать (нсв, пх)	[pomɔgát^j]
to hide (vt)	прятать (нсв, пх)	[pr^játat^j]

to hope (vi, vt)	надеяться (нсв, возв)	[nadéɪtsa]
to hunt (vi, vt)	охотиться (нсв, возв)	[ɔhótitsa]
to hurry (vi)	торопиться (нсв, возв)	[tɔrɔpítsa]

10. The most important verbs. Part 3

to inform (vt)	информировать (н/св, пх)	[infɔrmírɔvatʲ]
to insist (vi, vt)	настаивать (нсв, нпх)	[nastáivatʲ]
to insult (vt)	оскорблять (нсв, пх)	[ɔskɔrblʲátʲ]
to invite (vt)	приглашать (нсв, пх)	[priglaʃátʲ]
to joke (vi)	шутить (нсв, нпх)	[ʃutítʲ]

to keep (vt)	сохранять (нсв, пх)	[sɔhranʲátʲ]
to keep silent, to hush	молчать (нсв, нпх)	[mɔlʧátʲ]
to kill (vt)	убивать (нсв, пх)	[ubivátʲ]
to know (sb)	знать (нсв, пх)	[znátʲ]
to laugh (vi)	смеяться (нсв, возв)	[smejátsa]

to liberate (city, etc.)	освобождать (нсв, пх)	[ɔsvɔbɔʒdátʲ]
to like (I like ...)	нравиться (нсв, возв)	[nrávitsa]
to look for ... (search)	искать ... (нсв, пх)	[iskátʲ ...]
to love (sb)	любить (нсв, пх)	[lʲubítʲ]
to make a mistake	ошибаться (нсв, возв)	[ɔʃibátsa]

to manage, to run	руководить (нсв, пх)	[rukɔvɔdítʲ]
to mean (signify)	означать (нсв, пх)	[ɔznaʧátʲ]
to mention (talk about)	упоминать (нсв, пх)	[upɔminátʲ]
to miss (school, etc.)	пропускать (нсв, пх)	[prɔpuskátʲ]
to notice (see)	замечать (нсв, пх)	[zameʧátʲ]

to object (vi, vt)	возражать (нсв, н/пх)	[vɔzraʒátʲ]
to observe (see)	наблюдать (нсв, н/пх)	[nablʲudátʲ]
to open (vt)	открывать (нсв, пх)	[ɔtkrivátʲ]
to order (meal, etc.)	заказывать (нсв, пх)	[zakázivatʲ]
to order (mil.)	приказывать (нсв, пх)	[prikázivatʲ]
to own (possess)	владеть (нсв, пх)	[vladétʲ]

to participate (vi)	участвовать (нсв, нпх)	[uʧástvɔvatʲ]
to pay (vi, vt)	платить (нсв, н/пх)	[platítʲ]
to permit (vt)	разрешать (нсв, пх)	[razreʃátʲ]

| to plan (vt) | планировать (нсв, пх) | [planírɔvatʲ] |
| to play (children) | играть (нсв, нпх) | [igrátʲ] |

to pray (vi, vt)	молиться (нсв, возв)	[mɔlítsa]
to prefer (vt)	предпочитать (нсв, пх)	[pretpɔʧitátʲ]
to promise (vt)	обещать (н/св, пх)	[ɔbeʃátʲ]
to pronounce (vt)	произносить (нсв, пх)	[prɔiznɔsítʲ]
to propose (vt)	предлагать (нсв, пх)	[predlagátʲ]
to punish (vt)	наказывать (нсв, пх)	[nakázivatʲ]

11. The most important verbs. Part 4

to read (vi, vt)	читать (нсв, н/пх)	[tʃitátʲ]
to recommend (vt)	рекомендовать (нсв, пх)	[rekɔmendɔvátʲ]
to refuse (vi, vt)	отказываться (нсв, возв)	[ɔtkázivatsa]
to regret (be sorry)	сожалеть (нсв, нпх)	[sɔʒilétʲ]
to rent (sth from sb)	снимать (нсв, пх)	[snimátʲ]

to repeat (say again)	повторять (нсв, пх)	[pɔftɔrʲátʲ]
to reserve, to book	резервировать (н/св, пх)	[rezervírɔvatʲ]
to run (vi)	бежать (н/св, нпх)	[beʒátʲ]
to save (rescue)	спасать (нсв, пх)	[spasátʲ]
to say (~ thank you)	сказать (нсв, пх)	[skazátʲ]

to scold (vt)	ругать (нсв, пх)	[rugátʲ]
to see (vt)	видеть (нсв, пх)	[vídetʲ]
to sell (vt)	продавать (нсв, пх)	[prɔdavátʲ]
to send (vt)	отправлять (нсв, пх)	[ɔtpravlʲátʲ]
to shoot (vi)	стрелять (нсв, нпх)	[strelʲátʲ]

to shout (vi)	кричать (нсв, нпх)	[kritʃátʲ]
to show (vt)	показывать (нсв, пх)	[pɔkázivatʲ]
to sign (document)	подписывать (нсв, пх)	[pɔtpísivatʲ]
to sit down (vi)	садиться (нсв, возв)	[sadítsa]

to smile (vi)	улыбаться (нсв, возв)	[ulibátsa]
to speak (vi, vt)	говорить (нсв, н/пх)	[gɔvɔrítʲ]
to steal (money, etc.)	красть (нсв, н/пх)	[krástʲ]
to stop (for pause, etc.)	останавливаться (нсв, возв)	[ɔstanávlivatsa]
to stop (please ~ calling me)	прекращать (нсв, пх)	[prekraʃátʲ]

to study (vt)	изучать (нсв, пх)	[izutʃátʲ]
to swim (vi)	плавать (нсв, нпх)	[plávatʲ]
to take (vt)	брать (нсв), взять (св)	[brátʲ], [vzʲátʲ]
to think (vi, vt)	думать (нсв, н/пх)	[dúmatʲ]
to threaten (vt)	угрожать (нсв, пх)	[ugrɔʒátʲ]

to touch (with hands)	трогать (нсв, пх)	[trógatʲ]
to translate (vt)	переводить (нсв, пх)	[perevɔdítʲ]
to trust (vt)	доверять (нсв, пх)	[dɔverʲátʲ]
to try (attempt)	пробовать (нсв, пх)	[próbɔvatʲ]
to turn (e.g., ~ left)	поворачивать (нсв, нпх)	[pɔvɔrátʃivatʲ]

to underestimate (vt)	недооценивать (нсв, пх)	[nedɔɔtsǽnivatʲ]
to understand (vt)	понимать (нсв, пх)	[pɔnimátʲ]
to unite (vt)	объединять (нсв, пх)	[ɔbjedinʲátʲ]
to wait (vt)	ждать (нсв, пх)	[ʒdátʲ]
to want (wish, desire)	хотеть (нсв, пх)	[hɔtétʲ]
to warn (vt)	предупреждать (нсв, пх)	[predupreʒdátʲ]

to work (vi)	работать (нсв, нпх)	[rabótatʲ]
to write (vt)	писать (нсв, пх)	[pisátʲ]
to write down	записывать (нсв, пх)	[zapísivatʲ]

12. Colors

color	цвет (м)	[tsvét]
shade (tint)	оттенок (м)	[otténɔk]
hue	тон (м)	[tón]
rainbow	радуга (ж)	[ráduga]

white (adj)	белый	[bélij]
black (adj)	чёрный	[tʃórnij]
gray (adj)	серый	[sérij]

green (adj)	зелёный	[zelǿnij]
yellow (adj)	жёлтый	[ʒóltij]
red (adj)	красный	[krásnij]
blue (adj)	синий	[sínij]
light blue (adj)	голубой	[gɔlubój]
pink (adj)	розовый	[rózɔvij]
orange (adj)	оранжевый	[ɔránʒevij]
violet (adj)	фиолетовый	[fiɔlétɔvij]
brown (adj)	коричневый	[kɔrítʃnevij]

golden (adj)	золотой	[zɔlɔtój]
silvery (adj)	серебристый	[serebrístij]
beige (adj)	бежевый	[béʒevij]
cream (adj)	кремовый	[krémɔvij]
turquoise (adj)	бирюзовый	[birʲuzóvij]
cherry red (adj)	вишнёвый	[viʃnǿvij]
lilac (adj)	лиловый	[lilóvij]
crimson (adj)	малиновый	[malínɔvij]

light (adj)	светлый	[svétlij]
dark (adj)	тёмный	[tǿmnij]
bright, vivid (adj)	яркий	[járkij]

colored (pencils)	цветной	[tsvetnój]
color (e.g., ~ film)	цветной	[tsvetnój]
black-and-white (adj)	чёрно-белый	[tʃórnɔ-bélij]
plain (one-colored)	одноцветный	[ɔdnɔtsvétnij]
multicolored (adj)	разноцветный	[raznɔtsvétnij]

13. Questions

| Who? | Кто? | [któ?] |
| What? | Что? | [ʃtó?] |

Where? (at, in)	Где?	[gdé?]
Where (to)?	Куда?	[kudá?]
From where?	Откуда?	[ɔtkúda?]
When?	Когда?	[kɔgdá?]
Why? (What for?)	Зачем?	[zatʃém?]
Why? (~ are you crying?)	Почему?	[pɔtʃemú?]

What for?	Для чего?	[dlʲa tʃevó?]
How? (in what way)	Как?	[kák?]
What? (What kind of ...?)	Какой?	[kakój?]
Which?	Который?	[kɔtórij?]

To whom?	Кому?	[kɔmú?]
About whom?	О ком?	[ɔ kóm?]
About what?	О чём?	[ɔ tʃóm?]
With whom?	С кем?	[s kém?]

How many? How much?	Сколько?	[skólʲkɔ?]
Whose?	Чей?	[tʃéj?]
Whose? (fem.)	Чья?	[tʃjá?]
Whose? (pl)	Чьи?	[tʃjí?]

14. Function words. Adverbs. Part 1

Where? (at, in)	Где?	[gdé?]
here (adv)	здесь	[zdésʲ]
there (adv)	там	[tám]

| somewhere (to be) | где-то | [gdé-tɔ] |
| nowhere (not in any place) | нигде | [nigdé] |

| by (near, beside) | у, около | [u], [ókɔlɔ] |
| by the window | у окна | [u ɔkná] |

Where (to)?	Куда?	[kudá?]
here (e.g., come ~!)	сюда	[sʲudá]
there (e.g., to go ~)	туда	[tudá]
from here (adv)	отсюда	[ɔtsʲúda]
from there (adv)	оттуда	[ɔttúda]

| close (adv) | близко | [blískɔ] |
| far (adv) | далеко | [dalekó] |

near (e.g., ~ Paris)	около	[ókɔlɔ]
nearby (adv)	рядом	[rʲádɔm]
not far (adv)	недалеко	[nedalekó]

left (adj)	левый	[lévij]
on the left	слева	[sléva]
to the left	налево	[nalévɔ]

right (adj)	правый	[právij]
on the right	справа	[správa]
to the right	направо	[naprávɔ]

in front (adv)	спереди	[spéredi]
front (as adj)	передний	[perédnij]
ahead (the kids ran ~)	вперёд	[fperód]

behind (adv)	сзади	[szádi]
from behind	сзади	[szádi]
back (towards the rear)	назад	[nazád]

| middle | середина (ж) | [seredína] |
| in the middle | посередине | [pɔseredíne] |

at the side	сбоку	[zbóku]
everywhere (adv)	везде	[vezdé]
around (in all directions)	вокруг	[vɔkrúg]

from inside	изнутри	[iznutrí]
somewhere (to go)	куда-то	[kudá-tɔ]
straight (directly)	напрямик	[naprɪmík]
back (e.g., come ~)	обратно	[ɔbrátnɔ]

| from anywhere | откуда-нибудь | [ɔtkúda-nibutʲ] |
| from somewhere | откуда-то | [ɔtkúda-tɔ] |

firstly (adv)	во-первых	[vɔ-pérvɨh]
secondly (adv)	во-вторых	[vɔ-ftɔrɨ́h]
thirdly (adv)	в-третьих	[f trétjih]

suddenly (adv)	вдруг	[vdrúg]
at first (in the beginning)	вначале	[vnatʃále]
for the first time	впервые	[fpervíje]
long before …	задолго до …	[zadólgɔ dɔ …]
anew (over again)	заново	[zánɔvɔ]
for good (adv)	насовсем	[nasɔfsém]

never (adv)	никогда	[nikɔgdá]
again (adv)	опять	[ɔpʲátʲ]
now (at present)	теперь	[tepérʲ]
often (adv)	часто	[tʃástɔ]
then (adv)	тогда	[tɔgdá]
urgently (quickly)	срочно	[srótʃnɔ]
usually (adv)	обычно	[ɔbɨ́tʃnɔ]

by the way, …	кстати, …	[kstáti, …]
possibly	возможно	[vɔzmóʒnɔ]
probably (adv)	вероятно	[verɔjátnɔ]
maybe (adv)	может быть	[móʒet bɨ́tʲ]
besides …	кроме того, …	[króme tɔvó, …]
that's why …	поэтому …	[pɔǽtɔmu …]

in spite of ...	несмотря на ...	[nesmotrʲá na ...]
thanks to ...	благодаря ...	[blagɔdarʲá ...]
what (pron.)	что	[ʃtó]
that (conj.)	что	[ʃtó]
something	что-то	[ʃtó-tɔ]
anything (something)	что-нибудь	[ʃtó-nibutʲ]
nothing	ничего	[nitʃevó]
who (pron.)	кто	[któ]
someone	кто-то	[któ-tɔ]
somebody	кто-нибудь	[któ-nibutʲ]
nobody	никто	[niktó]
nowhere (a voyage to ~)	никуда	[nikudá]
nobody's	ничей	[nitʃéj]
somebody's	чей-нибудь	[tʃej-nibútʲ]
so (I'm ~ glad)	так	[ták]
also (as well)	также	[tágʒe]
too (as well)	тоже	[tóʒe]

15. Function words. Adverbs. Part 2

Why?	Почему?	[pɔtʃemú?]
for some reason	почему-то	[pɔtʃemú-tɔ]
because ...	потому, что ...	[pɔtɔmú, ʃtó ...]
for some purpose	зачем-то	[zatʃém-tɔ]
and	и	[i]
or	или	[íli]
but	но	[nó]
for (e.g., ~ me)	для	[dlʲá]
too (~ many people)	слишком	[slíʃkɔm]
only (exclusively)	только	[tólʲkɔ]
exactly (adv)	точно	[tótʃnɔ]
about (more or less)	около	[ókɔlɔ]
approximately (adv)	приблизительно	[priblizítelʲnɔ]
approximate (adj)	приблизительный	[priblizítelʲnij]
almost (adv)	почти	[pɔtʃtí]
the rest	остальное (c)	[ɔstalʲnóe]
each (adj)	каждый	[káʒdij]
any (no matter which)	любой	[lʲubój]
many, much (a lot of)	много	[mnógɔ]
many people	многие	[mnógie]
all (everyone)	все	[fsé]
in return for ...	в обмен на ...	[v ɔbmén na ...]

in exchange (adv)	взамен	[vzamén]
by hand (made)	вручную	[vrutʃnúju]
hardly (negative opinion)	вряд ли	[vrʲát lʲí]

probably (adv)	наверное	[navérnɔe]
on purpose (intentionally)	нарочно	[naróʃnɔ]
by accident (adv)	случайно	[slutʃájnɔ]

very (adv)	очень	[ótʃenʲ]
for example (adv)	например	[naprimér]
between	между	[méʒdu]
among	среди	[sredʲí]
so much (such a lot)	столько	[stólʲkɔ]
especially (adv)	особенно	[ɔsóbennɔ]

Basic concepts. Part 2

16. Opposites

rich (adj)	богатый	[bɔgátij]
poor (adj)	бедный	[bédnij]
ill, sick (adj)	больной	[bɔlʲnój]
well (not sick)	здоровый	[zdɔróvij]
big (adj)	большой	[bɔlʲʃój]
small (adj)	маленький	[málenʲkij]
quickly (adv)	быстро	[bĩstrɔ]
slowly (adv)	медленно	[médlenɔ]
fast (adj)	быстрый	[bĩstrij]
slow (adj)	медленный	[médlenij]
glad (adj)	весёлый	[vesǿlij]
sad (adj)	грустный	[grúsnij]
together (adv)	вместе	[vméste]
separately (adv)	отдельно	[ɔtdélʲnɔ]
aloud (to read)	вслух	[fslúh]
silently (to oneself)	про себя	[prɔ sebʲá]
tall (adj)	высокий	[vɨsókij]
low (adj)	низкий	[nískij]
deep (adj)	глубокий	[glubókij]
shallow (adj)	мелкий	[mélkij]
yes	да	[dá]
no	нет	[nét]
distant (in space)	далёкий	[dalǿkij]
nearby (adj)	близкий	[blískij]
far (adv)	далеко	[dalekó]
nearby (adv)	рядом	[rʲádɔm]
long (adj)	длинный	[dlínnij]
short (adj)	короткий	[kɔrótkij]
good (kindhearted)	добрый	[dóbrij]

evil (adj)	злой	[zlój]
married (adj)	женатый	[ʒenátij]
single (adj)	холостой	[holostój]

| to forbid (vt) | запретить (св, пх) | [zapretítʲ] |
| to permit (vt) | разрешить (св, пх) | [razreʃítʲ] |

| end | конец (м) | [konéts] |
| beginning | начало (с) | [natʃálo] |

| left (adj) | левый | [lévij] |
| right (adj) | правый | [právij] |

| first (adj) | первый | [pérvij] |
| last (adj) | последний | [poslédnij] |

| crime | преступление (с) | [prestuplénie] |
| punishment | наказание (с) | [nakazánie] |

| to order (vt) | приказать (св, пх) | [prikazátʲ] |
| to obey (vi, vt) | подчиниться (св, возв) | [pottʃinítsa] |

| straight (adj) | прямой | [prɪmój] |
| curved (adj) | кривой | [krivój] |

| paradise | рай (м) | [ráj] |
| hell | ад (м) | [ád] |

| to be born | родиться (св, возв) | [rodítsa] |
| to die (vi) | умереть (св, нпх) | [umerétʲ] |

| strong (adj) | сильный | [sílʲnij] |
| weak (adj) | слабый | [slábij] |

| old (adj) | старый | [stárij] |
| young (adj) | молодой | [molodój] |

| old (adj) | старый | [stárij] |
| new (adj) | новый | [nóvij] |

| hard (adj) | твёрдый | [tvǿrdij] |
| soft (adj) | мягкий | [mʲáhkij] |

| warm (tepid) | тёплый | [tǿplij] |
| cold (adj) | холодный | [holódnij] |

| fat (adj) | толстый | [tólstij] |
| thin (adj) | худой | [hudój] |

narrow (adj)	узкий	[úskij]
wide (adj)	широкий	[ʃirókij]
good (adj)	хороший	[horóʃij]

bad (adj)	плохой	[plɔhój]
brave (adj)	храбрый	[hrábrij]
cowardly (adj)	трусливый	[truslívij]

17. Weekdays

Monday	понедельник (м)	[pɔnedélʲnik]
Tuesday	вторник (м)	[ftórnik]
Wednesday	среда (ж)	[sredá]
Thursday	четверг (м)	[tʃetvérg]
Friday	пятница (ж)	[pʲátnitsa]
Saturday	суббота (ж)	[subóta]
Sunday	воскресенье (с)	[vɔskresénje]

today (adv)	сегодня	[sevódnʲa]
tomorrow (adv)	завтра	[záftra]
the day after tomorrow	послезавтра	[pɔslezáftra]
yesterday (adv)	вчера	[ftʃerá]
the day before yesterday	позавчера	[pɔzaftʃerá]

day	день (м)	[dénʲ]
working day	рабочий день (м)	[rabótʃij dénʲ]
public holiday	празник (м)	[práznik]
day off	выходной день (м)	[vihɔdnój dénʲ]
weekend	выходные (мн)	[vihɔdnĩje]

all day long	весь день	[vesʲ dénʲ]
the next day (adv)	на следующий день	[na sléduʃij dénʲ]
two days ago	2 дня назад	[dvá dnʲá nazád]
the day before	накануне	[nakanúne]
daily (adj)	ежедневный	[eʒednévnij]
every day (adv)	ежедневно	[eʒednévnɔ]

week	неделя (ж)	[nedélʲa]
last week (adv)	на прошлой неделе	[na próʃlɔj nedéle]
next week (adv)	на следующей неделе	[na sléduʃʲej nedéle]
weekly (adj)	еженедельный	[eʒenedélʲnij]
every week (adv)	еженедельно	[eʒenedélʲnɔ]
twice a week	2 раза в неделю	[dvá ráza v nedélʲu]
every Tuesday	каждый вторник	[káʒdij ftórnik]

18. Hours. Day and night

morning	утро (с)	[útrɔ]
in the morning	утром	[útrɔm]
noon, midday	полдень (м)	[pólpdenʲ]
in the afternoon	после обеда	[pósle ɔbéda]
evening	вечер (м)	[vétʃer]

in the evening	вечером (ж)	[vétʃerɔm]
night	ночь (ж)	[nótʃʲ]
at night	ночью	[nótʃʲu]
midnight	полночь (ж)	[pólnɔtʃʲ]

second	секунда (ж)	[sekúnda]
minute	минута (ж)	[minúta]
hour	час (м)	[tʃás]
half an hour	полчаса (мн)	[pɔltʃasá]
a quarter-hour	четверть (ж) часа	[tʃétvertʲ tʃása]
fifteen minutes	15 минут	[pitnátsatʲ minút]
24 hours	сутки (мн)	[sútki]

sunrise	восход (м) солнца	[vɔsxód sóntsa]
dawn	рассвет (м)	[rasvét]
early morning	раннее утро (с)	[ránnee útrɔ]
sunset	закат (м)	[zakát]

early in the morning	рано утром	[ránɔ útrɔm]
this morning	сегодня утром	[sevódnʲa útrɔm]
tomorrow morning	завтра утром	[záftra útrɔm]

this afternoon	сегодня днём	[sevódnʲa dnǿm]
in the afternoon	после обеда	[pósle ɔbéda]
tomorrow afternoon	завтра после обеда	[záftra pósle ɔbéda]

| tonight (this evening) | сегодня вечером | [sevódnʲa vétʃerɔm] |
| tomorrow night | завтра вечером | [záftra vetʃerɔm] |

at 3 o'clock sharp	ровно в 3 часа	[róvnɔ f trí tʃasá]
about 4 o'clock	около 4-х часов	[ókɔlɔ tʃetîrǿh tʃasóf]
by 12 o'clock	к 12-ти часам	[k dvenátsatí tʃasám]

in 20 minutes	через 20 минут	[tʃéres dvátsatʲ minút]
in an hour	через час	[tʃéres tʃás]
on time (adv)	вовремя	[vóvremʲa]

a quarter to …	без четверти …	[bes tʃétverti …]
within an hour	в течение часа	[f tetʃénie tʃása]
every 15 minutes	каждые 15 минут	[káʒdie pitnátsatʲ minút]
round the clock	круглые сутки	[krúglie sútki]

19. Months. Seasons

January	январь (м)	[jɪnvárʲ]
February	февраль (м)	[fevrálʲ]
March	март (м)	[márt]
April	апрель (м)	[aprélʲ]
May	май (м)	[máj]
June	июнь (м)	[ijúnʲ]

July	**июль** (м)	[ijúlʲ]
August	**август** (м)	[ávgust]
September	**сентябрь** (м)	[sentʲábrʲ]
October	**октябрь** (м)	[ɔktʲábrʲ]
November	**ноябрь** (м)	[nɔjábrʲ]
December	**декабрь** (м)	[dekábrʲ]
spring	**весна** (ж)	[vesná]
in spring	**весной**	[vesnój]
spring (as adj)	**весенний**	[vesénnij]
summer	**лето** (с)	[léto]
in summer	**летом**	[létɔm]
summer (as adj)	**летний**	[létnij]
fall	**осень** (ж)	[ósenʲ]
in fall	**осенью**	[ósenju]
fall (as adj)	**осенний**	[ɔsénnij]
winter	**зима** (ж)	[zimá]
in winter	**зимой**	[zimój]
winter (as adj)	**зимний**	[zímnij]
month	**месяц** (м)	[mésɪts]
this month	**в этом месяце**	[v ǽtom mésɪtse]
next month	**в следующем месяце**	[f sléduʃem mésɪtse]
last month	**в прошлом месяце**	[f próʃlom mésɪtse]
a month ago	**месяц назад**	[mésɪts nazád]
in a month (a month later)	**через месяц**	[tʃéres mésɪts]
in 2 months (2 months later)	**через 2 месяца**	[tʃéres dvá mésɪtsa]
the whole month	**весь месяц**	[vesʲ mésɪts]
all month long	**целый месяц**	[tsǽlij mésɪts]
monthly (~ magazine)	**ежемесячный**	[eʒemésɪtʃnij]
monthly (adv)	**ежемесячно**	[eʒemésɪtʃnɔ]
every month	**каждый месяц**	[káʒdij mésɪts]
twice a month	**2 раза в месяц**	[dvá ráza v mésɪts]
year	**год** (м)	[gód]
this year	**в этом году**	[v ǽtom gɔdú]
next year	**в следующем году**	[f sléduʃem gɔdú]
last year	**в прошлом году**	[f próʃlom gɔdú]
a year ago	**год назад**	[gót nazád]
in a year	**через год**	[tʃéres gód]
in two years	**через 2 года**	[tʃéres dvá góda]
the whole year	**весь год**	[vesʲ gód]
all year long	**целый год**	[tsǽlij gód]
every year	**каждый год**	[káʒdij gód]
annual (adj)	**ежегодный**	[eʒegódnij]

| annually (adv) | ежегодно | [eʒegódnɔ] |
| 4 times a year | 4 раза в год | [ʧetīre ráza v gód] |

date (e.g., today's ~)	число (с)	[ʧisló]
date (e.g., ~ of birth)	дата (ж)	[dáta]
calendar	календарь (м)	[kalendárʲ]

half a year	полгода	[pɔlgóda]
six months	полугодие (с)	[pɔlugódie]
season (summer, etc.)	сезон (м)	[sezón]
century	век (м)	[vék]

20. Time. Miscellaneous

time	время (с)	[vrémʲa]
moment	миг (м)	[míg]
instant (n)	мгновение (с)	[mgnɔvénie]
instant (adj)	мгновенный	[mgnɔvénnij]
lapse (of time)	отрезок (м)	[ɔtrézɔk]
life	жизнь (ж)	[ʒīznʲ]
eternity	вечность (ж)	[véʧnɔstʲ]

epoch	эпоха (ж)	[ɛpóha]
era	эра (ж)	[ǽra]
cycle	цикл (м)	[ʦīkl]
period	период (м)	[períud]
term (short-~)	срок (м)	[srók]

the future	будущее (с)	[búduʃee]
future (as adj)	будущий	[búduʃij]
next time	в следующий раз	[f sléduʃij rás]
the past	прошлое (с)	[próʃloe]
past (recent)	прошлый	[próʃlij]
last time	в прошлый раз	[f próʃlij rás]

later (adv)	позже	[póʒʒe]
after (prep.)	после	[pósle]
nowadays (adv)	теперь	[tepérʲ]
now (at this moment)	сейчас	[sejʧás]
immediately (adv)	немедленно	[nemédlenɔ]
soon (adv)	скоро	[skórɔ]
in advance (beforehand)	заранее	[zaránee]

a long time ago	давно	[davnó]
recently (adv)	недавно	[nedávnɔ]
destiny	судьба (ж)	[sutʲbá]
memories (childhood ~)	память (ж)	[pámɪtʲ]
archives	архив (м)	[arhíf]
during ...	во время ...	[vɔ vrémʲa ...]
long, a long time (adv)	долго	[dólgɔ]

not long (adv)	недолго	[nedólgɔ]
early (in the morning)	рано	[ránɔ]
late (not early)	поздно	[póznɔ]

forever (for good)	навсегда	[nafsegdá]
to start (begin)	начинать (нсв, пх)	[natʃinátʲ]
to postpone (vt)	перенести (св, пх)	[perenestí]

at the same time	одновременно	[ɔdnɔvreménnɔ]
permanently (adv)	постоянно	[pɔstɔjánnɔ]
constant (noise, pain)	постоянный	[pɔstɔjánnij]
temporary (adj)	временный	[vrémennij]

sometimes (adv)	иногда	[inɔgdá]
rarely (adv)	редко	[rétkɔ]
often (adv)	часто	[tʃástɔ]

21. Lines and shapes

square	квадрат (м)	[kvadrát]
square (as adj)	квадратный	[kvadrátnij]
circle	круг (м)	[krúg]
round (adj)	круглый	[krúglij]
triangle	треугольник (м)	[treugólʲnik]
triangular (adj)	треугольный	[treugólʲnij]

oval	овал (м)	[ɔvál]
oval (as adj)	овальный	[ɔválʲnij]
rectangle	прямоугольник (м)	[prımɔugólʲnik]
rectangular (adj)	прямоугольный	[prımɔugólʲnij]

pyramid	пирамида (ж)	[piramída]
rhombus	ромб (м)	[rómp]
trapezoid	трапеция (ж)	[trapétsija]
cube	куб (м)	[kúb]
prism	призма (ж)	[prízma]

circumference	окружность (ж)	[ɔkrúʒnostʲ]
sphere	сфера (ж)	[sféra]
ball (solid sphere)	шар (м)	[ʃár]
diameter	диаметр (м)	[diámetr]
radius	радиус (м)	[rádius]
perimeter (circle's ~)	периметр (м)	[perímetr]
center	центр (м)	[tsǽntr]

horizontal (adj)	горизонтальный	[gɔrizɔntálʲnij]
vertical (adj)	вертикальный	[vertikálʲnij]
parallel (n)	параллель (ж)	[paralélʲ]
parallel (as adj)	параллельный	[paralélʲnij]
line	линия (ж)	[línija]

stroke	черта (ж)	[tʃertá]
straight line	прямая (ж)	[prɪmája]
curve (curved line)	кривая (ж)	[krivája]
thin (line, etc.)	тонкий	[tónkij]
contour (outline)	контур (м)	[kóntur]

intersection	пересечение (с)	[peresetʃénie]
right angle	прямой угол (м)	[prɪmój úgɔl]
segment	сегмент (м)	[segmént]
sector (circular ~)	сектор (м)	[séktɔr]
side (of triangle)	сторона (ж)	[stɔrɔná]
angle	угол (м)	[úgɔl]

22. Units of measurement

weight	вес (м)	[vés]
length	длина (ж)	[dliná]
width	ширина (ж)	[ʃiriná]
height	высота (ж)	[visɔtá]
depth	глубина (ж)	[glubiná]
volume	объём (м)	[ɔbjóm]
area	площадь (ж)	[plóʃatʲ]

gram	грамм (м)	[grám]
milligram	миллиграмм (м)	[miligrám]
kilogram	килограмм (м)	[kilɔgrám]
ton	тонна (ж)	[tónna]
pound	фунт (м)	[fúnt]
ounce	унция (ж)	[úntsija]

meter	метр (м)	[métr]
millimeter	миллиметр (м)	[milimétr]
centimeter	сантиметр (м)	[santimétr]
kilometer	километр (м)	[kilɔmétr]
mile	миля (ж)	[mílʲa]

inch	дюйм (м)	[dʲújm]
foot	фут (м)	[fút]
yard	ярд (м)	[járd]

| square meter | квадратный метр (м) | [kvadrátnij métr] |
| hectare | гектар (м) | [gektár] |

liter	литр (м)	[lítr]
degree	градус (м)	[grádus]
volt	вольт (м)	[vólʲt]
ampere	ампер (м)	[ampér]
horsepower	лошадиная сила (ж)	[lɔʃidínaja síla]
quantity	количество (с)	[kɔlítʃestvɔ]
a little bit of ...	немного ...	[nemnógɔ ...]

half	половина (ж)	[pɔlɔvína]
dozen	дюжина (ж)	[dʲúʒina]
piece (item)	штука (ж)	[ʃtúka]

| size | размер (м) | [razmér] |
| scale (map ~) | масштаб (м) | [maʃtáb] |

minimal (adj)	минимальный	[minimálʲnij]
the smallest (adj)	наименьший	[naiménʲʃij]
medium (adj)	средний	[srédnij]
maximal (adj)	максимальный	[maksimálʲnij]
the largest (adj)	наибольший	[naibólʲʃij]

23. Containers

canning jar (glass ~)	банка (ж)	[bánka]
can	банка (ж)	[bánka]
bucket	ведро (с)	[vedró]
barrel	бочка (ж)	[bótʃka]

wash basin (e.g., plastic ~)	таз (м)	[tás]
tank (100L water ~)	бак (м)	[bák]
hip flask	фляжка (ж)	[flʲáʃka]
jerrycan	канистра (ж)	[kanístra]
tank (e.g., tank car)	цистерна (ж)	[tsistǽrna]

mug	кружка (ж)	[krúʃka]
cup (of coffee, etc.)	чашка (ж)	[tʃáʃka]
saucer	блюдце (с)	[blʲútse]
glass (tumbler)	стакан (м)	[stakán]
wine glass	бокал (м)	[bɔkál]
stock pot (soup pot)	кастрюля (ж)	[kastrʲúlʲa]

| bottle (~ of wine) | бутылка (ж) | [butîlka] |
| neck (of the bottle, etc.) | горлышко (с) | [górlɨʃkɔ] |

carafe (decanter)	графин (м)	[grafín]
pitcher	кувшин (м)	[kuʃʃîn]
vessel (container)	сосуд (м)	[sɔsúd]
pot (crock, stoneware ~)	горшок (м)	[gɔrʃók]
vase	ваза (ж)	[váza]

flacon, bottle (perfume ~)	флакон (м)	[flakón]
vial, small bottle	пузырёк (м)	[puzirǿk]
tube (of toothpaste)	тюбик (м)	[tʲúbik]

sack (bag)	мешок (м)	[meʃók]
bag (paper ~, plastic ~)	пакет (м)	[pakét]
pack (of cigarettes, etc.)	пачка (ж)	[pátʃka]
box (e.g., shoebox)	коробка (ж)	[kɔrópka]

| crate | ящик (м) | [jáʃik] |
| basket | корзина (ж) | [kɔrzína] |

24. Materials

material	материал (м)	[materjál]
wood (n)	дерево (c)	[dérevɔ]
wood-, wooden (adj)	деревянный	[derevʲánnij]

| glass (n) | стекло (c) | [steklɔ́] |
| glass (as adj) | стеклянный | [steklʲánnij] |

| stone (n) | камень (м) | [kámenʲ] |
| stone (as adj) | каменный | [kámennij] |

| plastic (n) | пластик (м) | [plástik] |
| plastic (as adj) | пластмассовый | [plastmásɔvij] |

| rubber (n) | резина (ж) | [rezína] |
| rubber (as adj) | резиновый | [rezínɔvij] |

| cloth, fabric (n) | ткань (ж) | [tkánʲ] |
| fabric (as adj) | из ткани | [is tkáni] |

| paper (n) | бумага (ж) | [bumága] |
| paper (as adj) | бумажный | [bumáʒnij] |

| cardboard (n) | картон (м) | [kartɔ́n] |
| cardboard (as adj) | картонный | [kartɔ́nnij] |

polyethylene	полиэтилен (м)	[pɔliɛtilén]
cellophane	целлофан (м)	[tsɛlɔfán]
linoleum	линолеум (м)	[linɔ́leum]
plywood	фанера (ж)	[fanéra]

porcelain (n)	фарфор (м)	[farfɔ́r]
porcelain (as adj)	фарфоровый	[farfɔ́rɔvij]
clay (n)	глина (ж)	[glína]
clay (as adj)	глиняный	[glínɪnij]
ceramic (n)	керамика (ж)	[kerámika]
ceramic (as adj)	керамический	[keramítʃeskij]

25. Metals

metal (n)	металл (м)	[metál]
metal (as adj)	металлический	[metalítʃeskij]
alloy (n)	сплав (м)	[spláf]
gold (n)	золото (c)	[zɔ́lɔtɔ]

gold, golden (adj)	золотой	[zɔlɔtój]
silver (n)	серебро (c)	[serebró]
silver (as adj)	серебряный	[serébrɪnɨj]
iron (n)	железо (c)	[ʒelézɔ]
iron-, made of iron (adj)	железный	[ʒeléznɨj]
steel (n)	сталь (ж)	[stálʲ]
steel (as adj)	стальной	[stalʲnój]
copper (n)	медь (ж)	[métʲ]
copper (as adj)	медный	[médnɨj]
aluminum (n)	алюминий (м)	[alʲumínij]
aluminum (as adj)	алюминиевый	[alʲumínievɨj]
bronze (n)	бронза (ж)	[brónza]
bronze (as adj)	бронзовый	[brónzɔvɨj]
brass	латунь (ж)	[latúnʲ]
nickel	никель (м)	[níkelʲ]
platinum	платина (ж)	[plátina]
mercury	ртуть (ж)	[rtútʲ]
tin	олово (c)	[ólɔvɔ]
lead	свинец (м)	[svinéʦ]
zinc	цинк (м)	[ʦɪ̆nk]

HUMAN BEING

Human being. The body

26. Humans. Basic concepts

human being	человек (м)	[ʧelɔvék]
man (adult male)	мужчина (м)	[muʃína]
woman	женщина (ж)	[ʒǽnʃina]
child	ребёнок (м)	[rebǿnɔk]
girl	девочка (ж)	[dévɔʧka]
boy	мальчик (м)	[málʲʧik]
teenager	подросток (м)	[pɔdróstɔk]
old man	старик (м)	[starík]
old woman	старая женщина (ж)	[stáraja ʒǽnʃina]

27. Human anatomy

organism (body)	организм (м)	[ɔrganízm]
heart	сердце (с)	[sérʦe]
blood	кровь (ж)	[krófʲ]
artery	артерия (ж)	[artǽrija]
vein	вена (ж)	[véna]
brain	мозг (м)	[mósg]
nerve	нерв (м)	[nérf]
nerves	нервы (мн)	[nérvi]
vertebra	позвонок (м)	[pɔzvɔnók]
spine (backbone)	позвоночник (м)	[pɔzvɔnóʧnik]
stomach (organ)	желудок (м)	[ʒelúdɔk]
intestines, bowels	кишечник (м)	[kiʃǽʧnik]
intestine (e.g., large ~)	кишка (ж)	[kiʃká]
liver	печень (ж)	[péʧenʲ]
kidney	почка (ж)	[póʧka]
bone	кость (ж)	[kóstʲ]
skeleton	скелет (м)	[skelét]
rib	ребро (с)	[rebró]
skull	череп (м)	[ʧérep]
muscle	мышца (ж)	[mɨ̀ʦa]
biceps	бицепс (м)	[bíʦɛps]

triceps	трицепс (м)	[trítsɛps]
tendon	сухожилие (с)	[suhɔʒílie]
joint	сустав (м)	[sustáf]
lungs	лёгкие (мн)	[lǿhkie]
genitals	половые органы (мн)	[pɔlɔvíe órganɨ]
skin	кожа (ж)	[kóʒa]

28. Head

head	голова (ж)	[gɔlɔvá]
face	лицо (с)	[litsó]
nose	нос (м)	[nós]
mouth	рот (м)	[rót]

eye	глаз (м)	[glás]
eyes	глаза (мн)	[glazá]
pupil	зрачок (м)	[zratʃók]
eyebrow	бровь (ж)	[bróf⁽ʲ⁾]
eyelash	ресница (ж)	[resnítsa]
eyelid	веко (с)	[vékɔ]

tongue	язык (м)	[jɪzík]
tooth	зуб (м)	[zúb]
lips	губы (мн)	[gúbɨ]
cheekbones	скулы (мн)	[skúlɨ]
gum	десна (ж)	[desná]
palate	нёбо (с)	[nǿbɔ]

nostrils	ноздри (мн)	[nózdri]
chin	подбородок (м)	[pɔdbɔródɔk]
jaw	челюсть (ж)	[tʃélʲustʲ]
cheek	щека (ж)	[ʃeká]

forehead	лоб (м)	[lób]
temple	висок (м)	[visók]
ear	ухо (с)	[úhɔ]
back of the head	затылок (м)	[zatílɔk]
neck	шея (ж)	[ʃǽja]
throat	горло (с)	[górlɔ]

hair	волосы (мн)	[vólɔsɨ]
hairstyle	причёска (ж)	[pritʃóska]
haircut	стрижка (ж)	[stríʃka]
wig	парик (м)	[parík]

mustache	усы (м мн)	[usí]
beard	борода (ж)	[bɔrɔdá]
to have (a beard, etc.)	носить (нсв, пх)	[nɔsítʲ]
braid	коса (ж)	[kɔsá]
sideburns	бакенбарды (мн)	[bakenbárdɨ]

red-haired (adj)	рыжий	[rɨ́ʒij]
gray (hair)	седой	[sedój]
bald (adj)	лысый	[lɨ́sij]
bald patch	лысина (ж)	[lɨ́sina]

| ponytail | хвост (м) | [hvóst] |
| bangs | чёлка (ж) | [ʧólka] |

29. Human body

| hand | кисть (ж) | [kístʲ] |
| arm | рука (ж) | [ruká] |

finger	палец (м)	[pálets]
thumb	большой палец (м)	[bolʲʃój pálets]
little finger	мизинец (м)	[mizínets]
nail	ноготь (м)	[nógotʲ]

fist	кулак (м)	[kulák]
palm	ладонь (ж)	[ladónʲ]
wrist	запястье (с)	[zapʲástje]
forearm	предплечье (с)	[pretplétʲje]
elbow	локоть (м)	[lókotʲ]
shoulder	плечо (с)	[pleʧó]

leg	нога (ж)	[nogá]
foot	ступня (ж)	[stupnʲá]
knee	колено (с)	[koléno]
calf (part of leg)	икра (ж)	[ikrá]
hip	бедро (с)	[bedró]
heel	пятка (ж)	[pʲátka]

body	тело (с)	[télo]
stomach	живот (м)	[ʒivót]
chest	грудь (ж)	[grútʲ]
breast	грудь (ж)	[grútʲ]
flank	бок (м)	[bók]
back	спина (ж)	[spiná]
lower back	поясница (ж)	[pojisnítsa]
waist	талия (ж)	[tálija]

navel (belly button)	пупок (м)	[pupók]
buttocks	ягодицы (мн)	[jágoditsi]
bottom	зад (м)	[zád]

beauty mark	родинка (ж)	[ródinka]
birthmark (café au lait spot)	родимое пятно (с)	[rodímoe pitnó]
tattoo	татуировка (ж)	[tatuirófka]
scar	шрам (м)	[ʃrám]

Clothing & Accessories

30. Outerwear. Coats

clothes	одежда (ж)	[ɔdéʒda]
outerwear	верхняя одежда (ж)	[vérhnʲaja ɔdéʒda]
winter clothing	зимняя одежда (ж)	[zímnʲaja ɔdéʒda]
coat (overcoat)	пальто (с)	[palʲtó]
fur coat	шуба (ж)	[ʃúba]
fur jacket	полушубок (м)	[pɔluʃúbɔk]
down coat	пуховик (м)	[puhɔvík]
jacket (e.g., leather ~)	куртка (ж)	[kúrtka]
raincoat (trenchcoat, etc.)	плащ (м)	[pláʃʲ]
waterproof (adj)	непромокаемый	[neprɔmɔkáemij]

31. Men's & women's clothing

shirt (button shirt)	рубашка (ж)	[rubáʃka]
pants	брюки (мн)	[brʲúki]
jeans	джинсы (мн)	[dʒínsi]
suit jacket	пиджак (м)	[pidʒák]
suit	костюм (м)	[kɔstʲúm]
dress (frock)	платье (с)	[plátje]
skirt	юбка (ж)	[júpka]
blouse	блузка (ж)	[blúska]
knitted jacket (cardigan, etc.)	кофта (ж)	[kófta]
jacket (of woman's suit)	жакет (м)	[ʒakét]
T-shirt	футболка (ж)	[futbólka]
shorts (short trousers)	шорты (мн)	[ʃórti]
tracksuit	спортивный костюм (м)	[spɔrtívnij kɔstʲúm]
bathrobe	халат (м)	[halát]
pajamas	пижама (ж)	[piʒáma]
sweater	свитер (м)	[svítɛr]
pullover	пуловер (м)	[pulóver]
vest	жилет (м)	[ʒiłét]
tailcoat	фрак (м)	[frák]
tuxedo	смокинг (м)	[smóking]

uniform	форма (ж)	[fórma]
workwear	рабочая одежда (ж)	[rabótʃaja odéʒda]
overalls	комбинезон (м)	[kɔmbinezón]
coat (e.g., doctor's smock)	халат (м)	[halát]

32. Clothing. Underwear

underwear	бельё (с)	[beljǿ]
boxers, briefs	трусы (м)	[trusɨ́]
panties	бельё (с)	[beljǿ]
undershirt (A-shirt)	майка (ж)	[májka]
socks	носки (мн)	[nɔskí]

nightdress	ночная рубашка (ж)	[nɔtʃnája rubáʃka]
bra	бюстгальтер (м)	[bʲusgálʲter]
knee highs (knee-high socks)	гольфы (мн)	[gólʲfɨ]
pantyhose	колготки (мн)	[kɔlgótki]
stockings (thigh highs)	чулки (мн)	[tʃulkí]
bathing suit	купальник (м)	[kupálʲnik]

33. Headwear

hat	шапка (ж)	[ʃápka]
fedora	шляпа (ж)	[ʃlʲápa]
baseball cap	бейсболка (ж)	[bejzbólka]
flatcap	кепка (ж)	[képka]

beret	берет (м)	[berét]
hood	капюшон (м)	[kapʲuʃón]
panama hat	панамка (ж)	[panámka]
knit cap (knitted hat)	вязаная шапочка (ж)	[vʲázanaja ʃápɔtʃka]

headscarf	платок (м)	[platók]
women's hat	шляпка (ж)	[ʃlʲápka]
hard hat	каска (ж)	[káska]
garrison cap	пилотка (ж)	[pilótka]
helmet	шлем (м)	[ʃlém]

derby	котелок (м)	[kɔtelók]
top hat	цилиндр (м)	[tsɨlíndr]

34. Footwear

footwear	обувь (ж)	[óbufʲ]
shoes (men's shoes)	ботинки (мн)	[bɔtínki]

shoes (women's shoes)	туфли (мн)	[túfli]
boots (e.g., cowboy ~)	сапоги (мн)	[sapɔgí]
slippers	тапочки (мн)	[tápɔtʃki]
tennis shoes (e.g., Nike ~)	кроссовки (мн)	[krɔsófki]
sneakers (e.g., Converse ~)	кеды (мн)	[kédi]
sandals	сандалии (мн)	[sandálii]
cobbler (shoe repairer)	сапожник (м)	[sapóʒnik]
heel	каблук (м)	[kablúk]
pair (of shoes)	пара (ж)	[pára]
shoestring	шнурок (м)	[ʃnurók]
to lace (vt)	шнуровать (нсв, пх)	[ʃnurɔvátʲ]
shoehorn	рожок (м)	[rɔʒók]
shoe polish	крем (м) для обуви	[krém dlʲa óbuvi]

35. Textile. Fabrics

cotton (n)	хлопок (м)	[hlópɔk]
cotton (as adj)	из хлопка	[is hlópka]
flax (n)	лён (м)	[lǿn]
flax (as adj)	из льна	[iz lʲná]
silk (n)	шёлк (м)	[ʃólk]
silk (as adj)	шёлковый	[ʃólkɔvij]
wool (n)	шерсть (ж)	[ʃǽrstʲ]
wool (as adj)	шерстяной	[ʃɛrstinój]
velvet	бархат (м)	[bárhat]
suede	замша (ж)	[zámʃa]
corduroy	вельвет (м)	[velʲvét]
nylon (n)	нейлон (м)	[nejlón]
nylon (as adj)	из нейлона	[iz nejlóna]
polyester (n)	полиэстер (м)	[poliǽstɛr]
polyester (as adj)	полиэстровый	[poliǽstrɔvij]
leather (n)	кожа (ж)	[kóʒa]
leather (as adj)	из кожи	[is kóʒi]
fur (n)	мех (м)	[méh]
fur (e.g., ~ coat)	меховой	[mehɔvój]

36. Personal accessories

gloves	перчатки (ж мн)	[pertʃátki]
mittens	варежки (ж мн)	[váreʃki]

scarf (muffler)	шарф (м)	[ʃárf]
glasses (eyeglasses)	очки (мн)	[ɔʧkí]
frame (eyeglass ~)	оправа (ж)	[ɔpráva]
umbrella	зонт (м)	[zónt]
walking stick	трость (ж)	[trósti]
hairbrush	щётка (ж) для волос	[ʃʲótka dlʲa vɔlós]
fan	веер (м)	[véer]

tie (necktie)	галстук (м)	[gálstuk]
bow tie	галстук-бабочка (м)	[gálstuk-bábɔʧka]
suspenders	подтяжки (мн)	[pottʲáʃki]
handkerchief	носовой платок (м)	[nɔsɔvój platók]

comb	расчёска (ж)	[raʃóska]
barrette	заколка (ж)	[zakólka]
hairpin	шпилька (ж)	[ʃpílʲka]
buckle	пряжка (ж)	[prʲáʃka]

| belt | пояс (м) | [pójas] |
| shoulder strap | ремень (м) | [reménʲ] |

bag (handbag)	сумка (ж)	[súmka]
purse	сумочка (ж)	[súmɔʧka]
backpack	рюкзак (м)	[rʲukzák]

37. Clothing. Miscellaneous

fashion	мода (ж)	[móda]
in vogue (adj)	модный	[módnij]
fashion designer	модельер (м)	[mɔdɛljér]

collar	воротник (м)	[vɔrɔtník]
pocket	карман (м)	[karmán]
pocket (as adj)	карманный	[karmánnij]
sleeve	рукав (м)	[rukáʃ]
hanging loop	вешалка (ж)	[véʃəlka]
fly (on trousers)	ширинка (ж)	[ʃirínka]

zipper (fastener)	молния (ж)	[mólnija]
fastener	застёжка (ж)	[zastóʃka]
button	пуговица (ж)	[púgɔvitsa]
buttonhole	петля (ж)	[petlʲá]
to come off (ab. button)	оторваться (св, возв)	[ɔtɔrvátsa]

to sew (vi, vt)	шить (нсв, н/пх)	[ʃiti]
to embroider (vi, vt)	вышивать (нсв, н/пх)	[viʃiváti]
embroidery	вышивка (ж)	[víʃifka]
sewing needle	иголка (ж)	[igólka]
thread	нитка (ж)	[nítka]
seam	шов (м)	[ʃóf]

to get dirty (vi)	испачкаться (св, возв)	[ispátʃkatsa]
stain (mark, spot)	пятно (с)	[pɪtnó]
to crease, crumple (vi)	помяться (нсв, возв)	[pomʲátsa]
to tear, to rip (vt)	порвать (св, пх)	[pɔrvátʲ]
clothes moth	моль (м)	[mólʲ]

38. Personal care. Cosmetics

toothpaste	зубная паста (ж)	[zubnája pásta]
toothbrush	зубная щётка (ж)	[zubnája ʃǿtka]
to brush one's teeth	чистить зубы	[tʃístitʲ zúbɨ]

razor	бритва (ж)	[brítva]
shaving cream	крем (м) для бритья	[krém dlʲa britjá]
to shave (vi)	бриться (нсв, возв)	[brítsa]

| soap | мыло (с) | [mɨ̄lɔ] |
| shampoo | шампунь (м) | [ʃampúnʲ] |

scissors	ножницы (мн)	[nóʒnitsɨ]
nail file	пилочка (ж) для ногтей	[pílotʃka dlʲa nɔktéj]
nail clippers	щипчики (мн)	[ʃíptʃiki]
tweezers	пинцет (м)	[pintsǽt]

cosmetics	косметика (ж)	[kɔsmétika]
face mask	маска (ж)	[máska]
manicure	маникюр (м)	[manikʲúr]
to have a manicure	делать маникюр	[délatʲ manikʲúr]
pedicure	педикюр (м)	[pedikʲúr]

make-up bag	косметичка (ж)	[kɔsmetítʃka]
face powder	пудра (ж)	[púdra]
powder compact	пудреница (ж)	[púdrenitsa]
blusher	румяна (ж)	[rumʲána]

perfume (bottled)	духи (мн)	[duhí]
toilet water (lotion)	туалетная вода (ж)	[tualétnaja vɔdá]
lotion	лосьон (м)	[lɔsjón]
cologne	одеколон (м)	[ɔdekɔlón]

eyeshadow	тени (мн) для век	[téni dlʲa vék]
eyeliner	карандаш (м) для глаз	[karandáʃ dlʲa glás]
mascara	тушь (ж)	[túʃ]

lipstick	губная помада (ж)	[gubnája pɔmáda]
nail polish, enamel	лак (м) для ногтей	[lák dlʲa nɔktéj]
hair spray	лак (м) для волос	[lák dlʲa vɔlós]
deodorant	дезодорант (м)	[dezɔdɔránt]
cream	крем (м)	[krém]
face cream	крем (м) для лица	[krém dlʲa litsá]

hand cream	крем (м) для рук	[krém dlʲa rúk]
anti-wrinkle cream	крем (м) против морщин	[krém prótif mɔrʃín]
day cream	дневной крем (м)	[dnevnój krém]
night cream	ночной крем (м)	[nɔtʃnój krém]
day (as adj)	дневной	[dnevnój]
night (as adj)	ночной	[nɔtʃnój]

tampon	тампон (м)	[tampón]
toilet paper (toilet roll)	туалетная бумага (ж)	[tualétnaja bumága]
hair dryer	фен (м)	[fén]

39. Jewelry

jewelry, jewels	драгоценности (мн)	[dragɔtsǽnnɔsti]
precious (e.g., ~ stone)	драгоценный	[dragɔtsǽnnij]
hallmark stamp	проба (ж)	[próba]

ring	кольцо (с)	[kɔlʲtsó]
wedding ring	обручальное кольцо (с)	[ɔbrutʃálʲnɔe kɔlʲtsó]
bracelet	браслет (м)	[braslét]

earrings	серьги (мн)	[sérʲgi]
necklace (~ of pearls)	ожерелье (с)	[ɔʒerélje]
crown	корона (ж)	[kɔróna]
bead necklace	бусы (мн)	[búsi]

diamond	бриллиант (м)	[briljánt]
emerald	изумруд (м)	[izumrúd]
ruby	рубин (м)	[rubín]
sapphire	сапфир (м)	[sapfír]
pearl	жемчуг (м)	[ʒǽmtʃʲug]
amber	янтарь (м)	[jɪntárʲ]

40. Watches. Clocks

watch (wristwatch)	часы (мн)	[tʃasɨ́]
dial	циферблат (м)	[tsiferblát]
hand (of clock, watch)	стрелка (ж)	[strélka]
metal watch band	браслет (м)	[braslét]
watch strap	ремешок (м)	[remeʃók]

battery	батарейка (ж)	[bataréjka]
to be dead (battery)	сесть (св, нпх)	[séstʲ]
to change a battery	поменять батарейку	[pɔmenʲátʲ bataréjku]
to run fast	спешить (нсв, нпх)	[speʃítʲ]
to run slow	отставать (нсв, нпх)	[ɔtstavátʲ]
wall clock	настенные часы (мн)	[nasténnie tʃasɨ́]
hourglass	песочные часы (мн)	[pesótʃnie tʃasɨ́]

sundial	**солнечные часы** (мн)	[sólnetʃnie tʃasī]
alarm clock	**будильник** (м)	[budílʲnik]
watchmaker	**часовщик** (м)	[tʃasofʃʲík]
to repair (vt)	**ремонтировать** (нсв, пх)	[remɔntírɔvatʲ]

Food. Nutricion

meat	мясо (с)	[mʲásɔ]
chicken	курица (ж)	[kúritsa]
Rock Cornish hen (poussin)	цыплёнок (м)	[ʦiplʲǿnɔk]
duck	утка (ж)	[útka]
goose	гусь (м)	[gúsʲ]
game	дичь (ж)	[díʧ]
turkey	индейка (ж)	[indéjka]
pork	свинина (ж)	[svinína]
veal	телятина (ж)	[telʲátina]
lamb	баранина (ж)	[baránina]
beef	говядина (ж)	[gɔvʲádina]
rabbit	кролик (м)	[królik]
sausage (bologna, etc.)	колбаса (ж)	[kɔlbasá]
vienna sausage (frankfurter)	сосиска (ж)	[sɔsíska]
bacon	бекон (м)	[bekón]
ham	ветчина (ж)	[vetʧiná]
gammon	окорок (м)	[ókɔrɔk]
pâté	паштет (м)	[paʃtét]
liver	печень (ж)	[pétʧenʲ]
hamburger (ground beef)	фарш (м)	[fárʃ]
tongue	язык (м)	[jɪzɪ̃k]
egg	яйцо (с)	[jɪjʦó]
eggs	яйца (мн)	[jájʦa]
egg white	белок (м)	[belók]
egg yolk	желток (м)	[ʒeltók]
fish	рыба (ж)	[rɪ̃ba]
seafood	морепродукты (мн)	[mɔre·prɔdúkti]
crustaceans	ракообразные (мн)	[rakɔɔbráznie]
caviar	икра (ж)	[ikrá]
crab	краб (м)	[kráb]
shrimp	креветка (ж)	[krevétka]
oyster	устрица (ж)	[ústriʦa]
spiny lobster	лангуст (м)	[langúst]
octopus	осьминог (м)	[ɔsʲminóg]

squid	кальмар (м)	[kalʲmár]
sturgeon	осетрина (ж)	[ɔsetrína]
salmon	лосось (м)	[lɔsósʲ]
halibut	палтус (м)	[páltus]
cod	треска (ж)	[treská]
mackerel	скумбрия (ж)	[skúmbrija]
tuna	тунец (м)	[tunéts]
eel	угорь (м)	[úgɔrʲ]
trout	форель (ж)	[fɔrǽlʲ]
sardine	сардина (ж)	[sardína]
pike	щука (ж)	[ʃʲúka]
herring	сельдь (ж)	[sélʲtʲ]
bread	хлеб (м)	[hléb]
cheese	сыр (м)	[sɪ̃r]
sugar	сахар (м)	[sáhar]
salt	соль (ж)	[sólʲ]
rice	рис (м)	[rís]
pasta (macaroni)	макароны (мн)	[makaróni]
noodles	лапша (ж)	[lapʃá]
butter	сливочное масло (с)	[slívɔtʃnɔe máslɔ]
vegetable oil	растительное масло (с)	[rastítelʲnɔe máslɔ]
sunflower oil	подсолнечное масло (с)	[pɔtsólnetʃnɔe máslɔ]
margarine	маргарин (м)	[margarín]
olives	оливки (мн)	[ɔlífki]
olive oil	оливковое масло (с)	[ɔlífkɔvɔe máslɔ]
milk	молоко (с)	[mɔlɔkó]
condensed milk	сгущённое молоко (с)	[sguʃʲǿnɔe mɔlɔkó]
yogurt	йогурт (м)	[jógurt]
sour cream	сметана (ж)	[smetána]
cream (of milk)	сливки (мн)	[slífki]
mayonnaise	майонез (м)	[majinǽs]
buttercream	крем (м)	[krém]
groats (barley ~, etc.)	крупа (ж)	[krupá]
flour	мука (ж)	[muká]
canned food	консервы (мн)	[kɔnsérvi]
cornflakes	кукурузные хлопья (мн)	[kukurúznie hlópja]
honey	мёд (м)	[mǿd]
jam	джем, конфитюр (м)	[dʒǽm], [kɔnfitʲúr]
chewing gum	жевательная резинка (м)	[ʒevátelʲnaja rezínka]

42. Drinks

water	вода (ж)	[vɔdá]
drinking water	питьевая вода (ж)	[pitjevája vɔdá]
mineral water	минеральная вода (ж)	[minerálʲnaja vɔdá]

still (adj)	без газа	[bez gáza]
carbonated (adj)	газированная	[gazirɔ́vanaja]
sparkling (adj)	с газом	[s gázɔm]
ice	лёд (м)	[lʲǿd]
with ice	со льдом	[sɔ lʲdóm]

non-alcoholic (adj)	безалкогольный	[bezalkɔgólʲnij]
soft drink	безалкогольный напиток (м)	[bezalkɔgólʲnij napítɔk]
refreshing drink	прохладительный напиток (м)	[prɔhladítelʲnij napítɔk]
lemonade	лимонад (м)	[limɔnád]

liquors	алкогольные напитки (мн)	[alkɔgólʲnie napítki]
wine	вино (с)	[vinó]
white wine	белое вино (с)	[bélɔe vinó]
red wine	красное вино (с)	[krásnɔe vinó]

liqueur	ликёр (м)	[likǿr]
champagne	шампанское (с)	[ʃampánskɔe]
vermouth	вермут (м)	[vérmut]

whiskey	виски (с)	[víski]
vodka	водка (ж)	[vótka]
gin	джин (м)	[dʒĩn]
cognac	коньяк (м)	[kɔnják]
rum	ром (м)	[róm]

coffee	кофе (м)	[kófe]
black coffee	чёрный кофе (м)	[tʃǿrnij kófe]
coffee with milk	кофе (м) с молоком	[kófe s mɔlɔkóm]
cappuccino	кофе (м) со сливками	[kófe sɔ slífkami]
instant coffee	растворимый кофе (м)	[rastvɔrímij kófe]

milk	молоко (с)	[mɔlɔkó]
cocktail	коктейль (м)	[kɔktǽjlʲ]
milkshake	молочный коктейль (м)	[mɔlótʃnij kɔktǽjlʲ]

juice	сок (м)	[sók]
tomato juice	томатный сок (м)	[tɔmátnij sók]
orange juice	апельсиновый сок (м)	[apelʲsínɔvij sók]
freshly squeezed juice	свежевыжатый сок (м)	[sveʒe·vĩʒatij sók]
beer	пиво (с)	[pívɔ]
light beer	светлое пиво (с)	[svétlɔe pívɔ]

dark beer	тёмное пиво (с)	[tǿmnɔe pívɔ]
tea	чай (м)	[ʧáj]
black tea	чёрный чай (м)	[ʧǿrnɨj ʧáj]
green tea	зелёный чай (м)	[zelǿnɨj ʧáj]

43. Vegetables

| vegetables | овощи (м мн) | [óvɔʃʲi] |
| greens | зелень (ж) | [zélenʲ] |

tomato	помидор (м)	[pɔmidór]
cucumber	огурец (м)	[ɔguréʦ]
carrot	морковь (ж)	[mɔrkófʲ]
potato	картофель (м)	[kartófelʲ]
onion	лук (м)	[lúk]
garlic	чеснок (м)	[ʧesnók]

cabbage	капуста (ж)	[kapústa]
cauliflower	цветная капуста (ж)	[ʦvetnája kapústa]
Brussels sprouts	брюссельская капуста (ж)	[brʲusélʲskaja kapústa]
broccoli	капуста брокколи (ж)	[kapústa brókɔli]

beet	свёкла (ж)	[svǿkla]
eggplant	баклажан (м)	[baklaʒán]
zucchini	кабачок (м)	[kabaʧók]
pumpkin	тыква (ж)	[tɨ̃kva]
turnip	репа (ж)	[répa]

parsley	петрушка (ж)	[petrúʃka]
dill	укроп (м)	[ukróp]
lettuce	салат (м)	[salát]
celery	сельдерей (м)	[selʲderéj]
asparagus	спаржа (ж)	[spárʒa]
spinach	шпинат (м)	[ʃpinát]

pea	горох (м)	[gɔróh]
beans	бобы (мн)	[bɔbɨ̃]
corn (maize)	кукуруза (ж)	[kukurúza]
kidney bean	фасоль (ж)	[fasólʲ]
bell pepper	перец (м)	[péreʦ]
radish	редис (м)	[redís]
artichoke	артишок (м)	[artiʃók]

44. Fruits. Nuts

| fruit | фрукт (м) | [frúkt] |
| apple | яблоко (с) | [jáblɔkɔ] |

pear	груша (ж)	[grúʃa]
lemon	лимон (м)	[limón]
orange	апельсин (м)	[apelʲsín]
strawberry (garden ~)	клубника (ж)	[klubníka]

mandarin	мандарин (м)	[mandarín]
plum	слива (ж)	[slíva]
peach	персик (м)	[pérsik]
apricot	абрикос (м)	[abrikós]
raspberry	малина (ж)	[malína]
pineapple	ананас (м)	[ananás]

banana	банан (м)	[banán]
watermelon	арбуз (м)	[arbús]
grape	виноград (м)	[vinɔgrád]
sour cherry	вишня (ж)	[víʃnʲa]
sweet cherry	черешня (ж)	[ʧeréʃnʲa]
melon	дыня (ж)	[dīnʲa]

grapefruit	грейпфрут (м)	[gréjpfrut]
avocado	авокадо (с)	[avɔkádɔ]
papaya	папайя (ж)	[papája]
mango	манго (с)	[mángɔ]
pomegranate	гранат (м)	[granát]

redcurrant	красная смородина (ж)	[krásnaja smɔródina]
blackcurrant	чёрная смородина (ж)	[ʧórnaja smɔródina]
gooseberry	крыжовник (м)	[kriʒóvnik]
bilberry	черника (ж)	[ʧerníka]
blackberry	ежевика (ж)	[eʒevíka]

raisin	изюм (м)	[izʲúm]
fig	инжир (м)	[inʒīr]
date	финик (м)	[fínik]

peanut	арахис (м)	[aráhis]
almond	миндаль (м)	[mindálʲ]
walnut	грецкий орех (м)	[grétskij ɔréh]
hazelnut	лесной орех (м)	[lesnój ɔréh]
coconut	кокосовый орех (м)	[kɔkósɔvij ɔréh]
pistachios	фисташки (мн)	[fistáʃki]

45. Bread. Candy

bakers' confectionery (pastry)	кондитерские изделия (мн)	[kɔndíterskie izdélija]
bread	хлеб (м)	[hléb]
cookies	печенье (с)	[peʧénje]
chocolate (n)	шоколад (м)	[ʃɔkɔlád]
chocolate (as adj)	шоколадный	[ʃɔkɔládnij]

candy (wrapped)	конфета (ж)	[kɔnféta]
cake (e.g., cupcake)	пирожное (c)	[piróʒnɔe]
cake (e.g., birthday ~)	торт (м)	[tórt]

| pie (e.g., apple ~) | пирог (м) | [piróg] |
| filling (for cake, pie) | начинка (ж) | [natʃínka] |

jam (whole fruit jam)	варенье (c)	[varénje]
marmalade	мармелад (м)	[marmelád]
wafers	вафли (мн)	[váfli]
ice-cream	мороженое (c)	[mɔróʒenɔe]
pudding	пудинг (м)	[púding]

46. Cooked dishes

course, dish	блюдо (c)	[blʲúdɔ]
cuisine	кухня (ж)	[kúhnʲa]
recipe	рецепт (м)	[retsǽpt]
portion	порция (ж)	[pórtsija]

| salad | салат (м) | [salát] |
| soup | суп (м) | [súp] |

clear soup (broth)	бульон (м)	[buljón]
sandwich (bread)	бутерброд (м)	[buterbród]
fried eggs	яичница (ж)	[iíʃnitsa]

| hamburger (beefburger) | гамбургер (м) | [gámburger] |
| beefsteak | бифштекс (м) | [bifʃtǽks] |

side dish	гарнир (м)	[garnír]
spaghetti	спагетти (мн)	[spagéti]
mashed potatoes	картофельное пюре (c)	[kartófelʲnɔe pʲuré]
pizza	пицца (ж)	[pítsa]
porridge (oatmeal, etc.)	каша (ж)	[káʃa]
omelet	омлет (м)	[ɔmlét]

boiled (e.g., ~ beef)	варёный	[varǿnij]
smoked (adj)	копчёный	[kɔptʃǿnij]
fried (adj)	жареный	[ʒárenij]
dried (adj)	сушёный	[suʃǿnij]
frozen (adj)	замороженный	[zamoróʒenij]
pickled (adj)	маринованный	[marinóvanij]

sweet (sugary)	сладкий	[slátkij]
salty (adj)	солёный	[sɔlǿnij]
cold (adj)	холодный	[hɔlódnij]
hot (adj)	горячий	[gɔrʲátʃij]
bitter (adj)	горький	[górʲkij]
tasty (adj)	вкусный	[fkúsnij]

to cook in boiling water	варить (нсв, пх)	[varítʲ]
to cook (dinner)	готовить (нсв, пх)	[gotóvitʲ]
to fry (vt)	жарить (нсв, пх)	[ʒáritʲ]
to heat up (food)	разогревать (нсв, пх)	[razɔgrevátʲ]

to salt (vt)	солить (нсв, пх)	[sɔlítʲ]
to pepper (vt)	перчить (нсв, пх)	[pértʃitʲ], [pertʃítʲ]
to grate (vt)	тереть (нсв, пх)	[terétʲ]
peel (n)	кожура (ж)	[kɔʒurá]
to peel (vt)	чистить (нсв, пх)	[tʃístitʲ]

47. Spices

salt	соль (ж)	[sólʲ]
salty (adj)	солёный	[sɔlǿnij]
to salt (vt)	солить (нсв, пх)	[sɔlítʲ]

black pepper	чёрный перец (м)	[tʃórnij pérets]
red pepper (milled ~)	красный перец (м)	[krásnij pérets]
mustard	горчица (ж)	[gɔrtʃítsa]
horseradish	хрен (м)	[hrén]

condiment	приправа (ж)	[pripráva]
spice	пряность (ж)	[prʲánɔstʲ]
sauce	соус (м)	[sóus]
vinegar	уксус (м)	[úksus]

anise	анис (м)	[anís]
basil	базилик (м)	[bazilík]
cloves	гвоздика (ж)	[gvɔzdíka]

ginger	имбирь (м)	[imbírʲ]
coriander	кориандр (м)	[kɔriándr]
cinnamon	корица (ж)	[kɔrítsa]

sesame	кунжут (м)	[kunʒút]
bay leaf	лавровый лист (м)	[lavróvij líst]
paprika	паприка (ж)	[páprika]
caraway	тмин (м)	[tmín]
saffron	шафран (м)	[ʃafrán]

48. Meals

food	еда (ж)	[edá]
to eat (vi, vt)	есть (нсв, н/пх)	[éstʲ]

breakfast	завтрак (м)	[záftrak]
to have breakfast	завтракать (нсв, нпх)	[záftrakatʲ]

lunch	обед (м)	[ɔbéd]
to have lunch	обедать (нсв, нпх)	[ɔbédatʲ]
dinner	ужин (м)	[úʒin]
to have dinner	ужинать (нсв, нпх)	[úʒinatʲ]

| appetite | аппетит (м) | [apetít] |
| Enjoy your meal! | Приятного аппетита! | [prijátnɔvɔ apetíta] |

to open (~ a bottle)	открывать (нсв, пх)	[ɔtkrivátʲ]
to spill (liquid)	пролить (св, пх)	[prɔlítʲ]
to spill out (vi)	пролиться (св, возв)	[prɔlítsa]

to boil (vi)	кипеть (нсв, нпх)	[kipétʲ]
to boil (vt)	кипятить (нсв, пх)	[kipɪtítʲ]
boiled (~ water)	кипячёный	[kipɪʧónij]
to chill, cool down (vt)	охладить (св, пх)	[ɔhladítʲ]
to chill (vi)	охлаждаться (нсв, возв)	[ɔhlaʒdátsa]

| taste, flavor | вкус (м) | [fkús] |
| aftertaste | привкус (м) | [prífkus] |

to slim down (lose weight)	худеть (нсв, нпх)	[hudétʲ]
diet	диета (ж)	[diéta]
vitamin	витамин (м)	[vitamín]
calorie	калория (ж)	[kalórija]

| vegetarian (n) | вегетарианец (м) | [vegetariánets] |
| vegetarian (adj) | вегетарианский | [vegetariánskij] |

fats (nutrient)	жиры (мн)	[ʒirí]
proteins	белки (мн)	[belkí]
carbohydrates	углеводы (мн)	[uglevódi]

slice (of lemon, ham)	ломтик (м)	[lómtik]
piece (of cake, pie)	кусок (м)	[kusók]
crumb (of bread, cake, etc.)	крошка (ж)	[króʃka]

49. Table setting

spoon	ложка (ж)	[lóʃka]
knife	нож (м)	[nóʃ]
fork	вилка (ж)	[vílka]

| cup (e.g., coffee ~) | чашка (ж) | [ʧáʃka] |
| plate (dinner ~) | тарелка (ж) | [tarélka] |

saucer	блюдце (с)	[blʲútse]
napkin (on table)	салфетка (ж)	[salfétka]
toothpick	зубочистка (ж)	[zubɔʧístka]

50. Restaurant

restaurant	ресторан (м)	[restɔrán]
coffee house	кофейня (ж)	[kɔféjnʲa]
pub, bar	бар (м)	[bár]
tearoom	чайный салон (м)	[ʧájnʲj salón]
waiter	официант (м)	[ɔfiʦiánt]
waitress	официантка (ж)	[ɔfiʦiántka]
bartender	бармен (м)	[bármɛn]
menu	меню (с)	[menʲú]
wine list	карта (ж) вин	[kárta vín]
to book a table	забронировать столик	[zabrɔnírɔvatʲ stólik]
course, dish	блюдо (с)	[blʲúdɔ]
to order (meal)	заказать (св, пх)	[zakazátʲ]
to make an order	сделать заказ	[zdélatʲ zakás]
aperitif	аперитив (м)	[aperitíf]
appetizer	закуска (ж)	[zakúska]
dessert	десерт (м)	[desért]
check	счёт (м)	[ʃǿt]
to pay the check	оплатить счёт	[ɔplatítʲ ʃǿt]
to give change	дать сдачу	[dátʲ zdáʧʲu]
tip	чаевые (мн)	[ʧaevĩe]

Family, relatives and friends

51. Personal information. Forms

name (first name)	**имя** (с)	[ím^ja]
surname (last name)	**фамилия** (ж)	[famílija]
date of birth	**дата** (ж) **рождения**	[dáta rɔʒdénija]
place of birth	**место** (с) **рождения**	[mésto rɔʒdénija]

nationality	**национальность** (ж)	[natsionálʲnostʲ]
place of residence	**место** (с) **жительства**	[mésto ʒítelʲstva]
country	**страна** (ж)	[straná]
profession (occupation)	**профессия** (ж)	[prɔfésija]

gender, sex	**пол** (м)	[pól]
height	**рост** (м)	[róst]
weight	**вес** (м)	[vés]

52. Family members. Relatives

mother	**мать** (ж)	[mátʲ]
father	**отец** (м)	[ɔtéts]
son	**сын** (м)	[sĩn]
daughter	**дочь** (ж)	[dótʃʲ]

younger daughter	**младшая дочь** (ж)	[mládʃaja dótʃʲ]
younger son	**младший сын** (м)	[mládʃij sĩn]
eldest daughter	**старшая дочь** (ж)	[stárʃaja dótʃʲ]
eldest son	**старший сын** (м)	[stárʃij sĩn]

brother	**брат** (м)	[brát]
sister	**сестра** (ж)	[sestrá]

cousin (masc.)	**двоюродный брат** (м)	[dvɔjúrɔdnij brát]
cousin (fem.)	**двоюродная сестра** (ж)	[dvɔjúrɔdnaja sestrá]
mom, mommy	**мама** (ж)	[máma]
dad, daddy	**папа** (м)	[pápa]
parents	**родители** (мн)	[rɔdíteli]
child	**ребёнок** (м)	[rebǿnɔk]
children	**дети** (мн)	[déti]

grandmother	**бабушка** (ж)	[bábuʃka]
grandfather	**дедушка** (м)	[déduʃka]
grandson	**внук** (м)	[vnúk]

| granddaughter | внучка (ж) | [vnútʃka] |
| grandchildren | внуки (мн) | [vnúki] |

uncle	дядя (м)	[dʲádʲa]
aunt	тётя (ж)	[tʲótʲa]
nephew	племянник (м)	[plemʲánik]
niece	племянница (ж)	[plemʲánitsa]
mother-in-law (wife's mother)	тёща (ж)	[tʲóʃʲa]

| father-in-law (husband's father) | свёкор (м) | [svʲókɔr] |

| son-in-law (daughter's husband) | зять (м) | [zʲátʲ] |

| stepmother | мачеха (ж) | [mátʃeha] |
| stepfather | отчим (м) | [óttʃim] |

infant	грудной ребёнок (м)	[grudnój rebʲónɔk]
baby (infant)	младенец (м)	[mladénets]
little boy, kid	малыш (м)	[maɫíʃ]

wife	жена (ж)	[ʒená]
husband	муж (м)	[múʃ]
spouse (husband)	супруг (м)	[suprúg]
spouse (wife)	супруга (ж)	[suprúga]

married (masc.)	женатый	[ʒenátij]
married (fem.)	замужняя	[zamúʒnʲaja]
single (unmarried)	холостой	[hɔɫɔstój]
bachelor	холостяк (м)	[hɔɫɔstʲák]
divorced (masc.)	разведённый	[razvedʲónnij]
widow	вдова (ж)	[vdɔvá]
widower	вдовец (м)	[vdɔvʲéts]

relative	родственник (м)	[rótstvenik]
close relative	близкий родственник (м)	[blískij rótstvenik]
distant relative	дальний родственник (м)	[dálʲnij rótstvenik]
relatives	родные (мн)	[rɔdnɨ̃je]

orphan (boy)	сирота (м)	[sirɔtá]
orphan (girl)	сирота (ж)	[sirɔtá]
guardian (of a minor)	опекун (м)	[ɔpekún]
to adopt (a boy)	усыновить (св, пх)	[usɨnɔvítʲ]
to adopt (a girl)	удочерить (св, пх)	[udɔtʃerítʲ]

53. Friends. Coworkers

| friend (masc.) | друг (м) | [drúg] |
| friend (fem.) | подруга (ж) | [pɔdrúga] |

| friendship | дружба (ж) | [drúʒba] |
| to be friends | дружить (нсв, нпх) | [druʒítʲ] |

buddy (masc.)	приятель (м)	[prijátelʲ]
buddy (fem.)	приятельница (ж)	[prijátelʲnitsa]
partner	партнёр (м)	[partnǿr]

chief (boss)	шеф (м)	[ʃǽf]
superior (n)	начальник (м)	[natʃálʲnik]
owner, proprietor	владелец (м)	[vladélets]
subordinate (n)	подчинённый (м)	[pɔttʃinǿnnij]
colleague	коллега (м)	[kɔléga]

acquaintance (person)	знакомый (м)	[znakómij]
fellow traveler	попутчик (м)	[pɔpúttʃik]
classmate	одноклассник (м)	[ɔdnɔklásnik]

neighbor (masc.)	сосед (м)	[sɔséd]
neighbor (fem.)	соседка (ж)	[sɔsétka]
neighbors	соседи (мн)	[sɔsédi]

54. Man. Woman

woman	женщина (ж)	[ʒǽnʃʲina]
girl (young woman)	девушка (ж)	[dévuʃka]
bride	невеста (ж)	[nevésta]

beautiful (adj)	красивая	[krasívaja]
tall (adj)	высокая	[visókaja]
slender (adj)	стройная	[strójnaja]
short (adj)	невысокого роста	[nevisókɔvɔ rósta]

| blonde (n) | блондинка (ж) | [blɔndínka] |
| brunette (n) | брюнетка (ж) | [brʲunétka] |

ladies' (adj)	дамский	[dámskij]
virgin (girl)	девственница (ж)	[défstvenitsa]
pregnant (adj)	беременная	[berémennaja]

man (adult male)	мужчина (м)	[muʃʲina]
blond (n)	блондин (м)	[blɔndín]
brunet (n)	брюнет (м)	[brʲunét]
tall (adj)	высокий	[visókij]
short (adj)	невысокого роста	[nevisókɔvɔ rósta]

rude (rough)	грубый	[grúbij]
stocky (adj)	коренастый	[kɔrenástij]
robust (adj)	крепкий	[krépkij]
strong (adj)	сильный	[sílʲnij]
strength	сила (ж)	[síla]

stout, fat (adj)	полный	[pólnɨj]
swarthy (adj)	смуглый	[smúglɨj]
slender (well-built)	стройный	[strójnɨj]
elegant (adj)	элегантный	[ɛlegántnɨj]

55. Age

age	возраст (м)	[vózrast]
youth (young age)	юность (ж)	[júnostʲ]
young (adj)	молодой	[mɔlɔdój]
younger (adj)	младше	[mládʃɛ]
older (adj)	старше	[stárʃɛ]
young man	юноша (м)	[júnɔʃa]
teenager	подросток (м)	[pɔdróstɔk]
guy, fellow	парень (м)	[párenʲ]
old man	старик (м)	[starík]
old woman	старая женщина (ж)	[stáraja ʒǽnʃʲina]
adult (adj)	взрослый	[vzróslɨj]
middle-aged (adj)	средних лет	[srédnih lét]
elderly (adj)	пожилой	[pɔʒɨlój]
old (adj)	старый	[stárɨj]
retirement	пенсия (ж)	[pénsija]
to retire (from job)	уйти на пенсию	[ujtí na pénsiju]
retiree	пенсионер (ж)	[pensiɔnér]

56. Children

child	ребёнок (м)	[rebǿnɔk]
children	дети (мн)	[déti]
twins	близнецы (мн)	[bliznetsɨ́]
cradle	люлька (ж), колыбель (ж)	[lʲúlʲka], [kɔlibélʲ]
rattle	погремушка (ж)	[pɔgremúʃka]
diaper	подгузник (м)	[pɔdgúznik]
pacifier	соска (ж)	[sóska]
baby carriage	коляска (ж)	[kɔlʲáska]
kindergarten	детский сад (м)	[détskij sád]
babysitter	няня (ж)	[nʲánʲa]
childhood	детство (с)	[détstvɔ]
doll	кукла (ж)	[kúkla]
toy	игрушка (ж)	[igrúʃka]

construction set (toy)	конструктор (м)	[kɔnstrúktɔr]
well-bred (adj)	воспитанный	[vɔspítanij]
ill-bred (adj)	невоспитанный	[nevɔspítanij]
spoiled (adj)	избалованный	[izbalóvannij]
to be naughty	шалить (нсв, нпх)	[ʃalítʲ]
mischievous (adj)	шаловливый	[ʃalɔvlívij]
mischievousness	шалость (ж)	[ʃálɔstʲ]
mischievous child	шалун (м)	[ʃalún]
obedient (adj)	послушный	[pɔslúʃnij]
disobedient (adj)	непослушный	[nepɔslúʃnij]
docile (adj)	умный, послушный	[úmnij], [pɔslúʃnij]
clever (smart)	умный, одарённый	[úmnij], [ɔdarǿnnij]
child prodigy	вундеркинд (м)	[vunderkínd]

57. Married couples. Family life

to kiss (vt)	целовать (нсв, пх)	[tsɛlɔvátʲ]
to kiss (vi)	целоваться (нсв, возв)	[tsɛlɔvátsa]
family (n)	семья (ж)	[semjá]
family (as adj)	семейный	[seméjnij]
couple	пара (ж), чета (ж)	[pára], [tʃetá]
marriage (state)	брак (м)	[brák]
hearth (home)	домашний очаг (м)	[dɔmáʃnij ɔtʃág]
dynasty	династия (ж)	[dinástija]
date	свидание (с)	[svidánie]
kiss	поцелуй (м)	[pɔtsɛlúj]
love (for sb)	любовь (ж)	[lʲubófʲ]
to love (sb)	любить (нсв, пх)	[lʲubítʲ]
beloved	любимый	[lʲubímij]
tenderness	нежность (ж)	[néʒnɔstʲ]
tender (affectionate)	нежный	[néʒnij]
faithfulness	верность (ж)	[vérnɔstʲ]
faithful (adj)	верный	[vérnij]
care (attention)	забота (ж)	[zabóta]
caring (~ father)	заботливый	[zabótlivij]
newlyweds	молодожёны (мн)	[mɔlɔdɔʒóni]
honeymoon	медовый месяц (м)	[medóvij mésɪts]
to get married (ab. woman)	выйти замуж	[vɨ́jti zámuʃ]
to get married (ab. man)	жениться (н/св, возв)	[ʒenítsa]
wedding	свадьба (ж)	[svátʲba]
golden wedding	золотая свадьба (ж)	[zɔlɔtája svátʲba]

anniversary	**годовщина** (ж)	[gɔdɔfʃína]
lover (masc.)	**любовник** (м)	[lʲubóvnik]
mistress (lover)	**любовница** (ж)	[lʲubóvnitsa]

adultery	**измена** (ж)	[izména]
to cheat on ... (commit adultery)	**изменить** (св, пх)	[izmenítʲ]
jealous (adj)	**ревнивый**	[revnívij]
to be jealous	**ревновать** (нсв, н/пх)	[revnɔvátʲ]
divorce	**развод** (м)	[razvód]
to divorce (vi)	**развестись** (св, возв)	[razvestísʲ]

to quarrel (vi)	**ссориться** (нсв, возв)	[ssóritsa]
to be reconciled (after an argument)	**мириться** (нсв, возв)	[mirítsa]
together (adv)	**вместе**	[vméste]
sex	**секс** (м)	[sǽks]

happiness	**счастье** (с)	[ʃʲástje]
happy (adj)	**счастливый**	[ʃʲislívij]
misfortune (accident)	**несчастье** (с)	[neʃʲástje]
unhappy (adj)	**несчастный**	[neʃʲásnij]

Character. Feelings. Emotions

58. Feelings. Emotions

feeling (emotion)	чувство (с)	[ʧústvɔ]
feelings	чувства (с мн)	[ʧústva]
to feel (vt)	чувствовать (нсв, пх)	[ʧústvɔvatʲ]

hunger	голод (м)	[gólɔd]
to be hungry	хотеть есть	[hɔtétʲ éstʲ]
thirst	жажда (ж)	[ʒáʒda]
to be thirsty	хотеть пить	[hɔtétʲ pítʲ]
sleepiness	сонливость (ж)	[sɔnlívɔstʲ]
to feel sleepy	хотеть спать	[hɔtétʲ spátʲ]

tiredness	усталость (ж)	[ustálɔstʲ]
tired (adj)	усталый	[ustálij]
to get tired	устать (св, нпх)	[ustátʲ]

mood (humor)	настроение (с)	[nastrɔénie]
boredom	скука (ж)	[skúka]
to be bored	скучать (нсв, нпх)	[skuʧátʲ]
seclusion	уединение (с)	[uedinénie]
to seclude oneself	уединиться (св, возв)	[uedinítsa]

to worry (make anxious)	беспокоить (нсв, пх)	[bespɔkóitʲ]
to be worried	беспокоиться (нсв, возв)	[bespɔkóitsa]
worrying (n)	беспокойство (с)	[bespɔkójstvɔ]
anxiety	тревога (ж)	[trevóga]
preoccupied (adj)	озабоченный	[ɔzabóʧenij]
to be nervous	нервничать (нсв, нпх)	[nérvniʧatʲ]
to panic (vi)	паниковать (нсв, нпх)	[panikɔvátʲ]

| hope | надежда (ж) | [nadéʒda] |
| to hope (vi, vt) | надеяться (нсв, возв) | [nadéitsa] |

certainty	уверенность (ж)	[uvérenɔstʲ]
certain, sure (adj)	уверенный	[uvérenij]
uncertainty	неуверенность (ж)	[neuvérenɔstʲ]
uncertain (adj)	неуверенный	[neuvérennij]

drunk (adj)	пьяный	[pjánij]
sober (adj)	трезвый	[trézvij]
weak (adj)	слабый	[slábij]
to scare (vt)	испугать (св, пх)	[ispugátʲ]
fury (madness)	бешенство (с)	[béʃɛnstvɔ]

rage (fury)	ярость (ж)	[járɔstʲ]
depression	депрессия (ж)	[deprésija]
discomfort (unease)	дискомфорт (м)	[diskɔmfórt]
comfort	комфорт (м)	[kɔmfórt]
to regret (be sorry)	сожалеть (нсв, нпх)	[sɔʒilétʲ]
regret	сожаление (с)	[sɔʒilénie]
bad luck	невезение (с)	[nevezénie]
sadness	огорчение (с)	[ɔgɔrtʃénie]

shame (remorse)	стыд (м)	[stĩd]
gladness	веселье (с)	[vesélje]
enthusiasm, zeal	энтузиазм (м)	[ɛntuziázm]
enthusiast	энтузиаст (м)	[ɛntuziást]
to show enthusiasm	проявить энтузиазм	[prɔjivítʲ ɛntuziázm]

59. Character. Personality

character	характер (м)	[harákter]
character flaw	недостаток (м)	[nedɔstátɔk]
mind	ум (м)	[úm]
reason	разум (м)	[rázum]

conscience	совесть (ж)	[sóvestʲ]
habit (custom)	привычка (ж)	[privĩtʃka]
ability (talent)	способность (ж)	[spɔsóbnɔstʲ]
can (e.g., ~ swim)	уметь	[umétʲ]

patient (adj)	терпеливый	[terpelívij]
impatient (adj)	нетерпеливый	[neterpelívij]
curious (inquisitive)	любопытный	[lʲubɔpĩtnij]
curiosity	любопытство (с)	[lʲubɔpĩtstvɔ]

modesty	скромность (ж)	[skrómnɔstʲ]
modest (adj)	скромный	[skrómnij]
immodest (adj)	нескромный	[neskrómnij]

laziness	лень (ж)	[lénʲ]
lazy (adj)	ленивый	[lenívij]
lazy person (masc.)	лентяй (м)	[lentʲáj]

cunning (n)	хитрость (ж)	[hítrɔstʲ]
cunning (as adj)	хитрый	[hítrij]
distrust	недоверие (с)	[nedɔvérie]
distrustful (adj)	недоверчивый	[nedɔvértʃivij]

generosity	щедрость (ж)	[ʃʲédrɔstʲ]
generous (adj)	щедрый	[ʃʲédrij]
talented (adj)	талантливый	[talántlivij]
talent	талант (м)	[talánt]
courageous (adj)	смелый	[smélij]

courage	смелость (ж)	[smélost']
honest (adj)	честный	[tʃésnij]
honesty	честность (ж)	[tʃésnost']
careful (cautious)	осторожный	[ɔstɔróʒnij]
brave (courageous)	отважный	[ɔtváʒnij]
serious (adj)	серьёзный	[serjǿznij]
strict (severe, stern)	строгий	[strógij]
decisive (adj)	решительный	[reʃítel'nij]
indecisive (adj)	нерешительный	[nereʃítel'nij]
shy, timid (adj)	робкий	[rópkij]
shyness, timidity	робость (ж)	[róbost']
confidence (trust)	доверие (с)	[dɔvérie]
to believe (trust)	верить (нсв, пх)	[vérit']
trusting (credulous)	доверчивый	[dɔvértʃivij]
sincerely (adv)	искренне	[ískrene]
sincere (adj)	искренний	[ískrenij]
sincerity	искренность (ж)	[ískrenost']
open (person)	открытый	[ɔtkrĩtij]
calm (adj)	тихий	[tíhij]
frank (sincere)	откровенный	[ɔtkrɔvénnij]
naïve (adj)	наивный	[naívnij]
absent-minded (adj)	рассеянный	[rasséinij]
funny (odd)	смешной	[smeʃnój]
greed, stinginess	жадность (ж)	[ʒádnost']
greedy, stingy (adj)	жадный	[ʒádnij]
stingy (adj)	скупой	[skupój]
evil (adj)	злой	[zlój]
stubborn (adj)	упрямый	[upr'ámij]
unpleasant (adj)	неприятный	[neprijátnij]
selfish person (masc.)	эгоист (м)	[ɛgɔíst]
selfish (adj)	эгоистичный	[ɛgɔistítʃnij]
coward	трус (м)	[trús]
cowardly (adj)	трусливый	[truslívij]

60. Sleep. Dreams

to sleep (vi)	спать (нсв, нпх)	[spát']
sleep, sleeping	сон (м)	[són]
dream	сон (м)	[són]
to dream (in sleep)	видеть сны	[vídet' snĩ]
sleepy (adj)	сонный	[sónnij]
bed	кровать (ж)	[krɔvát']
mattress	матрас (м)	[matrás]

blanket (comforter)	одеяло (c)	[ɔdejálɔ]
pillow	подушка (ж)	[pɔdúʃka]
sheet	простыня (ж)	[prɔstinʲá]

insomnia	бессонница (ж)	[bessónitsa]
sleepless (adj)	бессонный	[bessónij]
sleeping pill	снотворное (c)	[snɔtvórnɔe]
to take a sleeping pill	принять снотворное	[prinʲátʲ snɔtvórnɔe]

to feel sleepy	хотеть спать	[hɔtétʲ spátʲ]
to yawn (vi)	зевать (нсв, нпх)	[zevátʲ]
to go to bed	идти спать	[itʲtí spátʲ]
to make up the bed	стелить постель	[stelítʲ pɔstélʲ]
to fall asleep	заснуть (св, нпх)	[zasnútʲ]

nightmare	кошмар (м)	[kɔʃmár]
snore, snoring	храп (м)	[hráp]
to snore (vi)	храпеть (нсв, нпх)	[hrapétʲ]

alarm clock	будильник (м)	[budílʲnik]
to wake (vt)	разбудить (св, пх)	[razbudítʲ]
to wake up	просыпаться (св, возв)	[prɔsīpatsa]
to get up (vi)	вставать (нсв, нпх)	[fstavátʲ]
to wash up (wash face)	умываться (нсв, возв)	[umivátsa]

61. Humour. Laughter. Gladness

| humor (wit, fun) | юмор (м) | [júmɔr] |
| sense of humor | чувство юмора (c) | [ʧústvɔ júmɔra] |

to enjoy oneself	веселиться (нсв, возв)	[veselítsa]
cheerful (merry)	весёлый	[vesǿlij]
merriment (gaiety)	веселье (c)	[vesélje]

| smile | улыбка (ж) | [ulīpka] |
| to smile (vi) | улыбаться (нсв, возв) | [ulibátsa] |

to start laughing	засмеяться (св, возв)	[zasmejátsa]
to laugh (vi)	смеяться (нсв, возв)	[smejátsa]
laugh, laughter	смех (м)	[sméh]

anecdote	анекдот (м)	[anekdót]
funny (anecdote, etc.)	смешной	[smeʃnój]
funny (odd)	смешной	[smeʃnój]

to joke (vi)	шутить (нсв, нпх)	[ʃutítʲ]
joke (verbal)	шутка (ж)	[ʃútka]
joy (emotion)	радость (ж)	[rádɔstʲ]
to rejoice (vi)	радоваться (нсв, возв)	[rádɔvatsa]
joyful (adj)	радостный	[rádɔsnij]

62. Discussion, conversation. Part 1

communication	общение (c)	[ɔpʃénie]
to communicate	общаться (нсв, возв)	[ɔpʃátsa]
conversation	разговор (м)	[razgɔvór]
dialog	диалог (м)	[dialóg]
discussion (discourse)	дискуссия (ж)	[diskúsija]
dispute (debate)	спор (м)	[spór]
to dispute, debate	спорить (нсв, нпх)	[spóritʲ]
interlocutor	собеседник (м)	[sɔbesédnik]
topic (theme)	тема (ж)	[téma]
point of view	точка (ж) зрения	[tótʃka zrénija]
opinion (point of view)	мнение (c)	[mnénie]
speech (talk)	речь (ж)	[rétʃʲ]
discussion (of report, etc.)	обсуждение (c)	[ɔpsuʒdénie]
to discuss (vt)	обсуждать (нсв, пх)	[ɔpsuʒdátʲ]
talk (conversation)	беседа (ж)	[beséda]
to talk (to chat)	беседовать (нсв, нпх)	[besédɔvatʲ]
meeting (encounter)	встреча (ж)	[fstrétʃa]
to meet (vi, vt)	встречаться (нсв, возв)	[fstretʃátsa]
proverb	пословица (ж)	[pɔslóvitsa]
saying	поговорка (ж)	[pɔgɔvórka]
riddle (poser)	загадка (ж)	[zagátka]
to pose a riddle	загадывать загадку	[zagádivatʲ zagátku]
password	пароль (м)	[parólʲ]
secret	секрет (м)	[sekrét]
oath (vow)	клятва (ж)	[klʲátva]
to swear (an oath)	клясться (нсв, возв)	[klʲástsa]
promise	обещание (c)	[ɔbeʃánie]
to promise (vt)	обещать (н/св, пх)	[ɔbeʃátʲ]
advice (counsel)	совет (м)	[sɔvét]
to advise (vt)	советовать (нсв, пх)	[sɔvétɔvatʲ]
to follow one's advice	следовать совету	[slédɔvatʲ sɔvétu]
to listen to ... (obey)	слушаться (нсв, возв)	[slúʃatsa]
news	новость (ж)	[nóvɔstʲ]
sensation (news)	сенсация (ж)	[sensátsija]
information (report)	сведения (мн)	[svédenja]
conclusion (decision)	вывод (м)	[vīvɔd]
voice	голос (ж)	[gólɔs]
compliment	комплимент (м)	[kɔmplimént]
kind (nice)	любезный	[lʲubéznɨj]
word	слово (c)	[slóvɔ]
phrase	фраза (ж)	[fráza]

answer	ответ (м)	[ɔtvét]
truth	правда (ж)	[právda]
lie	ложь (ж)	[lóʃ]

| thought | мысль (ж) | [mɨslʲ] |
| fantasy | фантазия (ж) | [fantázija] |

63. Discussion, conversation. Part 2

respected (adj)	уважаемый	[uvaʒáemij]
to respect (vt)	уважать (нсв, пх)	[uvaʒátʲ]
respect	уважение (с)	[uvaʒǽnie]
Dear ... (letter)	Уважаемый ...	[uvaʒáemij ...]

| to introduce (sb to sb) | познакомить (св, пх) | [pɔznakómitʲ] |
| to make acquaintance | познакомиться (св, возв) | [pɔznakómitsa] |

intention	намерение (с)	[namérenie]
to intend (have in mind)	намереваться (нсв, возв)	[namerevátsa]
wish	пожелание (с)	[pɔʒelánie]
to wish (~ good luck)	пожелать (св, пх)	[pɔʒelátʲ]

surprise (astonishment)	удивление (с)	[udivlénie]
to surprise (amaze)	удивлять (нсв, пх)	[udivlʲátʲ]
to be surprised	удивляться (нсв, возв)	[udivlʲátsa]

to give (vt)	дать (св, пх)	[dátʲ]
to take (get hold of)	взять (св, пх)	[vzʲátʲ]
to give back	вернуть (св, пх)	[vernútʲ]
to return (give back)	отдать (св, пх)	[ɔtdátʲ]

to apologize (vi)	извиняться (нсв, возв)	[izvinʲátsa]
apology	извинение (с)	[izvinénie]
to forgive (vt)	прощать (нсв, пх)	[prɔʃátʲ]

to talk (speak)	разговаривать (нсв, нпх)	[razgɔvárivatʲ]
to listen (vi)	слушать (нсв, пх)	[slúʃatʲ]
to hear out	выслушать (св, пх)	[vɨsluʃatʲ]
to understand (vt)	понять (св, пх)	[ponʲátʲ]

to show (to display)	показать (св, пх)	[pokazátʲ]
to look at ...	глядеть на ... (нсв)	[glʲadétʲ na ...]
to call (yell for sb)	позвать (св, пх)	[pozvátʲ]
to distract (disturb)	беспокоить (нсв, пх)	[bespɔkóitʲ]
to disturb (vt)	мешать (нсв, пх)	[meʃátʲ]
to pass (to hand sth)	передать (св, пх)	[peredátʲ]

demand (request)	просьба (ж)	[prósʲba]
to request (ask)	просить (нсв, пх)	[prosítʲ]
demand (firm request)	требование (с)	[trébɔvanie]

to demand (request firmly)	**требовать** (нсв, пх)	[trébɔvatʲ]
to tease (call names)	**дразнить** (нсв, пх)	[draznítʲ]
to mock (make fun of)	**насмехаться** (нсв, возв)	[nasmehátsa]
mockery, derision	**насмешка** (ж)	[nasméʃka]
nickname	**прозвище** (с)	[prózviʃʲe]

insinuation	**намёк** (м)	[namǿk]
to insinuate (imply)	**намекать** (нсв, н/пх)	[namekátʲ]
to mean (vt)	**подразумевать** (нсв, пх)	[pɔdrazumevátʲ]

description	**описание** (с)	[ɔpisánie]
to describe (vt)	**описать** (нсв, пх)	[ɔpisátʲ]
praise (compliments)	**похвала** (ж)	[pɔhvalá]
to praise (vt)	**похвалить** (св, пх)	[pɔhvalítʲ]

disappointment	**разочарование** (с)	[razɔtʃarɔvánie]
to disappoint (vt)	**разочаровать** (св, пх)	[razɔtʃarɔvátʲ]
to be disappointed	**разочароваться** (св, возв)	[razɔtʃarɔvátsa]

supposition	**предположение** (с)	[pretpɔlɔʒǽnie]
to suppose (assume)	**предполагать** (нсв, пх)	[pretpɔlagátʲ]
warning (caution)	**предостережение** (с)	[predɔstereʒǽnie]
to warn (vt)	**предостеречь** (св, пх)	[predɔsterétʲʃʲ]

64. Discussion, conversation. Part 3

| to talk into (convince) | **уговорить** (св, пх) | [ugɔvorítʲ] |
| to calm down (vt) | **успокаивать** (нсв, пх) | [uspɔkáivatʲ] |

silence (~ is golden)	**молчание** (с)	[mɔltʃánie]
to be silent (not speaking)	**молчать** (нсв, нпх)	[mɔltʃátʲ]
to whisper (vi, vt)	**шепнуть** (св, пх)	[ʃɛpnútʲ]
whisper	**шёпот** (м)	[ʃópɔt]

| frankly, sincerely (adv) | **откровенно** | [ɔtkrɔvénnɔ] |
| in my opinion … | **по моему мнению …** | [pɔ mɔemú mnéniju …] |

detail (of the story)	**подробность** (ж)	[pɔdróbnɔstʲ]
detailed (adj)	**подробный**	[pɔdróbnij]
in detail (adv)	**подробно**	[pɔdróbnɔ]

| hint, clue | **подсказка** (ж) | [pɔtskáska] |
| to give a hint | **подсказать** (св, пх) | [pɔtskazátʲ] |

look (glance)	**взгляд** (м)	[vzglʲád]
to have a look	**взглянуть** (св, нпх)	[vzglınútʲ]
fixed (look)	**неподвижный**	[nepɔdvíʒnij]
to blink (vi)	**моргать** (нсв, нпх)	[mɔrgátʲ]
to wink (vi)	**мигнуть** (св, нпх)	[mignútʲ]
to nod (in assent)	**кивнуть** (св, н/пх)	[kivnútʲ]

sigh	вздох (м)	[vzdóh]
to sigh (vi)	вздохнуть (св, нпх)	[vzdɔhnútʲ]
to shudder (vi)	вздрагивать (нсв, нпх)	[vzdrágivatʲ]
gesture	жест (м)	[ʒǽst]
to touch (one's arm, etc.)	прикоснуться (св, возв)	[prikɔsnútsa]
to seize	хватать (нсв, пх)	[hvatátʲ]
(e.g., ~ by the arm)		
to tap (on the shoulder)	хлопать (нсв, нпх)	[hlópatʲ]

Look out!	Осторожно!	[ɔstɔróʒnɔ]
Really?	Неужели?	[neuʒǽli?]
Are you sure?	Ты уверен?	[tĭ uvéren?]
Good luck!	Удачи!	[udátʃi]
I see!	Ясно!	[jásnɔ]
What a pity!	Жаль!	[ʒálʲ]

65. Agreement. Refusal

consent	согласие (с)	[sɔglásie]
to consent (vi)	соглашаться (нсв, возв)	[sɔglaʃátsa]
approval	одобрение (с)	[ɔdobrénie]
to approve (vt)	одобрить (св, пх)	[ɔdóbritʲ]
refusal	отказ (м)	[ɔtkás]
to refuse (vi, vt)	отказываться (нсв, возв)	[ɔtkázivatsa]

Great!	Отлично!	[ɔtlítʃnɔ]
All right!	Хорошо!	[hɔrɔʃó]
Okay! (I agree)	Ладно!	[ládnɔ]

forbidden (adj)	запрещённый	[zapreʃǿnij]
it's forbidden	нельзя	[nelʲzʲá]
it's impossible	невозможно	[nevozmóʒnɔ]
incorrect (adj)	неправильный	[neprávilʲnij]

to reject (~ a demand)	отклонить (св, пх)	[ɔtklɔnítʲ]
to support (cause, idea)	поддержать (св, пх)	[pɔdderʒátʲ]
to accept (~ an apology)	принять (св, пх)	[prinʲátʲ]

to confirm (vt)	подтвердить (св, пх)	[pɔttverdítʲ]
confirmation	подтверждение (с)	[pɔttverʒdénie]
permission	разрешение (с)	[razreʃǽnie]
to permit (vt)	разрешить (св, пх)	[razreʃítʲ]
decision	решение (с)	[reʃǽnie]
to say nothing	промолчать (св, нпх)	[prɔmɔltʃátʲ]
(hold one's tongue)		

condition (term)	условие (с)	[uslóvie]
excuse (pretext)	отговорка (ж)	[ɔdgɔvórka]
praise (compliments)	похвала (ж)	[pɔhvalá]
to praise (vt)	похвалить (св, пх)	[pɔhvalítʲ]

66. Success. Good luck. Failure

success	успех (м)	[uspéh]
successfully (adv)	успешно	[uspéʃnɔ]
successful (adj)	успешный	[uspéʃnij]
luck (good luck)	удача (ж)	[udátʃa]
Good luck!	Удачи!	[udátʃi]
lucky (e.g., ~ day)	удачный	[udátʃnij]
lucky (fortunate)	удачливый	[udátʃlivij]
failure	неудача (ж)	[neudátʃa]
misfortune	неудача (ж)	[neudátʃa]
bad luck	невезение (с)	[nevezénie]
unsuccessful (adj)	неудачный	[neudátʃnij]
catastrophe	катастрофа (ж)	[katastrófa]
pride	гордость (ж)	[górdɔstʲ]
proud (adj)	гордый	[górdij]
to be proud	гордиться (нсв, возв)	[gɔrdítsa]
winner	победитель (м)	[pɔbedítelʲ]
to win (vi)	победить (св, нпх)	[pɔbedítʲ]
to lose (not win)	проиграть (св, нпх)	[prɔigrátʲ]
try	попытка (ж)	[pɔpïtka]
to try (vi)	пытаться (нсв, возв)	[pitátsa]
chance (opportunity)	шанс (м)	[ʃáns]

67. Quarrels. Negative emotions

shout (scream)	крик (м)	[krík]
to shout (vi)	кричать (нсв, нпх)	[kritʃátʲ]
to start to cry out	закричать (св, нпх)	[zakritʃátʲ]
quarrel	ссора (ж)	[ssóra]
to quarrel (vi)	ссориться (нсв, возв)	[ssóritsa]
fight (squabble)	скандал (м)	[skandál]
to make a scene	скандалить (нсв, нпх)	[skandálitʲ]
conflict	конфликт (м)	[kɔnflíkt]
misunderstanding	недоразумение (с)	[nedɔrazuménie]
insult	оскорбление (с)	[ɔskɔrblénie]
to insult (vt)	оскорблять (нсв, пх)	[ɔskɔrblʲátʲ]
insulted (adj)	оскорблённый	[ɔskɔrblɵnnij]
resentment	обида (ж)	[ɔbída]
to offend (vt)	обидеть (св, пх)	[ɔbídetʲ]
to take offense	обидеться (св, возв)	[ɔbídetsa]
indignation	возмущение (с)	[vɔzmuʃénie]
to be indignant	возмущаться (нсв, возв)	[vɔzmuʃátsa]

| complaint | жалоба (ж) | [ʒálɔba] |
| to complain (vi, vt) | жаловаться (нсв, возв) | [ʒálɔvatsa] |

apology	извинение (с)	[izvinénie]
to apologize (vi)	извиняться (нсв, возв)	[izvinʲátsa]
to beg pardon	просить прощения	[prɔsítʲ prɔʃénija]

criticism	критика (ж)	[krítika]
to criticize (vt)	критиковать (нсв, пх)	[kritikɔvátʲ]
accusation (charge)	обвинение (с)	[ɔbvinénie]
to accuse (vt)	обвинять (нсв, пх)	[ɔbvinʲátʲ]

revenge	месть (ж)	[méstʲ]
to avenge (get revenge)	мстить (нсв, пх)	[mstítʲ]
to pay back	отплатить (св, пх)	[ɔtplatítʲ]

disdain	презрение (с)	[prezrénie]
to despise (vt)	презирать (нсв, пх)	[prezirátʲ]
hatred, hate	ненависть (ж)	[nénavistʲ]
to hate (vt)	ненавидеть (нсв, пх)	[nenavídetʲ]

nervous (adj)	нервный	[nérvnij]
to be nervous	нервничать (нсв, нпх)	[nérvnitʃatʲ]
angry (mad)	сердитый	[serdítij]
to make angry	рассердить (св, пх)	[rasserdítʲ]

humiliation	унижение (с)	[uniʒǽnie]
to humiliate (vt)	унижать (нсв, пх)	[uniʒátʲ]
to humiliate oneself	унижаться (нсв, возв)	[uniʒátsa]

| shock | шок (м) | [ʃók] |
| to shock (vt) | шокировать (н/св, пх) | [ʃɔkírɔvatʲ] |

| trouble (e.g., serious ~) | неприятность (ж) | [neprijátnɔstʲ] |
| unpleasant (adj) | неприятный | [neprijátnij] |

fear (dread)	страх (м)	[stráh]
terrible (storm, heat)	страшный	[stráʃnij]
scary (e.g., ~ story)	страшный	[stráʃnij]
horror	ужас (м)	[úʒas]
awful (crime, news)	ужасный	[uʒásnij]

to begin to tremble	задрожать (нсв, нпх)	[zadrɔʒátʲ]
to cry (weep)	плакать (нсв, нпх)	[plákatʲ]
to start crying	заплакать (св, нпх)	[zaplákatʲ]
tear	слеза (мн)	[slezá]

fault	вина (ж)	[viná]
guilt (feeling)	вина (ж)	[viná]
dishonor (disgrace)	позор (м)	[pɔzór]
protest	протест (м)	[prɔtést]
stress	стресс (м)	[strés]

to disturb (vt)	**беспокоить** (нсв, пх)	[bespɔkóitʲ]
to be furious	**злиться** (нсв, возв)	[zlítsa]
mad, angry (adj)	**злой**	[zlój]
to end (~ a relationship)	**прекращать** (нсв, пх)	[prekraʃátʲ]
to swear (at sb)	**ругаться** (нсв, возв)	[rugátsa]
to scare (become afraid)	**пугаться** (нсв, возв)	[pugátsa]
to hit (strike with hand)	**ударить** (св, пх)	[udáritʲ]
to fight (street fight, etc.)	**драться** (нсв, возв)	[drátsa]
to settle (a conflict)	**урегулировать** (св, пх)	[uregulírɔvatʲ]
discontented (adj)	**недовольный**	[nedɔvólʲnij]
furious (adj)	**яростный**	[járɔsnij]
It's not good!	**Это нехорошо!**	[ǽtɔ nehɔrɔʃó]
It's bad!	**Это плохо!**	[ǽtɔ plóhɔ]

Medicine

sickness	**болезнь** (ж)	[bɔléznʲ]
to be sick	**болеть** (нсв, нпх)	[bɔlétʲ]
health	**здоровье** (с)	[zdɔróvje]

runny nose (coryza)	**насморк** (м)	[násmɔrk]
tonsillitis	**ангина** (ж)	[angína]
cold (illness)	**простуда** (ж)	[prɔstúda]
to catch a cold	**простудиться** (св, возв)	[prɔstudítsa]

bronchitis	**бронхит** (м)	[brɔnhít]
pneumonia	**воспаление** (с) **лёгких**	[vɔspalénie lɵ́hkih]
flu, influenza	**грипп** (м)	[gríp]

nearsighted (adj)	**близорукий**	[blizɔrúkij]
farsighted (adj)	**дальнозоркий**	[dalʲnɔzórkij]
strabismus (crossed eyes)	**косоглазие** (с)	[kɔsɔglázie]
cross-eyed (adj)	**косоглазый**	[kɔsɔglázij]
cataract	**катаракта** (ж)	[katarákta]
glaucoma	**глаукома** (ж)	[glaukóma]

stroke	**инсульт** (м)	[insúlʲt]
heart attack	**инфаркт** (м)	[infárkt]
myocardial infarction	**инфаркт** (м) **миокарда**	[infárkt miɔkárda]
paralysis	**паралич** (м)	[paralíʧ]
to paralyze (vt)	**парализовать** (нсв, пх)	[paralizɔvátʲ]

allergy	**аллергия** (ж)	[alergíja]
asthma	**астма** (ж)	[ástma]
diabetes	**диабет** (м)	[diabét]

toothache	**зубная боль** (ж)	[zubnája bólʲ]
caries	**кариес** (м)	[káries]

diarrhea	**диарея** (ж)	[diaréja]
constipation	**запор** (м)	[zapór]
stomach upset	**расстройство** (с) **желудка**	[rastrójstvɔ ʒelútka]
food poisoning	**отравление** (с)	[ɔtravlénie]
to get food poisoning	**отравиться** (св, возв)	[ɔtravítsa]

arthritis	**артрит** (м)	[artrít]
rickets	**рахит** (м)	[rahít]

| rheumatism | ревматизм (м) | [revmatízm] |
| atherosclerosis | атеросклероз (м) | [atɛrɔsklerós] |

gastritis	гастрит (м)	[gastrít]
appendicitis	аппендицит (м)	[apendiʦít]
cholecystitis	холецистит (м)	[hɔleʦistít]
ulcer	язва (ж)	[jázva]

measles	корь (ж)	[kórʲ]
rubella (German measles)	краснуха (ж)	[krasnúha]
jaundice	желтуха (ж)	[ʒeltúha]
hepatitis	гепатит (м)	[gepatít]

schizophrenia	шизофрения (ж)	[ʃizɔfreníja]
rabies (hydrophobia)	бешенство (с)	[béʃɛnstvɔ]
neurosis	невроз (м)	[nevrós]
concussion	сотрясение (с) мозга	[sɔtrɪsénie mózga]

cancer	рак (м)	[rák]
sclerosis	склероз (м)	[sklerós]
multiple sclerosis	рассеянный склероз (м)	[rasséɪnnij sklerós]

alcoholism	алкоголизм (м)	[alkɔgɔlízm]
alcoholic (n)	алкоголик (м)	[alkɔgólik]
syphilis	сифилис (м)	[sífilis]
AIDS	СПИД (м)	[spíd]

tumor	опухоль (ж)	[ópuhɔlʲ]
malignant (adj)	злокачественная	[zlɔkátʃestvenaja]
benign (adj)	доброкачественная	[dɔbrɔkátʃestvenaja]

fever	лихорадка (ж)	[lihɔrátka]
malaria	малярия (ж)	[malîrîja]
gangrene	гангрена (ж)	[gangréna]
seasickness	морская болезнь (ж)	[mɔrskája bɔléznʲ]
epilepsy	эпилепсия (ж)	[ɛpilépsija]

epidemic	эпидемия (ж)	[ɛpidémija]
typhus	тиф (м)	[tíf]
tuberculosis	туберкулёз (м)	[tuberkulǿs]
cholera	холера (ж)	[hɔléra]
plague (bubonic ~)	чума (ж)	[ʧʲumá]

69. Symptoms. Treatments. Part 1

symptom	симптом (м)	[simptóm]
temperature	температура (ж)	[temperatúra]
high temperature (fever)	высокая температура (ж)	[visókaja temperatúra]
pulse (heartbeat)	пульс (м)	[púlʲs]

dizziness (vertigo)	**головокружение** (c)	[gólovo·kruʒǽnie]
hot (adj)	**горячий**	[gorʲátʃij]
shivering	**озноб** (м)	[oznób]
pale (e.g., ~ face)	**бледный**	[blédnʲij]

cough	**кашель** (м)	[káʃelʲ]
to cough (vi)	**кашлять** (нсв, нпх)	[káʃlʲitʲ]
to sneeze (vi)	**чихать** (нсв, нпх)	[tʃihátʲ]
faint	**обморок** (м)	[óbmorok]
to faint (vi)	**упасть в обморок**	[upástʲ v óbmorok]

bruise (hématome)	**синяк** (м)	[sinʲák]
bump (lump)	**шишка** (ж)	[ʃʃka]
to bang (bump)	**удариться** (св, возв)	[udáritsa]
contusion (bruise)	**ушиб** (м)	[uʃíb]
to get a bruise	**ударить ...** (св, пх)	[udáritʲ ...]

to limp (vi)	**хромать** (нсв, нпх)	[hromátʲ]
dislocation	**вывих** (м)	[vívih]
to dislocate (vt)	**вывихнуть** (св, пх)	[vívihnutʲ]
fracture	**перелом** (м)	[perelóm]
to have a fracture	**получить перелом**	[polutʃítʲ perelóm]

cut (e.g., paper ~)	**порез** (м)	[porés]
to cut oneself	**порезаться** (св, возв)	[porézatsa]
bleeding	**кровотечение** (c)	[krovo·tetʃénie]

burn (injury)	**ожог** (м)	[oʒóg]
to get burned	**обжечься** (св, возв)	[obʒǽtʃsʲa]

to prick (vt)	**уколоть** (св, пх)	[ukolótʲ]
to prick oneself	**уколоться** (св, возв)	[ukolótsa]
to injure (vt)	**повредить** (св, пх)	[povredítʲ]
injury	**повреждение** (c)	[povreʒdénie]
wound	**рана** (ж)	[rána]
trauma	**травма** (ж)	[trávma]

to be delirious	**бредить** (нсв, нпх)	[bréditʲ]
to stutter (vi)	**заикаться** (нсв, возв)	[zaikátsa]
sunstroke	**солнечный удар** (м)	[sólnetʃnij udár]

70. Symptoms. Treatments. Part 2

pain, ache	**боль** (ж)	[bólʲ]
splinter (in foot, etc.)	**заноза** (ж)	[zanóza]

sweat (perspiration)	**пот** (м)	[pót]
to sweat (perspire)	**потеть** (нсв, нпх)	[potétʲ]
vomiting	**рвота** (ж)	[rvóta]
convulsions	**судороги** (ж мн)	[súdorogi]

pregnant (adj)	беременная	[berémennaja]
to be born	родиться (св, возв)	[rɔdítsa]
delivery, labor	роды (мн)	[ródi]
to deliver (~ a baby)	рожать (нсв, пх)	[rɔʒátʲ]
abortion	аборт (м)	[abórt]

breathing, respiration	дыхание (с)	[dihánie]
in-breath (inhalation)	вдох (м)	[vdóh]
out-breath (exhalation)	выдох (м)	[vĩdɔh]
to exhale (breathe out)	выдохнуть (св, пх)	[vĩdɔhnutʲ]
to inhale (vi)	вдыхать (нсв, нпх)	[vdihátʲ]

disabled person	инвалид (м)	[invalíd]
cripple	калека (с)	[kaléka]
drug addict	наркоман (м)	[narkɔmán]

deaf (adj)	глухой	[gluhój]
mute (adj)	немой	[nemój]
deaf mute (adj)	глухонемой	[gluhɔ·nemój]

mad, insane (adj)	сумасшедший	[sumaʃǽdʃɛj]
madman (demented person)	сумасшедший (м)	[sumaʃǽdʃɛj]
madwoman	сумасшедшая (ж)	[sumaʃǽdʃaja]
to go insane	сойти с ума	[sɔjtí s umá]

gene	ген (м)	[gén]
immunity	иммунитет (м)	[imunitét]
hereditary (adj)	наследственный	[naslétstvenij]
congenital (adj)	врождённый	[vrɔʒdǿnij]

virus	вирус (м)	[vírus]
microbe	микроб (м)	[mikrób]
bacterium	бактерия (ж)	[baktǽrija]
infection	инфекция (ж)	[inféktsija]

71. Symptoms. Treatments. Part 3

| hospital | больница (ж) | [bɔlʲnítsa] |
| patient | пациент (м) | [patsiǽnt] |

diagnosis	диагноз (м)	[diágnɔs]
cure	лечение (с)	[letʃénie]
medical treatment	лечение (с)	[letʃénie]
to get treatment	лечиться (нсв, возв)	[letʃítsa]
to treat (~ a patient)	лечить (нсв, пх)	[letʃítʲ]
to nurse (look after)	ухаживать (нсв, нпх)	[uháʒivatʲ]
care (nursing ~)	уход (м)	[uhód]
operation, surgery	операция (ж)	[ɔperátsija]
to bandage (head, limb)	перевязать (св, пх)	[perevizátʲ]

bandaging	перевязка (ж)	[perevʲázka]
vaccination	прививка (ж)	[privífka]
to vaccinate (vt)	делать прививку	[délatʲ privífku]
injection, shot	укол (м)	[ukól]
to give an injection	делать укол	[délatʲ ukól]

amputation	ампутация (ж)	[amputátsija]
to amputate (vt)	ампутировать (н/св, пх)	[amputírovatʲ]
coma	кома (ж)	[kóma]
to be in a coma	быть в коме	[bɨtʲ f kóme]
intensive care	реанимация (ж)	[reanimátsija]

to recover (~ from flu)	выздоравливать (нсв, нпх)	[vɨzdɔrávlivatʲ]
condition (patient's ~)	состояние (с)	[sɔstɔjánie]
consciousness	сознание (с)	[sɔznánie]
memory (faculty)	память (ж)	[pámʲtʲ]

to pull out (tooth)	удалять (нсв, пх)	[udalʲátʲ]
filling	пломба (ж)	[plómba]
to fill (a tooth)	пломбировать (нсв, пх)	[plɔmbirɔvátʲ]

| hypnosis | гипноз (м) | [gipnós] |
| to hypnotize (vt) | гипнотизировать (нсв, пх) | [gipnɔtizírovatʲ] |

72. Doctors

doctor	врач (м)	[vrátʃ]
nurse	медсестра (ж)	[metsestrá]
personal doctor	личный врач (м)	[lítʃnij vrátʃ]

dentist	стоматолог (м)	[stɔmatólɔg]
eye doctor	окулист (м)	[ɔkulíst]
internist	терапевт (м)	[terapévt]
surgeon	хирург (м)	[hirúrg]

psychiatrist	психиатр (м)	[psihiátr]
pediatrician	педиатр (м)	[pediátr]
psychologist	психолог (м)	[psihólɔg]
gynecologist	гинеколог (м)	[ginekólɔg]
cardiologist	кардиолог (м)	[kardiólɔg]

73. Medicine. Drugs. Accessories

medicine, drug	лекарство (с)	[lekárstvɔ]
remedy	средство (с)	[srétstvɔ]
to prescribe (vt)	прописать (нсв, пх)	[prɔpisátʲ]
prescription	рецепт (м)	[retsæpt]
tablet, pill	таблетка (ж)	[tablétka]

ointment	мазь (ж)	[másʲ]
ampule	ампула (ж)	[ámpula]
mixture, solution	микстура (ж)	[mikstúra]
syrup	сироп (м)	[siróp]
capsule	пилюля (ж)	[pilʲúlʲa]
powder	порошок (м)	[pɔrɔʃók]

gauze bandage	бинт (м)	[bínt]
cotton wool	вата (ж)	[váta]
iodine	йод (м)	[jód]

Band-Aid	лейкопластырь (м)	[lejkɔplástirʲ]
eyedropper	пипетка (ж)	[pipétka]
thermometer	градусник (м)	[grádusnik]
syringe	шприц (м)	[ʃpríts]

| wheelchair | коляска (ж) | [kɔlʲáska] |
| crutches | костыли (м мн) | [kɔstɨlʲí] |

painkiller	обезболивающее (с)	[ɔbezbólivajuʃee]
laxative	слабительное (с)	[slabítelʲnɔe]
spirits (ethanol)	спирт (м)	[spírt]
medicinal herbs	трава (ж)	[travá]
herbal (~ tea)	травяной	[travɪnój]

74. Smoking. Tobacco products

tobacco	табак (м)	[tabák]
cigarette	сигарета (ж)	[sigaréta]
cigar	сигара (ж)	[sigára]
pipe	трубка (ж)	[trúpka]
pack (of cigarettes)	пачка (ж)	[pátʃka]

matches	спички (ж мн)	[spítʃki]
matchbox	спичечный коробок (м)	[spítʃetʃnɨj kɔrɔbók]
lighter	зажигалка (ж)	[zaʒigálka]
ashtray	пепельница (ж)	[pépelʲnitsa]
cigarette case	портсигар (м)	[pɔrtsigár]

| cigarette holder | мундштук (м) | [munʃtúk] |
| filter (cigarette tip) | фильтр (м) | [fílʲtr] |

to smoke (vi, vt)	курить (нсв, н/пх)	[kurítʲ]
to light a cigarette	прикурить (св, н/пх)	[prikurítʲ]
smoking	курение (с)	[kurénie]
smoker	курильщик (м)	[kurílʲʃik]

stub, butt (of cigarette)	окурок (м)	[ɔkúrɔk]
smoke, fumes	дым (м)	[dɨ̃m]
ash	пепел (м)	[pépel]

HUMAN HABITAT

City

city, town	город (м)	[górɔd]
capital city	столица (ж)	[stɔlítsa]
village	деревня (ж)	[derévnʲa]
city map	план (м) города	[plán górɔda]
downtown	центр (м) города	[ʦæntr górɔda]
suburb	пригород (м)	[prígɔrɔd]
suburban (adj)	пригородный	[prígɔrɔdnij]
outskirts	окраина (ж)	[ɔkráina]
environs (suburbs)	окрестности (ж мн)	[ɔkrésnɔsti]
city block	квартал (м)	[kvartál]
residential block (area)	жилой квартал (м)	[ʒilój kvartál]
traffic	движение (с)	[dviʒǽnie]
traffic lights	светофор (м)	[svetɔfór]
public transportation	городской транспорт (м)	[gɔrɔtskój tránspɔrt]
intersection	перекрёсток (м)	[perekrǿstɔk]
crosswalk	переход (м)	[perehód]
pedestrian underpass	подземный переход (м)	[pɔdzémnij perehód]
to cross (~ the street)	переходить (нсв, н/пх)	[perehɔdítʲ]
pedestrian	пешеход (м)	[peʃɛhód]
sidewalk	тротуар (м)	[trɔtuár]
bridge	мост (м)	[móst]
embankment (river walk)	набережная (ж)	[nábereʒnaja]
fountain	фонтан (м)	[fɔntán]
allée (garden walkway)	аллея (ж)	[aléja]
park	парк (м)	[párk]
boulevard	бульвар (м)	[bulʲvár]
square	площадь (ж)	[plóʃʲatʲ]
avenue (wide street)	проспект (м)	[prɔspékt]
street	улица (ж)	[úliʦa]
side street	переулок (м)	[pereúlɔk]
dead end	тупик (м)	[tupík]
house	дом (м)	[dóm]
building	здание (с)	[zdánie]

skyscraper	небоскрёб (м)	[nebɔskrǿb]
facade	фасад (м)	[fasád]
roof	крыша (ж)	[krɨ́ʃa]
window	окно (с)	[ɔknó]
arch	арка (ж)	[árka]
column	колонна (ж)	[kɔlóna]
corner	угол (м)	[úgɔl]

store window	витрина (ж)	[vitrína]
signboard (store sign, etc.)	вывеска (ж)	[vɨ́veska]
poster (e.g., playbill)	афиша (ж)	[afíʃa]
advertising poster	рекламный плакат (м)	[reklámnij plakát]
billboard	рекламный щит (м)	[reklámnij ʃʲít]

garbage, trash	мусор (м)	[músɔr]
trash can (public ~)	урна (ж)	[úrna]
to litter (vi)	сорить (нсв, нпх)	[sɔrítʲ]
garbage dump	свалка (ж)	[swálka]

phone booth	телефонная будка (ж)	[telefónnaja bútka]
lamppost	фонарный столб (м)	[fɔnárnij stólb]
bench (park ~)	скамейка (ж)	[skaméjka]

police officer	полицейский (м)	[pɔlitsǽjskij]
police	полиция (ж)	[pɔlítsija]
beggar	нищий (м)	[níʃʲij]
homeless (n)	бездомный (м)	[bezdómnij]

76. Urban institutions

store	магазин (м)	[magazín]
drugstore, pharmacy	аптека (ж)	[aptéka]
eyeglass store	оптика (ж)	[óptika]
shopping mall	торговый центр (м)	[tɔrgóvij ʦǽntr]
supermarket	супермаркет (м)	[supermárket]

bakery	булочная (ж)	[búlɔʧnaja]
baker	пекарь (м)	[pékarʲ]
pastry shop	кондитерская (ж)	[kɔndíterskaja]
grocery store	продуктовый магазин (м)	[prɔduktóvij magazín]

| butcher shop | мясная лавка (ж) | [mɪsnája láfka] |

| produce store | овощная лавка (ж) | [ɔvɔʃʲnája láfka] |
| market | рынок (м) | [rɨ́nɔk] |

coffee house	кафе (с)	[kafǽ]
restaurant	ресторан (м)	[restɔrán]
pub, bar	пивная (ж)	[pivnája]
pizzeria	пиццерия (ж)	[pitsǽrija], [pitsɛríja]

hair salon	парикмахерская (ж)	[parihmáherskaja]
post office	почта (ж)	[pótʃta]
dry cleaners	химчистка (ж)	[himtʃístka]
photo studio	фотоателье (с)	[foto·atɛljé]

shoe store	обувной магазин (м)	[ɔbuvnój magazín]
bookstore	книжный магазин (м)	[kníʒnij magazín]
sporting goods store	спортивный магазин (м)	[sportívnij magazín]

clothes repair shop	ремонт (м) одежды	[remónt ɔdéʒdi]
formal wear rental	прокат (м) одежды	[prɔkát ɔdéʒdi]
video rental store	прокат (м) фильмов	[prɔkát fílʲmɔf]

circus	цирк (м)	[tsïrk]
zoo	зоопарк (м)	[zɔɔpárk]
movie theater	кинотеатр (м)	[kinɔteátr]
museum	музей (м)	[muzéj]
library	библиотека (ж)	[bibliɔtéka]

theater	театр (м)	[teátr]
opera (opera house)	опера (ж)·	[ópera]
nightclub	ночной клуб (м)	[nɔtʃnój klúb]
casino	казино (с)	[kazinó]

mosque	мечеть (ж)	[metʃétʲ]
synagogue	синагога (ж)	[sinagóga]
cathedral	собор (м)	[sɔbór]

| temple | храм (м) | [hrám] |
| church | церковь (ж) | [tsǽrkɔfʲ] |

college	институт (м)	[institút]
university	университет (м)	[universitét]
school	школа (ж)	[ʃkóla]

| prefecture | префектура (ж) | [prefektúra] |
| city hall | мэрия (ж) | [mǽrija] |

| hotel | гостиница (ж) | [gɔstínitsa] |
| bank | банк (м) | [bánk] |

| embassy | посольство (с) | [pɔsólʲstvɔ] |
| travel agency | турагентство (с) | [tur·agénstvɔ] |

| information office | справочное бюро (с) | [správɔtʃnɔe bʲuró] |
| currency exchange | обменный пункт (м) | [ɔbménnij púnkt] |

| subway | метро (с) | [metró] |
| hospital | больница (ж) | [bɔlʲnítsa] |

| gas station | автозаправка (ж) | [afto·zapráfka] |
| parking lot | стоянка (ж) | [stɔjánka] |

77. Urban transportation

bus	**автобус** (м)	[aftóbus]
streetcar	**трамвай** (м)	[tramváj]
trolley bus	**троллейбус** (м)	[trɔléjbus]
route (of bus, etc.)	**маршрут** (м)	[marʃrút]
number (e.g., bus ~)	**номер** (м)	[nómer]
to go by …	**ехать на …** (нсв)	[éhatʲ na …]
to get on (~ the bus)	**сесть на …** (св)	[séstʲ na …]
to get off …	**сойти с …** (св)	[sɔjtí s …]
stop (e.g., bus ~)	**остановка** (ж)	[ɔstanófka]
next stop	**следующая остановка** (ж)	[sléduʃaja ɔstanófka]
terminus	**конечная остановка** (ж)	[kɔnétʃnaja ɔstanófka]
schedule	**расписание** (с)	[raspisánie]
to wait (vt)	**ждать** (нсв, пх)	[ʒdátʲ]
ticket	**билет** (м)	[bilét]
fare	**стоимость** (ж) **билета**	[stóimɔstʲ biléta]
cashier (ticket seller)	**кассир** (м)	[kassír]
ticket inspection	**контроль** (м)	[kɔntrólʲ]
ticket inspector	**контролёр** (м)	[kɔntrɔlǿr]
to be late (for …)	**опаздывать на …** (нсв, нпх)	[ɔpázdivatʲ na …]
to miss (~ the train, etc.)	**опоздать на …** (св, нпх)	[ɔpɔzdátʲ na …]
to be in a hurry	**спешить** (нсв, нпх)	[speʃítʲ]
taxi, cab	**такси** (с)	[taksí]
taxi driver	**таксист** (м)	[taksíst]
by taxi	**на такси**	[na taksí]
taxi stand	**стоянка** (ж) **такси**	[stɔjánka taksí]
to call a taxi	**вызвать такси**	[vízvatʲ taksí]
to take a taxi	**взять такси**	[vzʲátʲ taksí]
traffic	**уличное движение** (с)	[úlitʃnɔe dviʒǽnie]
traffic jam	**пробка** (ж)	[própka]
rush hour	**часы пик** (м)	[tʃasí pík]
to park (vi)	**парковаться** (нсв, возв)	[parkɔvátsa]
to park (vt)	**парковать** (нсв, пх)	[parkɔvátʲ]
parking lot	**стоянка** (ж)	[stɔjánka]
subway	**метро** (с)	[metró]
station	**станция** (ж)	[stántsija]
to take the subway	**ехать на метро**	[éhatʲ na metró]
train	**поезд** (м)	[póezd]
train station	**вокзал** (м)	[vɔkzál]

to deposit (vt)	положить (св, пх)	[pɔlɔʒítʲ]
to deposit into the account	положить на счёт	[pɔlɔʒítʲ na ʃǿt]
to withdraw (vt)	снять со счёта	[snʲátʲ sɔ ʃǿta]

credit card	кредитная карта (ж)	[kredítnaja kárta]
cash	наличные деньги (мн)	[nalítʃnʲe dénʲgi]
check	чек (м)	[tʃék]
to write a check	выписать чек	[vīpisatʲ tʃék]
checkbook	чековая книжка (ж)	[tʃékɔvaja kníʃka]

wallet	бумажник (м)	[bumáʒnik]
change purse	кошелёк (м)	[kɔʃɛlǿk]
safe	сейф (м)	[séjf]

heir	наследник (м)	[naslédnik]
inheritance	наследство (с)	[naslétstvɔ]
fortune (wealth)	состояние (с)	[sɔstɔjánie]

lease	аренда (ж)	[arénda]
rent (money)	квартирная плата (ж)	[kvartírnaja pláta]
to rent (sth from sb)	снимать (нсв, пх)	[snimátʲ]

price	цена (ж)	[tsɛná]
cost	стоимость (ж)	[stóimɔstʲ]
sum	сумма (ж)	[súmma]

to spend (vt)	тратить (нсв, пх)	[trátitʲ]
expenses	расходы (мн)	[rasxódi]
to economize (vi, vt)	экономить (нсв, н/пх)	[ɛkɔnómitʲ]
economical	экономный	[ɛkɔnómnij]

to pay (vi, vt)	платить (нсв, н/пх)	[platítʲ]
payment	оплата (ж)	[ɔpláta]
change (give the ~)	сдача (ж)	[zdátʃa]

tax	налог (м)	[nalóg]
fine	штраф (м)	[ʃtráf]
to fine (vt)	штрафовать (нсв, пх)	[ʃtrafovátʲ]

81. Post. Postal service

post office	почта (ж)	[pótʃta]
mail (letters, etc.)	почта (ж)	[pótʃta]
mailman	почтальон (м)	[pɔtʃtaljón]
opening hours	часы (мн) работы	[tʃasī rabóti]

letter	письмо (с)	[pisʲmó]
registered letter	заказное письмо (с)	[zakaznóe pisʲmó]
postcard	открытка (ж)	[ɔtkrītka]
telegram	телеграмма (ж)	[telegráma]

| package (parcel) | посылка (ж) | [pɔsɨ́lka] |
| money transfer | денежный перевод (м) | [déneʒnij perevód] |

to receive (vt)	получить (св, пх)	[pɔlutʃítʲ]
to send (vt)	отправить (св, пх)	[ɔtprávitʲ]
sending	отправка (ж)	[ɔtpráfka]

address	адрес (м)	[ádres]
ZIP code	индекс (м)	[índɛks]
sender	отправитель (м)	[ɔtpravítelʲ]
receiver	получатель (м)	[pɔlutʃátelʲ]

| name (first name) | имя (с) | [ímʲa] |
| surname (last name) | фамилия (ж) | [famílija] |

postage rate	тариф (м)	[taríf]
standard (adj)	обычный	[ɔbɨ́tʃnij]
economical (adj)	экономичный	[ɛkɔnɔmítʃnij]

weight	вес (м)	[vés]
to weigh (~ letters)	взвешивать (нсв, пх)	[vzvéʃivatʲ]
envelope	конверт (м)	[kɔnvért]
postage stamp	марка (ж)	[márka]
to stamp an envelope	наклеивать марку	[nakléivatʲ márku]

Dwelling. House. Home

82. House. Dwelling

house	дом (м)	[dóm]
at home (adv)	дома	[dóma]
yard	двор (м)	[dvór]
fence (iron ~)	ограда (ж)	[ɔgráda]
brick (n)	кирпич (м)	[kirpítʃ]
brick (as adj)	кирпичный	[kirpítʃnij]
stone (n)	камень (м)	[kámenʲ]
stone (as adj)	каменный	[kámennij]
concrete (n)	бетон (м)	[betón]
concrete (as adj)	бетонный	[betónnij]
new (new-built)	новый	[nóvij]
old (adj)	старый	[stárij]
ramshackle	ветхий	[vétxij]
modern (adj)	современный	[sɔvreménnij]
multistory (adj)	многоэтажный	[mnɔgɔ·etáʒnij]
tall (~ building)	высокий	[vɨsókij]
floor, story	этаж (м)	[etáʃ]
single-story (adj)	одноэтажный	[ɔdnɔ·etáʒnij]
1st floor	нижний этаж (м)	[nízʒnij etáʃ]
top floor	верхний этаж (м)	[vérhnij etáʃ]
roof	крыша (ж)	[krɨʃa]
chimney	труба (ж)	[trubá]
roof tiles	черепица (ж)	[tʃerepítsa]
tiled (adj)	черепичный	[tʃerepítʃnij]
attic (storage place)	чердак (м)	[tʃerdák]
window	окно (с)	[ɔknó]
glass	стекло (с)	[stekló]
window ledge	подоконник (м)	[pɔdɔkónik]
shutters	ставни (ж мн)	[stávni]
wall	стена (ж)	[stená]
balcony	балкон (м)	[balkón]
downspout	водосточная труба (ж)	[vɔdɔstótʃnaja trubá]
upstairs (to be ~)	наверху	[naverhú]
to go upstairs	подниматься (нсв, возв)	[pɔdnimátsa]

| to come down (the stairs) | спускаться (нсв, возв) | [spuskátsa] |
| to move (to new premises) | переезжать (нсв, нпх) | [pereeʒʒátʲ] |

83. House. Entrance. Lift

entrance	подъезд (м)	[pɔdjézd]
stairs (stairway)	лестница (ж)	[lésnitsa]
steps	ступени (ж мн)	[stupéni]
banister	перила (мн)	[períla]
lobby (hotel ~)	холл (м)	[hól]
mailbox	почтовый ящик (м)	[pɔtʃtóvij jáʃik]
garbage can	мусорный бак (м)	[músɔrnij bák]
trash chute	мусоропровод (м)	[musɔrɔ·prɔvód]
elevator	лифт (м)	[líft]
freight elevator	грузовой лифт (м)	[gruzɔvój líft]
elevator cage	кабина (ж)	[kabína]
to take the elevator	ехать на лифте	[éhatʲ na lífte]
apartment	квартира (ж)	[kvartíra]
residents (~ of a building)	жильцы (мн)	[ʒilʲtsɨ]
neighbor (masc.)	сосед (м)	[sɔséd]
neighbor (fem.)	соседка (ж)	[sɔsétka]
neighbors	соседи (мн)	[sɔsédi]

84. House. Doors. Locks

door	дверь (ж)	[dvérʲ]
gate (vehicle ~)	ворота (мн)	[vɔróta]
handle, doorknob	ручка (ж)	[rútʃka]
to unlock (unbolt)	отпереть (св, н/пх)	[ɔtperétʲ]
to open (vt)	открывать (нсв, пх)	[ɔtkrivátʲ]
to close (vt)	закрывать (нсв, пх)	[zakrivátʲ]
key	ключ (м)	[klʲútʃ]
bunch (of keys)	связка (ж)	[svʲáska]
to creak (door, etc.)	скрипеть (нсв, нпх)	[skripétʲ]
creak	скрип (м)	[skríp]
hinge (door ~)	петля (ж)	[petlʲá]
doormat	коврик (м)	[kóvrik]
door lock	замок (м)	[zámɔk]
keyhole	замочная скважина (ж)	[zamótʃnaja skváʒina]
crossbar (sliding bar)	засов (м)	[zasóf]
door latch	задвижка (ж)	[zadvíʃka]
padlock	навесной замок (м)	[navesnój zamók]
to ring (~ the door bell)	звонить (нсв, нпх)	[zvɔnítʲ]

ringing (sound)	звонок (м)	[zvɔnók]
doorbell	звонок (м)	[zvɔnók]
doorbell button	кнопка (ж)	[knópka]
knock (at the door)	стук (м)	[stúk]
to knock (vi)	стучать (нсв, нпх)	[stutʃátʲ]

code	код (м)	[kód]
combination lock	кодовый замок (м)	[kódɔvij zamók]
intercom	домофон (м)	[dɔmɔfón]
number (on the door)	номер (м)	[nómerʲ]
doorplate	табличка (ж)	[tablítʃka]
peephole	глазок (м)	[glazók]

85. Country house

village	деревня (ж)	[derévnʲa]
vegetable garden	огород (м)	[ɔgɔród]
fence	забор (м)	[zabór]
picket fence	изгородь (ж)	[ízgɔrɔtʲ]
wicket gate	калитка (ж)	[kalítka]

granary	амбар (м)	[ambár]
root cellar	погреб (м)	[pógreb]
shed (garden ~)	сарай (м)	[saráj]
water well	колодец (м)	[kɔlódets]

stove (wood-fired ~)	печь (ж)	[pétʃʲ]
to stoke the stove	топить печь (нсв)	[tɔpítʲ pétʃʲ]
firewood	дрова (ж)	[drɔvá]
log (firewood)	полено (с)	[pɔlénɔ]

veranda	веранда (ж)	[veránda]
deck (terrace)	терраса (ж)	[terása]
stoop (front steps)	крыльцо (с)	[krilʲtsó]
swing (hanging seat)	качели (мн)	[katʃéli]

86. Castle. Palace

castle	замок (м)	[zámɔk]
palace	дворец (м)	[dvɔréts]
fortress	крепость (ж)	[krépɔstʲ]

wall (round castle)	стена (ж)	[stená]
tower	башня (ж)	[báʃnʲa]
keep, donjon	главная башня (ж)	[glávnaja báʃnʲa]

| portcullis | подъёмные ворота (мн) | [pɔdjómnʲe vɔróta] |
| underground passage | подземный ход (м) | [pɔdzémnij hód] |

moat	**ров** (м)	[róf]
chain	**цепь** (ж)	[tsæpʲ]
arrow loop	**бойница** (ж)	[bɔjnítsa]

magnificent (adj)	**великолепный**	[velikɔlépnij]
majestic (adj)	**величественный**	[velítʃestvenij]
impregnable (adj)	**неприступный**	[nepristúpnij]
medieval (adj)	**средневековый**	[srednevekóvij]

87. Apartment

apartment	**квартира** (ж)	[kvartíra]
room	**комната** (ж)	[kómnata]
bedroom	**спальня** (ж)	[spálʲnʲa]
dining room	**столовая** (ж)	[stɔlóvaja]
living room	**гостиная** (ж)	[gɔstínaja]
study (home office)	**кабинет** (м)	[kabinét]

entry room	**прихожая** (ж)	[prihóʒaja]
bathroom (room with a bath or shower)	**ванная комната** (ж)	[vánnaja kómnata]
half bath	**туалет** (м)	[tualét]

ceiling	**потолок** (м)	[pɔtɔlók]
floor	**пол** (м)	[pól]
corner	**угол** (м)	[úgɔl]

88. Apartment. Cleaning

to clean (vi, vt)	**убирать** (нсв, пх)	[ubirátʲ]
to put away (to stow)	**уносить** (нсв, пх)	[unɔsítʲ]
dust	**пыль** (ж)	[pɨlʲ]
dusty (adj)	**пыльный**	[pɨlʲnij]
to dust (vt)	**вытирать пыль**	[vitirátʲ pɨlʲ]

vacuum cleaner	**пылесос** (м)	[pilesós]
to vacuum (vt)	**пылесосить** (нсв, н/пх)	[pilesósitʲ]

to sweep (vi, vt)	**подметать** (нсв, н/пх)	[pɔdmetátʲ]
sweepings	**мусор** (м)	[músɔr]

order	**порядок** (м)	[pɔrʲádɔk]
disorder, mess	**беспорядок** (м)	[bespɔrʲádɔk]

mop	**швабра** (ж)	[ʃvábra]
dust cloth	**тряпка** (ж)	[trʲápka]
short broom	**веник** (м)	[vénik]
dustpan	**совок** (м) **для мусора**	[sɔvók dlʲa músɔra]

89. Furniture. Interior

furniture	мебель (ж)	[mébelʲ]
table	стол (м)	[stól]
chair	стул (м)	[stúl]
bed	кровать (ж)	[krɔvátʲ]
couch, sofa	диван (м)	[diván]
armchair	кресло (с)	[kréslɔ]

| bookcase | книжный шкаф (м) | [kníʒnij ʃkáf] |
| shelf | полка (ж) | [pólka] |

wardrobe	гардероб (м)	[garderób]
coat rack (wall-mounted ~)	вешалка (ж)	[véʃəlka]
coat stand	вешалка (ж)	[véʃəlka]

| bureau, dresser | комод (м) | [kɔmód] |
| coffee table | журнальный столик (м) | [ʒurnálʲnij stólik] |

mirror	зеркало (с)	[zérkalɔ]
carpet	ковёр (м)	[kɔvǿr]
rug, small carpet	коврик (м)	[kóvrik]

fireplace	камин (м)	[kamín]
candle	свеча (ж)	[svetʃá]
candlestick	подсвечник (м)	[pɔtsvétʃnik]

drapes	шторы (ж мн)	[ʃtóri]
wallpaper	обои (мн)	[ɔbói]
blinds (jalousie)	жалюзи (мн)	[ʒalʲuzí]

table lamp	настольная лампа (ж)	[nastólʲnaja lámpa]
wall lamp (sconce)	светильник (м)	[svetílʲnik]
floor lamp	торшер (м)	[tɔrʃǽr]
chandelier	люстра (ж)	[lʲústra]

leg (of chair, table)	ножка (ж)	[nóʃka]
armrest	подлокотник (м)	[pɔdlɔkótnik]
back (backrest)	спинка (ж)	[spínka]
drawer	ящик (м)	[jáʃʲik]

90. Bedding

bedclothes	постельное бельё (с)	[pɔstélʲnɔe beljǿ]
pillow	подушка (ж)	[pɔdúʃka]
pillowcase	наволочка (ж)	[návɔlɔtʃka]
duvet, comforter	одеяло (с)	[ɔdejálɔ]
sheet	простыня (ж)	[prɔstinʲá]
bedspread	покрывало (с)	[pɔkriválɔ]

91. Kitchen

kitchen	кухня (ж)	[kúhnʲa]
gas	газ (м)	[gás]
gas stove (range)	газовая плита (ж)	[gázɔvaja plitá]
electric stove	электроплита (ж)	[ɛléktrɔ·plitá]
oven	духовка (ж)	[duhófka]
microwave oven	микроволновая печь (ж)	[mikrɔ·vɔlnóvaja pétʃʲ]

refrigerator	холодильник (м)	[hɔlɔdílʲnik]
freezer	морозильник (м)	[mɔrɔzílʲnik]
dishwasher	посудомоечная машина (ж)	[pɔsúdɔ·móetʃnaja maʃína]

meat grinder	мясорубка (ж)	[mɪsɔrúpka]
juicer	соковыжималка (ж)	[sɔkɔ·viʒimálka]
toaster	тостер (м)	[tóstɛr]
mixer	миксер (м)	[míkser]

coffee machine	кофеварка (ж)	[kɔfevárka]
coffee pot	кофейник (м)	[kɔféjnik]
coffee grinder	кофемолка (ж)	[kɔfemólka]

kettle	чайник (м)	[tʃájnik]
teapot	чайник (м)	[tʃájnik]
lid	крышка (ж)	[kríʃka]
tea strainer	ситечко (с)	[sítetʃkɔ]

spoon	ложка (ж)	[lóʃka]
teaspoon	чайная ложка (ж)	[tʃájnaja lóʃka]
soup spoon	столовая ложка (ж)	[stɔlóvaja lóʃka]
fork	вилка (ж)	[vílka]
knife	нож (м)	[nóʃ]

tableware (dishes)	посуда (ж)	[pɔsúda]
plate (dinner ~)	тарелка (ж)	[tarélka]
saucer	блюдце (с)	[blʲútse]

shot glass	рюмка (ж)	[rʲúmka]
glass (tumbler)	стакан (м)	[stakán]
cup	чашка (ж)	[tʃáʃka]

sugar bowl	сахарница (ж)	[sáharnitsa]
salt shaker	солонка (ж)	[sɔlónka]
pepper shaker	перечница (ж)	[péretʃnitsa]
butter dish	маслёнка (ж)	[maslǿnka]

stock pot (soup pot)	кастрюля (ж)	[kastrʲúlʲa]
frying pan (skillet)	сковородка (ж)	[skɔvɔrótka]
ladle	половник (м)	[pɔlóvnik]
colander	дуршлаг (м)	[durʃlág]

tray (serving ~)	поднос (м)	[pɔdnós]
bottle	бутылка (ж)	[butílka]
jar (glass)	банка (ж)	[bánka]
can	банка (ж)	[bánka]

bottle opener	открывалка (ж)	[ɔtkriválka]
can opener	открывалка (ж)	[ɔtkriválka]
corkscrew	штопор (м)	[ʃtópɔr]
filter	фильтр (м)	[fílʲtr]
to filter (vt)	фильтровать (нсв, пх)	[filʲtrɔvátʲ]

| trash, garbage (food waste, etc.) | мусор (м) | [músɔr] |
| trash can (kitchen ~) | мусорное ведро (с) | [músɔrnɔe vedró] |

92. Bathroom

bathroom	ванная комната (ж)	[vánnaja kómnata]
water	вода (ж)	[vɔdá]
faucet	кран (м)	[krán]
hot water	горячая вода (ж)	[gɔrʲátʃaja vɔdá]
cold water	холодная вода (ж)	[hɔlódnaja vɔdá]

toothpaste	зубная паста (ж)	[zubnája pásta]
to brush one's teeth	чистить зубы	[tʃístitʲ zúbɨ]
toothbrush	зубная щётка (ж)	[zubnája ʃʲǿtka]

to shave (vi)	бриться (нсв, возв)	[brítsa]
shaving foam	пена (ж) для бритья	[péna dlʲa britjá]
razor	бритва (ж)	[brítva]

to wash (one's hands, etc.)	мыть (нсв, пх)	[mɨtʲ]
to take a bath	мыться (нсв, возв)	[mɨtsa]
shower	душ (м)	[dúʃ]
to take a shower	принимать душ	[prinimátʲ dúʃ]

bathtub	ванна (ж)	[vánna]
toilet (toilet bowl)	унитаз (м)	[unitás]
sink (washbasin)	раковина (ж)	[rákɔvina]

| soap | мыло (с) | [mɨlɔ] |
| soap dish | мыльница (ж) | [mɨlʲnitsa] |

sponge	губка (ж)	[gúpka]
shampoo	шампунь (м)	[ʃampúnʲ]
towel	полотенце (с)	[pɔloténtse]
bathrobe	халат (м)	[halát]

| laundry (laundering) | стирка (ж) | [stírka] |
| washing machine | стиральная машина (ж) | [stirálʲnaja maʃína] |

| to do the laundry | стирать бельё | [stirátʲ beljǿ] |
| laundry detergent | стиральный порошок (м) | [stirálʲnij pɔrɔʃók] |

93. Household appliances

TV set	телевизор (м)	[televízɔr]
tape recorder	магнитофон (м)	[magnitɔfón]
VCR (video recorder)	видеомагнитофон (м)	[vídeɔ·magnitɔfón]
radio	приёмник (м)	[prijómnik]
player (CD, MP3, etc.)	плеер (м)	[plǽjer]

video projector	видеопроектор (м)	[vídeɔ·prɔǽktɔr]
home movie theater	домашний кинотеатр (м)	[dɔmáʃnij kinɔteátr]
DVD player	DVD проигрыватель (м)	[di·vi·dí prɔígrivatelʲ]
amplifier	усилитель (м)	[usílitelʲ]
video game console	игровая приставка (ж)	[igrɔvája pristáfka]

video camera	видеокамера (ж)	[vídeɔ·kámera]
camera (photo)	фотоаппарат (м)	[fɔtɔ·aparát]
digital camera	цифровой фотоаппарат (м)	[ʦifrɔvój fɔtɔaparát]

vacuum cleaner	пылесос (м)	[pilesós]
iron (e.g., steam ~)	утюг (м)	[utʲúg]
ironing board	гладильная доска (ж)	[gladílʲnaja dɔská]

telephone	телефон (м)	[telefón]
cell phone	мобильный телефон (м)	[mɔbílʲnij telefón]
sewing machine	швейная машинка (ж)	[ʃvejnaja maʃínka]

microphone	микрофон (м)	[mikrɔfón]
headphones	наушники (м мн)	[naúʃniki]
remote control (TV)	пульт (м)	[púlʲt]

CD, compact disc	компакт-диск (м)	[kɔmpákt-dísk]
cassette, tape	кассета (ж)	[kaséta]
vinyl record	пластинка (ж)	[plastínka]

94. Repairs. Renovation

renovations	ремонт (м)	[remónt]
to renovate (vt)	делать ремонт	[délatʲ remónt]
to repair, to fix (vt)	ремонтировать (нсв, пх)	[remɔntírovatʲ]
to put in order	приводить в порядок	[privɔdítʲ f pɔrʲádɔk]
to redo (do again)	переделывать (нсв, пх)	[peredélivatʲ]
paint	краска (ж)	[kráska]
to paint (~ a wall)	красить (нсв, пх)	[krásitʲ]

| house painter | маляр (м) | [malʲár] |
| paintbrush | кисть (ж) | [kístʲ] |

| whitewash | побелка (ж) | [pɔbélka] |
| to whitewash (vt) | белить (нсв, пх) | [belítʲ] |

wallpaper	обои (мн)	[ɔbói]
to wallpaper (vt)	оклеить обоями	[ɔkléitʲ ɔbójɪmi]
varnish	лак (м)	[lák]
to varnish (vt)	покрывать лаком	[pɔkrivátʲ lákɔm]

95. Plumbing

water	вода (ж)	[vɔdá]
hot water	горячая вода (ж)	[gɔrʲátʃaja vɔdá]
cold water	холодная вода (ж)	[hɔlódnaja vɔdá]
faucet	кран (м)	[krán]

drop (of water)	капля (ж)	[káplʲa]
to drip (vi)	капать (нсв, нпх)	[kápatʲ]
to leak (ab. pipe)	течь (нсв, нпх)	[tétʃʲ]
leak (pipe ~)	течь (ж)	[tétʃʲ]
puddle	лужа (ж)	[lúʒa]

pipe	труба (ж)	[trubá]
valve (e.g., ball ~)	вентиль (м)	[véntilʲ]
to be clogged up	засориться (св, возв)	[zasorítsa]

tools	инструменты (м мн)	[instruménti]
adjustable wrench	разводной ключ (м)	[razvɔdnój klʲútʃ]
to unscrew (lid, filter, etc.)	открутить (св, пх)	[ɔtkrutítʲ]
to screw (tighten)	закрутить (св, пх)	[zakrutítʲ]

to unclog (vt)	прочищать (нсв, пх)	[prɔtʃiʃʲátʲ]
plumber	сантехник (м)	[santéhnik]
basement	подвал (м)	[pɔdvál]
sewerage (system)	канализация (ж)	[kanalizátsija]

96. Fire. Conflagration

fire (accident)	пожар (м)	[pɔʒár]
flame	пламя (ж)	[plámʲa]
spark	искра (ж)	[ískra]
smoke (from fire)	дым (м)	[dĩm]
torch (flaming stick)	факел (м)	[fákel]
campfire	костёр (м)	[kɔstǿr]
gas, gasoline	бензин (м)	[benzín]
kerosene (type of fuel)	керосин (м)	[kerɔsín]

flammable (adj)	горючий	[gɔrʲútʃij]
explosive (adj)	взрывоопасный	[vzrivɔˑopásnij]
NO SMOKING	НЕ КУРИТЬ!	[ne kurítʲ]

safety	безопасность (ж)	[bezɔpásnɔstʲ]
danger	опасность (ж)	[ɔpásnɔstʲ]
dangerous (adj)	опасный	[ɔpásnij]

to catch fire	загореться (св, возв)	[zagɔrétsa]
explosion	взрыв (м)	[vzrîf]
to set fire	поджечь (св, пх)	[pɔdʒǽtʃʲ]
arsonist	поджигатель (м)	[pɔdʒigátelʲ]
arson	поджог (м)	[pɔdʒóg]

to blaze (vi)	пылать (нсв, нпх)	[pilátʲ]
to burn (be on fire)	гореть (нсв, нпх)	[gɔrétʲ]
to burn down	сгореть (св, нпх)	[sgɔrétʲ]

to call the fire department	вызвать пожарных	[vîzvatʲ pɔʒárnih]
firefighter, fireman	пожарный (м)	[pɔʒárnij]
fire truck	пожарная машина (ж)	[pɔʒárnaja maʃína]
fire department	пожарная команда (ж)	[pɔʒárnaja kɔmánda]
fire truck ladder	пожарная лестница (ж)	[pɔʒárnaja lésnitsa]

fire hose	шланг (м)	[ʃláng]
fire extinguisher	огнетушитель (м)	[ɔgnetuʃítelʲ]
helmet	каска (ж)	[káska]
siren	сирена (ж)	[siréna]

to cry (for help)	кричать (нсв, нпх)	[kritʃátʲ]
to call for help	звать на помощь	[zvátʲ na pómɔʃʲ]
rescuer	спасатель (м)	[spasátelʲ]
to rescue (vt)	спасать (нсв, пх)	[spasátʲ]

to arrive (vi)	приехать (св, нпх)	[priéhatʲ]
to extinguish (vt)	тушить (нсв, пх)	[tuʃítʲ]
water	вода (ж)	[vɔdá]
sand	песок (м)	[pesók]

ruins (destruction)	руины (мн)	[ruíni]
to collapse (building, etc.)	рухнуть (св, нпх)	[rúhnutʲ]
to fall down (vi)	обвалиться (св, возв)	[ɔbvalítsa]
to cave in (ceiling, floor)	обрушиться (св, возв)	[ɔbrúʃitsa]

| piece of debris | обломок (м) | [ɔblómɔk] |
| ash | пепел (м) | [pépel] |

| to suffocate (die) | задохнуться (св, возв) | [zadɔhnútsa] |
| to be killed (perish) | погибнуть (св, нпх) | [pɔgíbnutʲ] |

HUMAN ACTIVITIES

Job. Business. Part 1

97. Banking

bank	банк (м)	[bánk]
branch (of bank, etc.)	отделение (с)	[ɔtdelénie]
bank clerk, consultant	консультант (м)	[kɔnsulʲtánt]
manager (director)	управляющий (м)	[upravlʲájuʃij]
bank account	счёт (м)	[ʃǿt]
account number	номер (м) счёта	[nómer ʃǿta]
checking account	текущий счёт (м)	[tekúʃij ʃǿt]
savings account	накопительный счёт (м)	[nakɔpítelʲnij ʃǿt]
to open an account	открыть счёт	[ɔtkrítʲ ʃǿt]
to close the account	закрыть счёт	[zakrítʲ ʃǿt]
to deposit into the account	положить на счёт	[pɔlɔʒítʲ na ʃǿt]
to withdraw (vt)	снять со счёта	[snʲátʲ sɔ ʃǿta]
deposit	вклад (м)	[fklád]
to make a deposit	сделать вклад	[zdélatʲ fklád]
wire transfer	перевод (м)	[perevód]
to wire, to transfer	сделать перевод	[zdélatʲ perevód]
sum	сумма (ж)	[súmma]
How much?	Сколько?	[skólʲkɔ?]
signature	подпись (ж)	[pótpisʲ]
to sign (vt)	подписать (св, пх)	[pɔtpisátʲ]
credit card	кредитная карта (ж)	[kredítnaja kárta]
code (PIN code)	код (м)	[kód]
credit card number	номер (м) кредитной карты	[nómer kredítnɔj kárti]
ATM	банкомат (м)	[bankɔmát]
check	чек (м)	[ʧék]
to write a check	выписать чек	[vípisatʲ ʧék]
checkbook	чековая книжка (ж)	[ʧékɔvaja kníʃka]
loan (bank ~)	кредит (м)	[kredít]
to apply for a loan	обращаться за кредитом	[ɔbraʃátsa za kredítɔm]

to get a loan	брать кредит	[brátʲ kredít]
to give a loan	предоставлять кредит	[predostavlʲátʲ kredít]
guarantee	гарантия (ж)	[garántija]

98. Telephone. Phone conversation

telephone	телефон (м)	[telefón]
cell phone	мобильный телефон (м)	[mobílʲnij telefón]
answering machine	автоответчик (м)	[áfto·otvéttʃik]

| to call (by phone) | звонить (нсв, н/пх) | [zvonítʲ] |
| phone call | звонок (м) | [zvonók] |

to dial a number	набрать номер	[nabrátʲ nómer]
Hello!	Алло!	[aló]
to ask (vt)	спросить (св, пх)	[sprositʲ]
to answer (vi, vt)	ответить (св, пх)	[otvétitʲ]

to hear (vt)	слышать (нсв, пх)	[slíʃatʲ]
well (adv)	хорошо	[horoʃó]
not well (adv)	плохо	[plóho]
noises (interference)	помехи (ж мн)	[poméhi]

receiver	трубка (ж)	[trúpka]
to pick up (~ the phone)	снять трубку	[snʲátʲ trúpku]
to hang up (~ the phone)	положить трубку	[poloʒítʲ trúpku]

busy (engaged)	занятый	[zánıtij]
to ring (ab. phone)	звонить (нсв, нпх)	[zvonítʲ]
telephone book	телефонная книга (ж)	[telefónnaja kníga]

local (adj)	местный	[mésnij]
local call	местный звонок (м)	[mésnij zvonók]
long distance (~ call)	междугородний	[meʒdugoródnij]
long-distance call	междугородний звонок (м)	[meʒdugoródnij zvonók]
international (adj)	международный	[meʒdunaródnij]
international call	международный звонок	[meʒdunaródnij zvonók]

99. Cell phone

cell phone	мобильный телефон (м)	[mobílʲnij telefón]
display	дисплей (м)	[displǽj]
button	кнопка (ж)	[knópka]
SIM card	SIM-карта (ж)	[sim-kárta]
battery	батарея (ж)	[bataréja]
to be dead (battery)	разрядиться (св, возв)	[razrıdítsa]

charger	зарядное устройство (c)	[zarʲádnɔe ustrójstvɔ]
menu	меню (c)	[menʲú]
settings	настройки (ж мн)	[nastrójki]
tune (melody)	мелодия (ж)	[melódija]
to select (vt)	выбрать (св, пх)	[vībratʲ]

calculator	калькулятор (м)	[kalʲkulʲátɔr]
voice mail	голосовая почта (ж)	[gɔlɔsɔvája pótʃta]
alarm clock	будильник (м)	[budílʲnik]
contacts	телефонная книга (ж)	[telefónnaja kníga]

| SMS (text message) | SMS-сообщение (c) | [ɛs·ɛm·ǽs-sɔɔpʃénie] |
| subscriber | абонент (м) | [abɔnént] |

100. Stationery

| ballpoint pen | шариковая ручка (ж) | [ʃárikɔvaja rútʃka] |
| fountain pen | перьевая ручка (ж) | [perjevája rútʃka] |

pencil	карандаш (м)	[karandáʃ]
highlighter	маркер (м)	[márker]
felt-tip pen	фломастер (м)	[flɔmáster]

| notepad | блокнот (м) | [blɔknót] |
| agenda (diary) | ежедневник (м) | [eʒednévnik] |

ruler	линейка (ж)	[linéjka]
calculator	калькулятор (м)	[kalʲkulʲátɔr]
eraser	ластик (м)	[lástik]
thumbtack	кнопка (ж)	[knópka]
paper clip	скрепка (ж)	[skrépka]

glue	клей (м)	[kléj]
stapler	степлер (м)	[stǽpler]
hole punch	дырокол (м)	[dirɔkól]
pencil sharpener	точилка (ж)	[tɔtʃílka]

Job. Business. Part 2

101. Mass Media

newspaper	газета (ж)	[gazéta]
magazine	журнал (м)	[ʒurnál]
press (printed media)	пресса (ж)	[présa]
radio	радио (с)	[rádiɔ]
radio station	радиостанция (ж)	[radiɔ·stántsija]
television	телевидение (с)	[televídenje]
presenter, host	ведущий (м)	[vedúʃij]
newscaster	диктор (м)	[díktɔr]
commentator	комментатор (м)	[kɔmentátɔr]
journalist	журналист (м)	[ʒurnalíst]
correspondent (reporter)	корреспондент (м)	[kɔrespɔndént]
press photographer	фотокорреспондент (м)	[fɔtɔ·kɔrespɔndént]
reporter	репортёр (м)	[repɔrtǿr]
editor	редактор (м)	[redáktɔr]
editor-in-chief	главный редактор (м)	[glávnij redáktɔr]
to subscribe (to …)	подписаться (св, возв)	[pɔtpisátsa]
subscription	подписка (ж)	[pɔtpíska]
subscriber	подписчик (м)	[pɔtpíʃik]
to read (vi, vt)	читать (нсв, н/пх)	[tʃitátʲ]
reader	читатель (м)	[tʃitátelʲ]
circulation (of newspaper)	тираж (м)	[tiráʃ]
monthly (adj)	ежемесячный	[eʒemésɪtʃnij]
weekly (adj)	еженедельный	[eʒenedélʲnij]
issue (edition)	номер (м)	[nómer]
new (~ issue)	свежий	[svéʒij]
headline	заголовок (м)	[zagɔlóvɔk]
short article	заметка (ж)	[zamétka]
column (regular article)	рубрика (ж)	[rúbrika]
article	статья (ж)	[statjá]
page	страница (ж)	[stranítsa]
reportage, report	репортаж (м)	[repɔrtáʃ]
event (happening)	событие (с)	[sɔbītie]
sensation (news)	сенсация (ж)	[sensátsija]
scandal	скандал (м)	[skandál]
scandalous (adj)	скандальный	[skandálʲnij]

great (~ scandal)	громкий	[grómkij]
show (e.g., cooking ~)	передача (ж)	[peredátʃa]
interview	интервью (с)	[intɛrvjú]
live broadcast	прямая трансляция (ж)	[primája translʲátsija]
channel	канал (м)	[kanál]

102. Agriculture

agriculture	сельское хозяйство (с)	[sélʲskɔe hɔzʲájstvɔ]
peasant (masc.)	крестьянин (м)	[krestjánin]
peasant (fem.)	крестьянка (ж)	[krestjánka]
farmer	фермер (м)	[férmer]

| tractor (farm ~) | трактор (м) | [tráktɔr] |
| combine, harvester | комбайн (м) | [kɔmbájn] |

plow	плуг (м)	[plúg]
to plow (vi, vt)	пахать (нсв, н/пх)	[pahátʲ]
plowland	пашня (ж)	[páʃnʲa]
furrow (in field)	борозда (ж)	[bɔrɔzdá]

to sow (vi, vt)	сеять (нсв, пх)	[séjatʲ]
seeder	сеялка (ж)	[séjalka]
sowing (process)	посев (м)	[pɔséf]

| scythe | коса (ж) | [kɔsá] |
| to mow, to scythe | косить (нсв, н/пх) | [kɔsítʲ] |

| spade (tool) | лопата (ж) | [lɔpáta] |
| to till (vt) | копать (нсв, пх) | [kɔpátʲ] |

hoe	тяпка (ж)	[tʲápka]
to hoe, to weed	полоть (нсв, пх)	[pɔlótʲ]
weed (plant)	сорняк (м)	[sɔrnʲák]

watering can	лейка (ж)	[léjka]
to water (plants)	поливать (нсв, пх)	[pɔlivátʲ]
watering (act)	полив (м)	[pɔlíf]

| pitchfork | вилы (мн) | [víli] |
| rake | грабли (мн) | [grábli] |

fertilizer	удобрение (с)	[udɔbrénie]
to fertilize (vt)	удобрять (нсв, пх)	[udɔbrʲátʲ]
manure (fertilizer)	навоз (м)	[navós]

field	поле (с)	[póle]
meadow	луг (м)	[lúg]
vegetable garden	огород (м)	[ɔgɔród]
orchard (e.g., apple ~)	сад (м)	[sád]

to graze (vt)	пасти (нсв, пх)	[pastí]
herder (herdsman)	пастух (м)	[pastúh]
pasture	пастбище (с)	[pázbiʲe]

| cattle breeding | животноводство (с) | [ʒivɔtnɔvótstvɔ] |
| sheep farming | овцеводство (с) | [ɔftsɛvótstvɔ] |

plantation	плантация (ж)	[plantátsija]
row (garden bed ~s)	грядка (ж)	[grʲátka]
hothouse	парник (м)	[parník]

| drought (lack of rain) | засуха (ж) | [zásuha] |
| dry (~ summer) | засушливый | [zasúʃlivij] |

grain	зерно (с)	[zernó]
cereal crops	зерновые (мн)	[zernɔvʲije]
to harvest, to gather	убирать (нсв, пх)	[ubirátʲ]

miller (person)	мельник (м)	[mélʲnik]
mill (e.g., gristmill)	мельница (ж)	[mélʲnitsa]
to grind (grain)	молоть (нсв, пх)	[mɔlótʲ]
flour	мука (ж)	[muká]
straw	солома (ж)	[sɔlóma]

103. Building. Building process

construction site	стройка (ж)	[strójka]
to build (vt)	строить (нсв, пх)	[stróitʲ]
construction worker	строитель (м)	[strɔítelʲ]

project	проект (м)	[prɔǽkt]
architect	архитектор (м)	[arhitéktɔr]
worker	рабочий (м)	[rabótʃij]

foundation (of a building)	фундамент (м)	[fundáment]
roof	крыша (ж)	[krɨ̄ʃa]
foundation pile	свая (ж)	[svája]
wall	стена (ж)	[stená]

| reinforcing bars | арматура (ж) | [armatúra] |
| scaffolding | строительные леса (мн) | [strɔítelʲnie lesá] |

concrete	бетон (м)	[betón]
granite	гранит (м)	[granít]
stone	камень (м)	[kámenʲ]
brick	кирпич (м)	[kirpítʃ]

sand	песок (м)	[pesók]
cement	цемент (м)	[tsɛmént]
plaster (for walls)	штукатурка (ж)	[ʃtukatúrka]

to plaster (vt)	штукатурить (нсв, пх)	[ʃtukatúritʲ]
paint	краска (ж)	[kráska]
to paint (~ a wall)	красить (нсв, пх)	[krásitʲ]
barrel	бочка (ж)	[bótʃka]

crane	кран (м)	[krán]
to lift, to hoist (vt)	поднимать (нсв, пх)	[pɔdnimátʲ]
to lower (vt)	опускать (нсв, пх)	[ɔpuskátʲ]

bulldozer	бульдозер (м)	[bulʲdózer]
excavator	экскаватор (м)	[ɛkskavátɔr]
scoop, bucket	ковш (м)	[kóvʃ]
to dig (excavate)	копать (нсв, пх)	[kɔpátʲ]
hard hat	каска (ж)	[káska]

Professions and occupations

job	работа (ж)	[rabóta]
staff (work force)	сотрудники (мн)	[sɔtrúdniki]
personnel	персонал (м)	[persɔnál]

career	карьера (ж)	[karjéra]
prospects (chances)	перспектива (ж)	[perspektíva]
skills (mastery)	мастерство (с)	[masterstvó]

selection (screening)	подбор (м)	[pɔdbór]
employment agency	кадровое агентство (с)	[kádrɔvɔe agénstvɔ]
résumé	резюме (с)	[rezʲumé]
job interview	собеседование (с)	[sɔbesédɔvanie]
vacancy, opening	вакансия (ж)	[vakánsija]

salary, pay	зарплата (ж)	[zarpláta]
fixed salary	оклад (м)	[ɔklád]
pay, compensation	оплата (ж)	[ɔpláta]

position (job)	должность (ж)	[dólʒnɔstʲ]
duty (of employee)	обязанность (ж)	[ɔbʲázanɔstʲ]
range of duties	круг (м)	[krúg]
busy (I'm ~)	занятой	[zanɪtój]

| to fire (dismiss) | уволить (св, пх) | [uvólitʲ] |
| dismissal | увольнение (с) | [uvɔlʲnénie] |

unemployment	безработица (ж)	[bezrabótitsa]
unemployed (n)	безработный (м)	[bezrabótnɪj]
retirement	пенсия (ж)	[pénsija]
to retire (from job)	уйти на пенсию	[ujtí na pénsiju]

director	директор (м)	[diréktɔr]
manager (director)	управляющий (м)	[upravlʲájuʃij]
boss	руководитель, шеф (м)	[rukɔvɔdítelʲ], [ʃǽf]

superior	начальник (м)	[natʃálʲnik]
superiors	начальство (с)	[natʃálʲstvɔ]
president	президент (м)	[prezidént]

chairman	председатель (м)	[pretsedátelʲ]
deputy (substitute)	заместитель (м)	[zamestítelʲ]
assistant	помощник (м)	[pɔmóʃnik]
secretary	секретарь (м)	[sekretárʲ]
personal assistant	личный секретарь (м)	[líʧnij sekretárʲ]

businessman	бизнесмен (м)	[biznɛsmén]
entrepreneur	предприниматель (м)	[pretprinimátelʲ]
founder	основатель (м)	[ɔsnɔvátelʲ]
to found (vt)	основать (св, пх)	[ɔsnɔvátʲ]

incorporator	учредитель (м)	[uʧredítelʲ]
partner	партнёр (м)	[partnǿr]
stockholder	акционер (м)	[aktsiɔnér]

millionaire	миллионер (м)	[miliɔnér]
billionaire	миллиардер (м)	[miliardér]
owner, proprietor	владелец (м)	[vladélets]
landowner	землевладелец (м)	[zemle·vladélets]

client	клиент (м)	[kliént]
regular client	постоянный клиент (м)	[pɔstɔjánnij kliént]
buyer (customer)	покупатель (м)	[pɔkupátelʲ]
visitor	посетитель (м)	[pɔsetítelʲ]

professional (n)	профессионал (м)	[prɔfesiɔnál]
expert	эксперт (м)	[ɛkspért]
specialist	специалист (м)	[spetsialíst]

| banker | банкир (м) | [bankír] |
| broker | брокер (м) | [bróker] |

cashier, teller	кассир (м)	[kassír]
accountant	бухгалтер (м)	[buhgálter]
security guard	охранник (м)	[ɔhránnik]

investor	инвестор (м)	[invéstɔr]
debtor	должник (м)	[dɔlʒník]
creditor	кредитор (м)	[kreditór]
borrower	заёмщик (м)	[zajómʃik]

| importer | импортёр (м) | [impɔrtǿr] |
| exporter | экспортёр (м) | [ɛkspɔrtǿr] |

manufacturer	производитель (м)	[prɔizvɔdítelʲ]
distributor	дистрибьютор (м)	[distribjútor]
middleman	посредник (м)	[pɔsrédnik]

consultant	консультант (м)	[kɔnsulʲtánt]
sales representative	представитель (м)	[pretstavítelʲ]
agent	агент (м)	[agént]
insurance agent	страховой агент (м)	[strahɔvój agént]

106. Service professions

cook	повар (м)	[póvar]
chef (kitchen chef)	шеф-повар (м)	[ʃæf-póvar]
baker	пекарь (м)	[pékarʲ]
bartender	бармен (м)	[bármɛn]
waiter	официант (м)	[ɔfitsiánt]
waitress	официантка (ж)	[ɔfitsiántka]
lawyer, attorney	адвокат (м)	[advɔkát]
lawyer (legal expert)	юрист (м)	[juríst]
notary public	нотариус (м)	[nɔtárius]
electrician	электрик (м)	[ɛléktrik]
plumber	сантехник (м)	[santéhnik]
carpenter	плотник (м)	[plótnik]
masseur	массажист (м)	[masaʒĩst]
masseuse	массажистка (ж)	[masaʒĩstka]
doctor	врач (м)	[vrátʃ]
taxi driver	таксист (м)	[taksíst]
driver	шофёр (м)	[ʃɔfǿr]
delivery man	курьер (м)	[kurjér]
chambermaid	горничная (ж)	[górnitʃnaja]
security guard	охранник (м)	[ɔhránnik]
flight attendant (fem.)	стюардесса (ж)	[stʲuardǽsa]
schoolteacher	учитель (м)	[utʃítelʲ]
librarian	библиотекарь (м)	[bibliotékarʲ]
translator	переводчик (м)	[perevóttʃik]
interpreter	переводчик (м)	[perevóttʃik]
guide	гид (м)	[gíd]
hairdresser	парикмахер (м)	[parikmáher]
mailman	почтальон (м)	[pɔtʃtaljón]
salesman (store staff)	продавец (м)	[prɔdavéts]
gardener	садовник (м)	[sadóvnik]
domestic servant	слуга (ж)	[slugá]
maid (female servant)	служанка (ж)	[sluʒánka]
cleaner (cleaning lady)	уборщица (ж)	[ubórʃitsa]

107. Military professions and ranks

private	рядовой (м)	[rɪdɔvój]
sergeant	сержант (м)	[serʒánt]

| lieutenant | лейтенант (м) | [lejtenánt] |
| captain | капитан (м) | [kapitán] |

major	майор (м)	[majór]
colonel	полковник (м)	[polkóvnik]
general	генерал (м)	[generál]
marshal	маршал (м)	[márʃal]
admiral	адмирал (м)	[admirál]

military (n)	военный (м)	[vɔénnij]
soldier	солдат (м)	[sɔldát]
officer	офицер (м)	[ɔfitsǽr]
commander	командир (м)	[kɔmandír]

border guard	пограничник (м)	[pɔgraníʧnik]
radio operator	радист (м)	[radíst]
scout (searcher)	разведчик (м)	[razvétʧik]
pioneer (sapper)	сапёр (м)	[sapǿr]
marksman	стрелок (м)	[strelók]
navigator	штурман (м)	[ʃtúrman]

108. Officials. Priests

| king | король (м) | [kɔrólʲ] |
| queen | королева (ж) | [kɔrɔléva] |

| prince | принц (м) | [prínts] |
| princess | принцесса (ж) | [printsǽsa] |

| czar | царь (м) | [tsárʲ] |
| czarina | царица (ж) | [tsarítsa] |

president	президент (м)	[prezidént]
Secretary (minister)	министр (м)	[minístr]
prime minister	премьер-министр (м)	[premjér-minístr]
senator	сенатор (м)	[senátor]

diplomat	дипломат (м)	[diplɔmát]
consul	консул (м)	[kónsul]
ambassador	посол (м)	[pɔsól]
counselor (diplomatic officer)	советник (м)	[sɔvétnik]

official, functionary (civil servant)	чиновник (м)	[ʧinóvnik]
prefect	префект (м)	[prefékt]
mayor	мэр (м)	[mǽr]
judge	судья (ж)	[sudjá]
prosecutor (e.g., district attorney)	прокурор (м)	[prɔkurór]

missionary	миссионер (м)	[misionér]
monk	монах (м)	[monáh]
abbot	аббат (м)	[abát]
rabbi	раввин (м)	[ravín]

vizier	визирь (м)	[vizírʲ]
shah	шах (м)	[ʃáh]
sheikh	шейх (м)	[ʃǽjh]

109. Agricultural professions

beekeeper	пчеловод (м)	[ptʃelovód]
herder, shepherd	пастух (м)	[pastúh]
agronomist	агроном (м)	[agronóm]
cattle breeder	животновод (м)	[ʒivotnovód]
veterinarian	ветеринар (м)	[veterinár]

farmer	фермер (м)	[férmer]
winemaker	винодел (м)	[vinodél]
zoologist	зоолог (м)	[zoólog]
cowboy	ковбой (м)	[kovbój]

110. Art professions

| actor | актёр (м) | [aktór] |
| actress | актриса (ж) | [aktrísa] |

| singer (masc.) | певец (м) | [pevéts] |
| singer (fem.) | певица (ж) | [pevítsa] |

| dancer (masc.) | танцор (м) | [tantsór] |
| dancer (fem.) | танцовщица (ж) | [tantsófʃʲitsa] |

| performer (masc.) | артист (м) | [artíst] |
| performer (fem.) | артистка (ж) | [artístka] |

musician	музыкант (м)	[muzikánt]
pianist	пианист (м)	[pianíst]
guitar player	гитарист (м)	[gitaríst]

conductor (orchestra ~)	дирижёр (м)	[diriʒór]
composer	композитор (м)	[kompozítor]
impresario	импресарио (м)	[impresário]

film director	режиссёр (м)	[reʒisór]
producer	продюсер (м)	[prodʲúsɛr]
scriptwriter	сценарист (м)	[stsɛnaríst]
critic	критик (м)	[krítik]

writer	писатель (м)	[pisátelʲ]
poet	поэт (м)	[pɔǽt]
sculptor	скульптор (м)	[skúlʲptɔr]
artist (painter)	художник (м)	[hudóʒnik]

juggler	жонглёр (м)	[ʒɔnglǿr]
clown	клоун (м)	[klóun]
acrobat	акробат (м)	[akrɔbát]
magician	фокусник (м)	[fókusnik]

111. Various professions

doctor	врач (м)	[vrátʃ]
nurse	медсестра (ж)	[metsestrá]
psychiatrist	психиатр (м)	[psihiátr]
dentist	стоматолог (м)	[stɔmatólɔg]
surgeon	хирург (м)	[hirúrg]

| astronaut | астронавт (м) | [astrɔnávt] |
| astronomer | астроном (м) | [astrɔnóm] |

driver (of taxi, etc.)	водитель (м)	[vɔdítelʲ]
engineer (train driver)	машинист (м)	[maʃiníst]
mechanic	механик (м)	[mehánik]

miner	шахтёр (м)	[ʃahtǿr]
worker	рабочий (м)	[rabótʃij]
locksmith	слесарь (м)	[slésarʲ]
joiner (carpenter)	столяр (м)	[stɔlʲár]
turner (lathe operator)	токарь (м)	[tókarʲ]
construction worker	строитель (м)	[strɔítelʲ]
welder	сварщик (м)	[svárʲʃik]

professor (title)	профессор (м)	[prɔfésɔr]
architect	архитектор (м)	[arhitéktɔr]
historian	историк (м)	[istórik]
scientist	учёный (м)	[utʃónɨj]
physicist	физик (м)	[fízik]
chemist (scientist)	химик (м)	[hímik]

archeologist	археолог (м)	[arheólɔg]
geologist	геолог (м)	[geólɔg]
researcher (scientist)	исследователь (м)	[islédɔvatelʲ]

| babysitter | няня (ж) | [nʲánʲa] |
| teacher, educator | учитель (м) | [utʃítelʲ] |

editor	редактор (м)	[redáktɔr]
editor-in-chief	главный редактор (м)	[glávnij redáktɔr]
correspondent	корреспондент (м)	[kɔrespɔndént]

typist (fem.)	машинистка (ж)	[maʃinístka]
designer	дизайнер (м)	[dizájner]
computer expert	компьютерщик (м)	[kɔmpjútɛrʃik]
programmer	программист (м)	[prɔgramíst]
engineer (designer)	инженер (м)	[inʒenér]
sailor	моряк (м)	[mɔrʲák]
seaman	матрос (м)	[matrós]
rescuer	спасатель (м)	[spasátelʲ]
fireman	пожарный (м)	[pɔʒárnij]
police officer	полицейский (м)	[pɔliʦǽjskij]
watchman	сторож (м)	[stórɔʃ]
detective	сыщик (м)	[sɨ̃ʃik]
customs officer	таможенник (м)	[tamóʒenik]
bodyguard	телохранитель (м)	[telɔhranítelʲ]
prison guard	охранник (м)	[ɔhránnik]
inspector	инспектор (м)	[inspéktɔr]
sportsman	спортсмен (м)	[sportsmén]
trainer, coach	тренер (м)	[tréner]
butcher	мясник (м)	[mɪsník]
cobbler (shoe repairer)	сапожник (м)	[sapóʒnik]
merchant	коммерсант (м)	[kɔmersánt]
loader (person)	грузчик (м)	[grúʃik]
fashion designer	модельер (м)	[mɔdɛljér]
model (fem.)	модель (ж)	[mɔdǽlʲ]

112. Occupations. Social status

schoolboy	школьник (м)	[ʃkólʲnik]
student (college ~)	студент (м)	[studént]
philosopher	философ (м)	[filósɔf]
economist	экономист (м)	[ɛkɔnɔmíst]
inventor	изобретатель (м)	[izɔbretátelʲ]
unemployed (n)	безработный (м)	[bezrabótnij]
retiree	пенсионер (м)	[pensiɔnér]
spy, secret agent	шпион (м)	[ʃpión]
prisoner	заключённый (м)	[zaklʲuʧónnij]
striker	забастовщик (м)	[zabastófʃik]
bureaucrat	бюрократ (м)	[bʲurɔkrát]
traveler (globetrotter)	путешественник (м)	[puteʃǽstvenik]
gay, homosexual (n)	гомосексуалист (м)	[gɔmɔ·sɛksualíst]
hacker	хакер (м)	[háker]

hippie	**хиппи** (м)	[híppi]
bandit	**бандит** (м)	[bandít]
hit man, killer	**наёмный убийца** (м)	[najómnij ubíjtsa]
drug addict	**наркоман** (м)	[narkomán]
drug dealer	**торговец** (м) **наркотиками**	[torgóvets narkótikami]
prostitute (fem.)	**проститутка** (ж)	[prostitútka]
pimp	**сутенёр** (м)	[sutenǿr]
sorcerer	**колдун** (м)	[koldún]
sorceress (evil ~)	**колдунья** (ж)	[koldúnja]
pirate	**пират** (м)	[pirát]
slave	**раб** (м)	[ráb]
samurai	**самурай** (м)	[samuráj]
savage (primitive)	**дикарь** (м)	[dikárʲ]

Sports

| sportsman | спортсмен (м) | [sportsmén] |
| kind of sports | вид (м) спорта | [víd spórta] |

| basketball | баскетбол (м) | [basketból] |
| basketball player | баскетболист (м) | [basketbolíst] |

| baseball | бейсбол (м) | [bejzból] |
| baseball player | бейсболист (м) | [bejzbolíst] |

soccer	футбол (м)	[futból]
soccer player	футболист (м)	[futbolíst]
goalkeeper	вратарь (м)	[vratárʲ]

| hockey | хоккей (м) | [hɔkéj] |
| hockey player | хоккеист (м) | [hɔkeíst] |

| volleyball | волейбол (м) | [vɔlejból] |
| volleyball player | волейболист (м) | [vɔlejbolíst] |

| boxing | бокс (м) | [bóks] |
| boxer | боксёр (м) | [bɔksǿr] |

| wrestling | борьба (ж) | [borʲbá] |
| wrestler | борец (м) | [boréts] |

| karate | карате (с) | [karatǽ] |
| karate fighter | каратист (м) | [karatíst] |

| judo | дзюдо (с) | [dzʲudó] |
| judo athlete | дзюдоист (м) | [dzʲudɔíst] |

| tennis | теннис (м) | [tǽnis] |
| tennis player | теннисист (м) | [tɛnisíst] |

| swimming | плавание (с) | [plávanie] |
| swimmer | пловец (м) | [plɔvéts] |

| fencing | фехтование (с) | [fehtɔvánie] |
| fencer | фехтовальщик (м) | [fehtɔválʲʃik] |

| chess | шахматы (мн) | [ʃáhmati] |
| chess player | шахматист (м) | [ʃahmatíst] |

| alpinism | альпинизм (м) | [alʲpinízm] |
| alpinist | альпинист (м) | [alʲpiníst] |

| running | бег (м) | [bég] |
| runner | бегун (м) | [begún] |

| athletics | лёгкая атлетика (ж) | [lǿhkaja atlétika] |
| athlete | атлет (м) | [atlét] |

| horseback riding | конный спорт (м) | [kónnij spórt] |
| horse rider | наездник (м) | [naéznik] |

figure skating	фигурное катание (с)	[figúrnɔe katánie]
figure skater (masc.)	фигурист (м)	[figuríst]
figure skater (fem.)	фигуристка (ж)	[figурístka]

| powerlifting | тяжёлая атлетика (ж) | [tɪʒólaja atlétika] |
| powerlifter | штангист (м) | [ʃtangíst] |

| car racing | автогонки (ж мн) | [aftɔ·gónki] |
| racer (driver) | гонщик (м) | [gónʃik] |

| cycling | велоспорт (м) | [velɔspórt] |
| cyclist | велосипедист (м) | [velɔsipedíst] |

broad jump	прыжки (м мн) в длину	[priʃkí v dlinú]
pole vault	прыжки (м мн) с шестом	[priʃkí s ʃestóm]
jumper	прыгун (м)	[prigún]

114. Kinds of sports. Miscellaneous

football	американский футбол (м)	[amerikánskij futból]
badminton	бадминтон (м)	[badmintón]
biathlon	биатлон (м)	[biatlón]
billiards	бильярд (м)	[biljárd]

bobsled	бобслей (м)	[bɔbsléj]
bodybuilding	бодибилдинг (м)	[bɔdibílding]
water polo	водное поло (с)	[vódnɔe pólɔ]
handball	гандбол (м)	[ganból]
golf	гольф (м)	[gólʲf]

rowing, crew	гребля (ж)	[gréblʲa]
scuba diving	дайвинг (м)	[dájving]
cross-country skiing	лыжные гонки (ж мн)	[lĩʒnʲe gónki]
table tennis (ping-pong)	настольный теннис (м)	[nastólʲnij tǽnis]

| sailing | парусный спорт (м) | [párusnij spórt] |
| rally racing | ралли (с) | [ráli] |

rugby	регби (c)	[rǽgbi]
snowboarding	сноуборд (м)	[snɔubórd]
archery	стрельба (ж) из лука	[strelʲbá iz lúka]

115. Gym

| barbell | штанга (ж) | [ʃtánga] |
| dumbbells | гантели (ж мн) | [gantéli] |

training machine	тренажёр (м)	[trenaʒór]
exercise bicycle	велотренажёр (м)	[velɔ·trenaʒór]
treadmill	беговая дорожка (ж)	[begɔvája dɔrójka]

horizontal bar	перекладина (ж)	[perekládina]
parallel bars	брусья (мн)	[brúsja]
vault (vaulting horse)	конь (м)	[kónʲ]
mat (exercise ~)	мат (м)	[mát]

jump rope	скакалка (ж)	[skakálka]
aerobics	аэробика (ж)	[aɛróbika]
yoga	йога (ж)	[jóga]

116. Sports. Miscellaneous

Olympic Games	Олимпийские игры (ж мн)	[ɔlimpíjskie ígri]
winner	победитель (м)	[pɔbedítelʲ]
to be winning	побеждать (нсв, нпх)	[pɔbeʒdátʲ]
to win (vi)	выиграть (св, нпх)	[vīigratʲ]

| leader | лидер (м) | [líder] |
| to lead (vi) | лидировать (нсв, нпх) | [lidírɔvatʲ] |

first place	первое место (c)	[pérvɔe méstɔ]
second place	второе место (c)	[ftɔróe méstɔ]
third place	третье место (c)	[trétje méstɔ]

medal	медаль (ж)	[medálʲ]
trophy	трофей (м)	[trɔféj]
prize cup (trophy)	кубок (м)	[kúbɔk]
prize (in game)	приз (м)	[prís]
main prize	главный приз (м)	[glávnij prís]

| record | рекорд (м) | [rekórd] |
| to set a record | ставить рекорд | [stávitʲ rekórd] |

final	финал (м)	[finál]
final (adj)	финальный	[finálʲnij]
champion	чемпион (м)	[tʃempión]

championship	чемпионат (м)	[ʧempiɔnát]
stadium	стадион (м)	[stadión]
stand (bleachers)	трибуна (ж)	[tribúna]
fan, supporter	болельщик (м)	[bɔlélʲʃik]
opponent, rival	противник (м)	[prɔtívnik]

| start (start line) | старт (м) | [stárt] |
| finish line | финиш (м) | [fíniʃ] |

| defeat | поражение (с) | [pɔraʒǽnie] |
| to lose (not win) | проиграть (св, нпх) | [prɔigrátʲ] |

referee	судья (ж)	[sudjá]
jury (judges)	жюри (с)	[ʒurí]
score	счёт (м)	[ʃǿt]
tie	ничья (ж)	[nitʃjá]
to tie (vi)	сыграть вничью	[sigrátʲ vnitʃjú]
point	очко (с)	[ɔʧkó]
result (final score)	результат (м)	[rezulʲtát]

half-time	перерыв (м)	[pererɨ́f]
doping	допинг (м)	[dóping]
to penalize (vt)	штрафовать (нсв, пх)	[ʃtrafɔvátʲ]
to disqualify (vt)	дисквалифицировать (нсв, пх)	[diskvalifitsɪ́rɔvatʲ]

apparatus	снаряд (м)	[snarʲád]
javelin	копьё (с)	[kɔpjǿ]
shot (metal ball)	ядро (с)	[jɪdró]
ball (snooker, etc.)	шар (м)	[ʃár]

aim (target)	цель (ж)	[tsǽlʲ]
target	мишень (ж)	[miʃǽnʲ]
to shoot (vi)	стрелять (нсв, нпх)	[strelʲátʲ]
accurate (~ shot)	точный	[tóʧnɨj]

trainer, coach	тренер (м)	[tréner]
to train (sb)	тренировать (нсв, пх)	[trenirɔvátʲ]
to train (vi)	тренироваться (нсв, возв)	[trenirɔvátsa]
training	тренировка (ж)	[trenirófka]

gym	спортзал (м)	[spɔrtzál]
exercise (physical)	упражнение (с)	[upraʒnénie]
warm-up (athlete ~)	разминка (ж)	[razmínka]

Education

school	школа (ж)	[ʃkóla]
principal (headmaster)	директор (м) школы	[diréktɔr ʃkóli]
pupil (boy)	ученик (м)	[utʃeník]
pupil (girl)	ученица (ж)	[utʃenítsa]
schoolboy	школьник (м)	[ʃkólʲnik]
schoolgirl	школьница (ж)	[ʃkólʲnitsa]
to teach (sb)	учить (нсв, пх)	[utʃítʲ]
to learn (language, etc.)	учить (нсв, пх)	[utʃítʲ]
to learn by heart	учить наизусть	[utʃítʲ naizústʲ]
to learn (~ to count, etc.)	учиться (нсв, возв)	[utʃítsa]
to be in school	учиться (нсв, возв)	[utʃítsa]
to go to school	идти в школу	[itʲtí f ʃkólu]
alphabet	алфавит (м)	[alfavít]
subject (at school)	предмет (м)	[predmét]
classroom	класс (м)	[klás]
lesson	урок (м)	[urók]
recess	перемена (ж)	[pereména]
school bell	звонок (м)	[zvɔnók]
school desk	парта (ж)	[párta]
chalkboard	доска (ж)	[dɔská]
grade	отметка (ж)	[ɔtmétka]
good grade	хорошая отметка (ж)	[hɔróʃaja ɔtmétka]
bad grade	плохая отметка (ж)	[plɔhája ɔtmétka]
to give a grade	ставить отметку	[stávitʲ ɔtmétku]
mistake, error	ошибка (ж)	[ɔʃípka]
to make mistakes	делать ошибки	[délatʲ ɔʃípki]
to correct (an error)	исправлять (нсв, пх)	[ispravlʲátʲ]
cheat sheet	шпаргалка (ж)	[ʃpargálka]
homework	домашнее задание (с)	[dɔmáʃnee zadánie]
exercise (in education)	упражнение (с)	[upraʒnénie]
to be present	присутствовать (нсв, нпх)	[prisútstvɔvatʲ]
to be absent	отсутствовать (нсв, нпх)	[ɔtsútstvɔvatʲ]
to miss school	пропускать уроки	[prɔpuskátʲ uróki]

to punish (vt)	наказывать (нсв, пх)	[nakázivatʲ]
punishment	наказание (с)	[nakazánie]
conduct (behavior)	поведение (с)	[povedénie]

report card	дневник (м)	[dnevník]
pencil	карандаш (м)	[karandáʃ]
eraser	ластик (м)	[lástik]
chalk	мел (м)	[mél]
pencil case	пенал (м)	[penál]

schoolbag	портфель (м)	[portfélʲ]
pen	ручка (ж)	[rútʃka]
school notebook	тетрадь (ж)	[tetrátʲ]
textbook	учебник (м)	[utʃébnik]
drafting compass	циркуль (м)	[tsírkulʲ]

| to make technical drawings | чертить (нсв, пх) | [tʃertítʲ] |
| technical drawing | чертёж (м) | [tʃertǿʃ] |

poem	стихотворение (с)	[stihotvorénie]
by heart (adv)	наизусть	[naizústʲ]
to learn by heart	учить наизусть	[utʃítʲ naizústʲ]

school vacation	каникулы (мн)	[kaníkuli]
to be on vacation	быть на каникулах	[bítʲ na kaníkulah]
to spend one's vacation	провести каникулы	[provestí kaníkuli]

test (written math ~)	контрольная работа (ж)	[kontrólʲnaja rabóta]
essay (composition)	сочинение (с)	[sotʃinénie]
dictation	диктант (м)	[diktánt]
exam (examination)	экзамен (м)	[ɛkzámen]
to take an exam	сдавать экзамены	[zdavátʲ ɛkzámeni]
experiment (e.g., chemistry ~)	опыт (м)	[ópit]

118. College. University

academy	академия (ж)	[akadémija]
university	университет (м)	[universitét]
faculty (e.g., ~ of Medicine)	факультет (м)	[fakulʲtét]

student (masc.)	студент (м)	[studént]
student (fem.)	студентка (ж)	[studéntka]
lecturer (teacher)	преподаватель (м)	[prepodavátelʲ]

lecture hall, room	аудитория (ж)	[auditórija]
graduate	выпускник (м)	[vípuskník]
diploma	диплом (м)	[diplóm]

dissertation	диссертация (ж)	[disertátsija]
study (report)	исследование (с)	[islédɔvanie]
laboratory	лаборатория (ж)	[labɔratórija]

lecture	лекция (ж)	[léktsija]
coursemate	однокурсник (м)	[ɔdnɔkúrsnik]
scholarship	стипендия (ж)	[stipéndija]
academic degree	учёная степень (ж)	[utʃónaja stépenʲ]

119. Sciences. Disciplines

mathematics	математика (ж)	[matemátika]
algebra	алгебра (ж)	[álgebra]
geometry	геометрия (ж)	[geɔmétrija]

astronomy	астрономия (ж)	[astrɔnómija]
biology	биология (ж)	[biɔlógija]
geography	география (ж)	[geɔgráfija]
geology	геология (ж)	[geɔlógija]
history	история (ж)	[istórija]

medicine	медицина (ж)	[meditsīna]
pedagogy	педагогика (ж)	[pedagógika]
law	право (с)	[právɔ]

physics	физика (ж)	[fízika]
chemistry	химия (ж)	[hímija]
philosophy	философия (ж)	[filɔsófija]
psychology	психология (ж)	[psihɔlógija]

120. Writing system. Orthography

grammar	грамматика (ж)	[gramátika]
vocabulary	лексика (ж)	[léksika]
phonetics	фонетика (ж)	[fɔnǽtika]

noun	существительное (с)	[suʃestvítelʲnɔe]
adjective	прилагательное (с)	[prilagátelʲnɔe]
verb	глагол (м)	[glagól]
adverb	наречие (с)	[narétʃie]

pronoun	местоимение (с)	[mestɔiménie]
interjection	междометие (с)	[meʒdɔmétie]
preposition	предлог (м)	[predlóg]

root	корень (м) слова	[kórenʲ slóva]
ending	окончание (с)	[ɔkɔntʃánie]
prefix	приставка (ж)	[pristáfka]

syllable	слог (м)	[slóg]
suffix	суффикс (м)	[súfiks]
stress mark	ударение (с)	[udarénie]
apostrophe	апостроф (м)	[apóstrof]
period, dot	точка (ж)	[tótʃka]
comma	запятая (ж)	[zapıtája]
semicolon	точка (ж) с запятой	[tótʃka s zapıtój]
colon	двоеточие (с)	[dvɔetótʃie]
ellipsis	многоточие (с)	[mnɔgɔtótʃie]
question mark	вопросительный знак (м)	[vɔprɔsítelʲnij znák]
exclamation point	восклицательный знак (м)	[vɔsklitsátelʲnij znák]
quotation marks	кавычки (ж мн)	[kavítʃki]
in quotation marks	в кавычках	[f kavítʃkah]
parenthesis	скобки (ж мн)	[skópki]
in parenthesis	в скобках	[f skópkah]
hyphen	дефис (м)	[defís]
dash	тире (с)	[tirǽ]
space (between words)	пробел (м)	[prɔbél]
letter	буква (ж)	[búkva]
capital letter	большая буква (ж)	[bɔlʲʃája búkva]
vowel (n)	гласный звук (м)	[glásnij zvúk]
consonant (n)	согласный звук (м)	[sɔglásnij zvúk]
sentence	предложение (с)	[predlɔʒǽnie]
subject	подлежащее (с)	[pɔdleʒáʃʲee]
predicate	сказуемое (с)	[skazúemɔe]
line	строка (ж)	[strɔká]
on a new line	с новой строки	[s nóvɔj strɔkí]
paragraph	абзац (м)	[abzáts]
word	слово (с)	[slóvɔ]
group of words	словосочетание (с)	[slɔvɔ·sɔtʃetánie]
expression	выражение (с)	[viraʒǽnie]
synonym	синоним (м)	[sinónim]
antonym	антоним (м)	[antónim]
rule	правило (с)	[právilɔ]
exception	исключение (с)	[isklʲutʃénie]
correct (adj)	верный	[vérnij]
conjugation	спряжение (с)	[sprıʒǽnie]
declension	склонение (с)	[sklɔnénie]

nominal case	падеж (м)	[padéʃ]
question	вопрос (м)	[vɔprós]
to underline (vt)	подчеркнуть (св, пх)	[pɔtʃerknútʲ]
dotted line	пунктир (м)	[punktír]

121. Foreign languages

language	язык (м)	[jɪzīk]
foreign (adj)	иностранный	[inɔstránnij]
foreign language	иностранный язык (м)	[inɔstránnij jɪzīk]
to study (vt)	изучать (нсв, пх)	[izuʧátʲ]
to learn (language, etc.)	учить (нсв, пх)	[uʧítʲ]

to read (vi, vt)	читать (нсв, н/пх)	[ʧitátʲ]
to speak (vi, vt)	говорить (нсв, н/пх)	[gɔvɔrítʲ]
to understand (vt)	понимать (нсв, пх)	[pɔnimátʲ]
to write (vt)	писать (нсв, пх)	[pisátʲ]

fast (adv)	быстро	[bīstrɔ]
slowly (adv)	медленно	[médlenɔ]
fluently (adv)	свободно	[svɔbódnɔ]

rules	правила (с мн)	[právila]
grammar	грамматика (ж)	[gramátika]
vocabulary	лексика (ж)	[léksika]
phonetics	фонетика (ж)	[fɔnǽtika]

textbook	учебник (м)	[uʧébnik]
dictionary	словарь (м)	[slɔvárʲ]
teach-yourself book	самоучитель (м)	[samɔuʧítelʲ]
phrasebook	разговорник (м)	[razgɔvórnik]

cassette, tape	кассета (ж)	[kaséta]
videotape	видеокассета (ж)	[vídeɔ·kaséta]
CD, compact disc	компакт-диск (м)	[kɔmpákt-dísk]
DVD	DVD-диск (м)	[di·vi·dí dísk]

alphabet	алфавит (м)	[alfavít]
to spell (vt)	говорить по буквам	[gɔvɔrítʲ pɔ búkvam]
pronunciation	произношение (с)	[prɔiznɔʃǽnie]

accent	акцент (м)	[aktsǽnt]
with an accent	с акцентом	[s aktsǽntɔm]
without an accent	без акцента	[bez aktsǽnta]

| word | слово (с) | [slóvɔ] |
| meaning | смысл (м) | [smīsl] |

| course (e.g., a French ~) | курсы (мн) | [kúrsɨ] |
| to sign up | записаться (св, возв) | [zapisátsa] |

teacher	преподаватель (м)	[prepɔdavátelʲ]
translation (process)	перевод (м)	[perevód]
translation (text, etc.)	перевод (м)	[perevód]

| translator | переводчик (м) | [perevóttʃik] |
| interpreter | переводчик (м) | [perevóttʃik] |

| polyglot | полиглот (м) | [pɔliglót] |
| memory | память (ж) | [pámɪtʲ] |

122. Fairy tale characters

Santa Claus	Санта Клаус (м)	[sánta kláus]
Cinderella	Золушка (ж)	[zóluʃka]
mermaid	русалка (ж)	[rusálka]
Neptune	Нептун (м)	[neptún]

magician, wizard	волшебник (м)	[vɔlʃǽbnik]
fairy	волшебница (ж)	[vɔlʃǽbnitsa]
magic (adj)	волшебный	[vɔlʃǽbnij]
magic wand	волшебная палочка (ж)	[vɔlʃǽbnaja pálɔtʃka]

fairy tale	сказка (ж)	[skáska]
miracle	чудо (с)	[tʃúdɔ]
dwarf	гном (м)	[gnóm]
to turn into ...	превратиться в ... (св)	[prevratítsa f ...]

ghost	привидение (с)	[prividénie]
phantom	призрак (м)	[prízrak]
monster	чудовище (с)	[tʃʲudóviʃʲe]
dragon	дракон (м)	[drakón]
giant	великан (м)	[velikán]

123. Zodiac Signs

Aries	Овен (м)	[ɔven]
Taurus	Телец (м)	[teléts]
Gemini	Близнецы (мн)	[bliznetsɪ̃]
Cancer	Рак (м)	[rák]
Leo	Лев (м)	[léf]
Virgo	Дева (ж)	[déva]

Libra	Весы (мн)	[vesɪ̃]
Scorpio	Скорпион (м)	[skɔrpión]
Sagittarius	Стрелец (м)	[streléts]
Capricorn	Козерог (м)	[kɔzeróg]
Aquarius	Водолей (м)	[vɔdɔléj]
Pisces	Рыбы (мн)	[rɪ̃bi]

character	**характер** (м)	[harákter]
character traits	**черты** (ж мн) **характера**	[tʃertí haráktera]
behavior	**поведение** (с)	[pɔvedénie]
to tell fortunes	**гадать** (нсв, нпх)	[gadátʲ]
fortune-teller	**гадалка** (ж)	[gadálka]
horoscope	**гороскоп** (м)	[gɔrɔskóp]

Arts

theater	театр (м)	[teátr]
opera	опера (ж)	[ópera]
operetta	оперетта (ж)	[ɔperétta]
ballet	балет (м)	[balét]

theater poster	афиша (ж)	[afíʃa]
troupe	труппа (ж)	[trúpa]
(theatrical company)		

tour	гастроли (мн)	[gastróli]
to be on tour	гастролировать (нсв, нпх)	[gastrɔlírovatʲ]
to rehearse (vi, vt)	репетировать (нсв, н/пх)	[repetírovatʲ]
rehearsal	репетиция (ж)	[repetítsija]
repertoire	репертуар (м)	[repertuár]

performance	представление (с)	[pretstavlénie]
theatrical show	спектакль (м)	[spektáklʲ]
play	пьеса (ж)	[pjésa]

ticket	билет (м)	[bilét]
box office (ticket booth)	билетная касса (ж)	[bilétnaja kássa]
lobby, foyer	холл (м)	[hól]
coat check (cloakroom)	гардероб (м)	[garderób]
coat check tag	номерок (м)	[nɔmerók]
binoculars	бинокль (м)	[binóklʲ]
usher	контролёр (м)	[kɔntrɔlǿr]

orchestra seats	партер (м)	[partǽr]
balcony	балкон (м)	[balkón]
dress circle	бельэтаж (м)	[beljetáʃ]
box	ложа (ж)	[lóʒa]
row	ряд (м)	[rʲád]
seat	место (с)	[méstɔ]

audience	публика (ж)	[públika]
spectator	зритель (м)	[zrítelʲ]
to clap (vi, vt)	хлопать (нсв, нпх)	[hlópatʲ]
applause	аплодисменты (мн)	[aplɔdisménti]
ovation	овации (ж мн)	[ɔvátsii]

stage	сцена (ж)	[stsǽna]
curtain	занавес (м)	[zánaves]
scenery	декорация (ж)	[dekɔrátsija]

backstage	кулисы (мн)	[kulísi]
scene (e.g., the last ~)	сцена (ж)	[stsǽna]
act	акт (м)	[ákt]
intermission	антракт (м)	[antrákt]

125. Cinema

| actor | актёр (м) | [aktǿr] |
| actress | актриса (ж) | [aktrísa] |

movies (industry)	кино (с)	[kinó]
movie	кино, фильм (м)	[kinó], [fíl'm]
episode	серия (ж)	[sérija]

detective movie	детектив (м)	[dɛtɛktíf]
action movie	боевик (м)	[bɔevík]
adventure movie	приключенческий фильм (м)	[prikl'utʃéntʃeskij fíl'm]
sci-fi movie	фантастический фильм (м)	[fantastítʃeskij fíl'm]
horror movie	фильм (м) ужасов	[fíl'm úʒasɔf]

comedy movie	кинокомедия (ж)	[kinɔ·kɔmédija]
melodrama	мелодрама (ж)	[melɔdráma]
drama	драма (ж)	[dráma]

fictional movie	художественный фильм (м)	[hudóʒestvenij fíl'm]
documentary	документальный фильм (м)	[dɔkumentál'nij fíl'm]
cartoon	мультфильм (м)	[mul'tfíl'm]
silent movies	немое кино (с)	[nemóe kinó]

role (part)	роль (ж)	[ról']
leading role	главная роль (ж)	[glávnaja ról']
to play (vi, vt)	играть (нсв, н/пх)	[igrát']

movie star	кинозвезда (ж)	[kinɔ·zvezdá]
well-known (adj)	известный	[izvésnij]
famous (adj)	знаменитый	[znamenítij]
popular (adj)	популярный	[pɔpul'árnij]

script (screenplay)	сценарий (м)	[stsɛnárij]
scriptwriter	сценарист (м)	[stsɛnaríst]
movie director	режиссёр (м)	[reʒisǿr]
producer	продюсер (м)	[prɔd'úsɛr]
assistant	ассистент (м)	[asistént]
cameraman	оператор (м)	[ɔperátɔr]
stuntman	каскадёр (м)	[kaskadǿr]
double (stand-in)	дублёр (м)	[dublǿr]

to shoot a movie	снимать фильм	[snimátʲ fílʲm]
audition, screen test	пробы (мн)	[próbɨ]
shooting	съёмки (мн)	[sjómki]
movie crew	съёмочная группа (ж)	[sjómətʃnaja grúpa]
movie set	съёмочная площадка (ж)	[sjómətʃnaja plɔʃátka]
camera	кинокамера (ж)	[kinɔ·kámera]

movie theater	кинотеатр (м)	[kinɔteátr]
screen (e.g., big ~)	экран (м)	[ɛkrán]
to show a movie	показывать фильм	[pɔkázivatʲ fílʲm]

soundtrack	звуковая дорожка (ж)	[zvukɔvája dɔróʃka]
special effects	специальные эффекты (м мн)	[spetsiálʲnɨe ɛfékti]
subtitles	субтитры (мн)	[suptítri]
credits	титры (мн)	[títri]
translation	перевод (м)	[perevód]

126. Painting

| art | искусство (с) | [iskústvɔ] |
| fine arts | изящные искусства (с мн) | [izʲáʃnie iskústva] |

| art gallery | арт-галерея (ж) | [art-galeréja] |
| art exhibition | выставка (ж) картин | [vɨstafka kartín] |

painting (art)	живопись (ж)	[ʒɨvɔpisʲ]
graphic art	графика (ж)	[gráfika]
abstract art	абстракционизм (м)	[abstraktsɨonízm]
impressionism	импрессионизм (м)	[impresɨonízm]

picture (painting)	картина (ж)	[kartína]
drawing	рисунок (м)	[risúnɔk]
poster	постер (м)	[póstɛr]

illustration (picture)	иллюстрация (ж)	[ilʲustrátsija]
miniature	миниатюра (ж)	[miniatʲúra]
copy (of painting, etc.)	копия (ж)	[kópija]
reproduction	репродукция (ж)	[reprɔdúktsija]

mosaic	мозаика (ж)	[mɔzáika]
stained glass window	витраж (м)	[vitráʃ]
fresco	фреска (ж)	[fréska]
engraving	гравюра (ж)	[gravʲúra]

bust (sculpture)	бюст (м)	[bʲúst]
sculpture	скульптура (ж)	[skulʲptúra]
statue	статуя (ж)	[státuja]
plaster of Paris	гипс (м)	[gíps]
plaster (as adj)	из гипса	[iz gípsa]

portrait	портрет (м)	[portrét]
self-portrait	автопортрет (м)	[afto·portrét]
landscape painting	пейзаж (м)	[pejzáʃ]
still life	натюрморт (м)	[natʲurmórt]
caricature	карикатура (ж)	[karikatúra]
sketch	набросок (м)	[nabrósɔk]

paint	краска (ж)	[kráska]
watercolor paint	акварель (ж)	[akvarélʲ]
oil (paint)	масло (с)	[máslɔ]
pencil	карандаш (м)	[karandáʃ]
India ink	тушь (ж)	[túʃ]
charcoal	уголь (м)	[úgɔlʲ]

to draw (vi, vt)	рисовать (нсв, н/пх)	[risɔvátʲ]
to paint (vi, vt)	рисовать (нсв, н/пх)	[risɔvátʲ]
to pose (vi)	позировать (нсв, нпх)	[pozírɔvatʲ]
artist's model (masc.)	натурщик (м)	[natúrʃik]
artist's model (fem.)	натурщица (ж)	[natúrʃitsa]

artist (painter)	художник (м)	[hudóʒnik]
work of art	произведение (с)	[prɔizvedénie]
masterpiece	шедевр (м)	[ʃɛdǽvr]
studio (artist's workroom)	мастерская (ж)	[masterskája]

canvas (cloth)	холст (м)	[hólst]
easel	мольберт (м)	[mɔlʲbért]
palette	палитра (ж)	[palítra]

frame (picture ~, etc.)	рама (ж)	[ráma]
restoration	реставрация (ж)	[restavrátsija]
to restore (vt)	реставрировать (нсв, пх)	[restavrírɔvatʲ]

127. Literature & Poetry

literature	литература (ж)	[literatúra]
author (writer)	автор (м)	[áftɔr]
pseudonym	псевдоним (м)	[psevdɔním]

book	книга (ж)	[kníga]
volume	том (м)	[tóm]
table of contents	оглавление (с)	[ɔglavlénie]
page	страница (ж)	[stranítsa]
main character	главный герой (м)	[glávnij gerój]
autograph	автограф (м)	[aftógraf]

short story	рассказ (м)	[raskás]
story (novella)	повесть (ж)	[póvestʲ]
novel	роман (м)	[rɔmán]
work (writing)	сочинение (с)	[sɔtʃinénie]

| fable | басня (ж) | [básnʲa] |
| detective novel | детектив (м) | [dɛtɛktíf] |

poem (verse)	стихотворение (с)	[stihotvorénie]
poetry	поэзия (ж)	[poǽzija]
poem (epic, ballad)	поэма (ж)	[poǽma]
poet	поэт (м)	[poǽt]

fiction	беллетристика (ж)	[beletrístika]
science fiction	научная фантастика (ж)	[naútʃnaja fantástika]
adventures	приключения (ж)	[priklʲutʃénija]
educational literature	учебная литература (ж)	[utʃébnaja literatúra]
children's literature	детская литература (ж)	[détskaja literatúra]

128. Circus

| circus | цирк (м) | [tsɪrk] |
| traveling circus | цирк-шапито (м) | [tsɪrk-ʃapitó] |

| program | программа (ж) | [prográma] |
| performance | представление (с) | [pretstavlénie] |

| act (circus ~) | номер (м) | [nómer] |
| circus ring | арена (ж) | [aréna] |

| pantomime (act) | пантомима (ж) | [pantomíma] |
| clown | клоун (м) | [klóun] |

acrobat	акробат (м)	[akrobát]
acrobatics	акробатика (ж)	[akrobátika]
gymnast	гимнаст (м)	[gimnást]

| acrobatic gymnastics | гимнастика (ж) | [gimnástika] |
| somersault | сальто (с) | [sálʲto] |

| athlete (strongman) | атлет (м) | [atlét] |
| tamer (e.g., lion ~) | укротитель (м) | [ukrotítelʲ] |

| rider (circus horse ~) | наездник (м) | [naéznik] |
| assistant | ассистент (м) | [asistént] |

stunt	трюк (м)	[trʲúk]
magic trick	фокус (м)	[fókus]
conjurer, magician	фокусник (м)	[fókusnik]

juggler	жонглёр (м)	[ʒonglǿr]
to juggle (vi, vt)	жонглировать (нсв, н/пх)	[ʒonglírovatʲ]
animal trainer	дрессировщик (м)	[dresiróffʲik]
animal training	дрессировка (ж)	[dresirófka]
to train (animals)	дрессировать (нсв, пх)	[dresirovátʲ]

129. Music. Pop music

music	музыка (ж)	[múzika]
musician	музыкант (м)	[muzikánt]
musical instrument	музыкальный инструмент (м)	[muzikálʲnij instrumént]
to play ...	играть на ... (нсв)	[igrátʲ na ...]
guitar	гитара (ж)	[gitára]
violin	скрипка (ж)	[skrípka]
cello	виолончель (ж)	[violontʃélʲ]
double bass	контрабас (м)	[kontrabás]
harp	арфа (ж)	[árfa]
piano	пианино (с)	[pianíno]
grand piano	рояль (м)	[rojálʲ]
organ	орган (м)	[orgán]
wind instruments	духовые инструменты (м мн)	[duhovíe instruménti]
oboe	гобой (м)	[gobój]
saxophone	саксофон (м)	[saksofón]
clarinet	кларнет (м)	[klarnét]
flute	флейта (ж)	[fléjta]
trumpet	труба (ж)	[trubá]
accordion	аккордеон (м)	[akordeón]
drum	барабан (м)	[barabán]
duo	дуэт (м)	[duǽt]
trio	трио (с)	[trío]
quartet	квартет (м)	[kvartét]
choir	хор (м)	[hór]
orchestra	оркестр (м)	[orkéstr]
pop music	поп-музыка (ж)	[póp-múzika]
rock music	рок-музыка (ж)	[rók-múzika]
rock group	рок-группа (ж)	[rok-grúpa]
jazz	джаз (м)	[dʒás]
idol	кумир (м)	[kumír]
admirer, fan	поклонник (м)	[poklónnik]
concert	концерт (м)	[kontsǽrt]
symphony	симфония (ж)	[simfónija]
composition	сочинение (с)	[sotʃinénie]
to compose (write)	сочинить (св, пх)	[sotʃinítʲ]
singing (n)	пение (с)	[pénie]
song	песня (ж)	[pésnʲa]
tune (melody)	мелодия (ж)	[melódija]

| rhythm | ритм (м) | [rítm] |
| blues | блюз (м) | [blʲús] |

sheet music	ноты (ж мн)	[nóti]
baton	палочка (ж)	[pálɔtʃka]
bow	смычок (м)	[smitʃók]
string	струна (ж)	[struná]
case (e.g., guitar ~)	футляр (м)	[futlʲár]

Rest. Entertainment. Travel

130. Trip. Travel

tourism, travel	туризм (м)	[turízm]
tourist	турист (м)	[turíst]
trip, voyage	путешествие (с)	[puteʃǽstvie]
adventure	приключение (с)	[priklʲutʃénie]
trip, journey	поездка (ж)	[pɔéstka]
vacation	отпуск (м)	[ótpusk]
to be on vacation	быть в отпуске	[bĭtʲ v ótpuske]
rest	отдых (м)	[ótdɨh]
train	поезд (м)	[póezd]
by train	поездом	[póezdɔm]
airplane	самолёт (м)	[samɔlǿt]
by airplane	самолётом	[samɔlǿtɔm]
by car	на автомобиле	[na aftɔmɔbíle]
by ship	на корабле	[na kɔrablé]
luggage	багаж (м)	[bagáʃ]
suitcase	чемодан (м)	[tʃemɔdán]
luggage cart	тележка (ж) для багажа	[teléʃka dlʲa bagaʒá]
passport	паспорт (м)	[páspɔrt]
visa	виза (ж)	[víza]
ticket	билет (м)	[bilét]
air ticket	авиабилет (м)	[aviabilét]
guidebook	путеводитель (м)	[putevɔdítelʲ]
map (tourist ~)	карта (ж)	[kárta]
area (rural ~)	местность (ж)	[mésnɔstʲ]
place, site	место (с)	[méstɔ]
exotica (n)	экзотика (ж)	[ɛkzótika]
exotic (adj)	экзотический	[ɛkzɔtítʃeskij]
amazing (adj)	удивительный	[udivítelʲnij]
group	группа (ж)	[grúpa]
excursion, sightseeing tour	экскурсия (ж)	[ɛkskúrsija]
guide (person)	экскурсовод (м)	[ɛkskursɔvód]

131. Hotel

hotel	гостиница (ж)	[gɔstínitsa]
motel	мотель (м)	[mɔtǽlʲ]
three-star (~ hotel)	3 звезды	[trí zvezdī]
five-star	5 звёзд	[pʲátʲ zvǿzd]
to stay (in a hotel, etc.)	остановиться (св, возв)	[ɔstanɔvítsa]
room	номер (м)	[nómer]
single room	одноместный номер (м)	[ɔdnɔ·mésnij nómer]
double room	двухместный номер (м)	[dvuh·mésnij nómer]
to book a room	бронировать номер	[brɔnírɔvatʲ nómer]
half board	полупансион (м)	[pɔlu·pansión]
full board	полный пансион (м)	[pólnij pansión]
with bath	с ванной	[s vánnɔj]
with shower	с душем	[s dúʃɛm]
satellite television	спутниковое телевидение (с)	[spútnikɔvɔe televídenie]
air-conditioner	кондиционер (м)	[kɔnditsiɔnér]
towel	полотенце (с)	[pɔloténtse]
key	ключ (м)	[klʲútʃ]
administrator	администратор (м)	[administrátɔr]
chambermaid	горничная (ж)	[górnitʃnaja]
porter, bellboy	носильщик (м)	[nɔsílʲʃik]
doorman	портье (с)	[pɔrtjé]
restaurant	ресторан (м)	[restɔrán]
pub, bar	бар (м)	[bár]
breakfast	завтрак (м)	[záftrak]
dinner	ужин (м)	[úʒin]
buffet	шведский стол (м)	[ʃvétskij stól]
lobby	вестибюль (м)	[vestibʲúlʲ]
elevator	лифт (м)	[líft]
DO NOT DISTURB	НЕ БЕСПОКОИТЬ	[ne bespɔkóitʲ]
NO SMOKING	НЕ КУРИТЬ!	[ne kurítʲ]

132. Books. Reading

book	книга (ж)	[kníga]
author	автор (м)	[áftɔr]
writer	писатель (м)	[pisátelʲ]
to write (~ a book)	написать (св, пх)	[napisátʲ]
reader	читатель (м)	[tʃitátelʲ]

| to read (vi, vt) | читать (нсв, н/пх) | [tʃitátʲ] |
| reading (activity) | чтение (с) | [tʃténie] |

| silently (to oneself) | про себя | [prɔ sebʲá] |
| aloud (adv) | вслух | [fslúh] |

to publish (vt)	издавать (нсв, пх)	[izdavátʲ]
publishing (process)	издание (с)	[izdánie]
publisher	издатель (м)	[izdátelʲ]
publishing house	издательство (с)	[izdátelʲstvɔ]

to come out (be released)	выйти (св, нпх)	[vɨ́jti]
release (of a book)	выход (м)	[vɨ́hɔd]
print run	тираж (м)	[tiráʃ]

| bookstore | книжный магазин (м) | [kníʒnij magazín] |
| library | библиотека (ж) | [bibliotéka] |

story (novella)	повесть (ж)	[póvestʲ]
short story	рассказ (м)	[raskás]
novel	роман (м)	[rɔmán]
detective novel	детектив (м)	[dɛtɛktíf]

memoirs	мемуары (мн)	[memuári]
legend	легенда (ж)	[legénda]
myth	миф (м)	[míf]

poetry, poems	стихи (м мн)	[stihí]
autobiography	автобиография (ж)	[áftɔ·biográfija]
selected works	избранное (с)	[ízbrannɔe]
science fiction	фантастика (ж)	[fantástika]

title	название (с)	[nazvánie]
introduction	введение (с)	[vvedénie]
title page	титульный лист (м)	[títulʲnij líst]

chapter	глава (ж)	[glavá]
extract	отрывок (м)	[ɔtrɨ́vɔk]
episode	эпизод (м)	[ɛpizód]

plot (storyline)	сюжет (м)	[sʲuʒǽt]
contents	содержание (с)	[sɔderʒánie]
table of contents	оглавление (с)	[ɔglavlénie]
main character	главный герой (м)	[glávnij gerój]

volume	том (м)	[tóm]
cover	обложка (ж)	[ɔblóʃka]
binding	переплёт (м)	[pereplót]
bookmark	закладка (ж)	[zaklátka]

| page | страница (ж) | [straníʦa] |
| to page through | листать (нсв, пх) | [listátʲ] |

margins	поля (ж)	[polʲá]
annotation (marginal note, etc.)	пометка (ж)	[pɔmétka]
footnote	примечание (с)	[primetʃánie]

text	текст (м)	[tékst]
type, font	шрифт (м)	[ʃríft]
misprint, typo	опечатка (ж)	[ɔpetʃátka]

translation	перевод (м)	[perevód]
to translate (vt)	переводить (нсв, пх)	[perevɔdítʲ]
original (n)	подлинник (м)	[pódlinik]

famous (adj)	знаменитый	[znamenítij]
unknown (not famous)	неизвестный	[neizvésnij]
interesting (adj)	интересный	[interésnij]
bestseller	бестселлер (м)	[bessǽler]

dictionary	словарь (м)	[slɔvárʲ]
textbook	учебник (м)	[utʃébnik]
encyclopedia	энциклопедия (ж)	[ɛntsiklɔpédija]

133. Hunting. Fishing

hunting	охота (ж)	[ɔhóta]
to hunt (vi, vt)	охотиться (нсв, возв)	[ɔhótitsa]
hunter	охотник (м)	[ɔhótnik]

to shoot (vi)	стрелять (нсв, нпх)	[strelʲátʲ]
rifle	ружьё (с)	[ruʒjǿ]
bullet (shell)	патрон (м)	[patrón]
shot (lead balls)	дробь (ж)	[drópʲ]

steel trap	капкан (м)	[kapkán]
snare (for birds, etc.)	ловушка (ж)	[lɔvúʃka]
to fall into the steel trap	попасться в капкан	[pɔpástsa f kapkán]
to lay a steel trap	ставить капкан	[stávitʲ kapkán]

poacher	браконьер (м)	[brakɔnjér]
game (in hunting)	дичь (ж)	[dítʃ]
hound dog	охотничья собака (ж)	[ɔhótnitʃja sɔbáka]
safari	сафари (с)	[safári]
mounted animal	чучело (с)	[tʃútʃelɔ]

fisherman, angler	рыбак (м)	[ribák]
fishing (angling)	рыбалка (ж)	[ribálka]
to fish (vi)	ловить рыбу	[lɔvítʲ rîbu]

| fishing rod | удочка (ж) | [údɔtʃka] |
| fishing line | леска (ж) | [léska] |

hook	крючок (м)	[krʲutʃók]
float, bobber	поплавок (м)	[pɔplavók]
bait	наживка (ж)	[naʒĭfka]

to cast a line	забросить удочку	[zabrósitʲ údɔtʃku]
to bite (ab. fish)	клевать (нсв, нпх)	[klevátʲ]
catch (of fish)	улов (м)	[ulóf]
ice-hole	прорубь (ж)	[prórupʲ]

fishing net	сеть (ж)	[sétʲ]
boat	лодка (ж)	[lótka]
to net (to fish with a net)	ловить сетью	[lɔvítʲ sétju]
to cast[throw] the net	забрасывать сеть	[zabrásivatʲ sétʲ]
to haul the net in	вытаскивать сеть	[vitáskivatʲ sétʲ]

whaler (person)	китобой (м)	[kitɔbój]
whaleboat	китобойное судно (с)	[kitɔbójnɔe súdnɔ]
harpoon	гарпун (м)	[garpún]

134. Games. Billiards

billiards	бильярд (м)	[biljárd]
billiard room, hall	бильярдная (ж)	[biljárdnaja]
ball (snooker, etc.)	бильярдный шар (м)	[biljárdnij ʃár]

to pocket a ball	загнать шар	[zagnátʲ ʃár]
cue	кий (м)	[kíj]
pocket	луза (ж)	[lúza]

135. Games. Playing cards

diamonds	бубны (мн)	[búbnĭ]
spades	пики (мн)	[píki]
hearts	черви (мн)	[tʃérvi]
clubs	трефы (мн)	[tréfĭ]

ace	туз (м)	[tús]
king	король (м)	[kɔrólʲ]
queen	дама (ж)	[dáma]
jack, knave	валет (м)	[valét]

playing card	игральная карта (ж)	[igrálʲnaja kárta]
cards	карты (ж мн)	[kárti]
trump	козырь (м)	[kózirʲ]
deck of cards	колода (ж)	[kɔlóda]

| point | очко (с) | [ɔtʃkó] |
| to deal (vi, vt) | сдавать (нсв, н/пх) | [zdavátʲ] |

to shuffle (cards)	тасовать (нсв, пх)	[tasɔvátʲ]
lead, turn (n)	ход (м)	[hód]
cardsharp	шулер (м)	[ʃúler]

136. Rest. Games. Miscellaneous

to stroll (vi, vt)	гулять (нсв, нпх)	[gulʲátʲ]
stroll (leisurely walk)	прогулка (ж)	[prɔgúlka]
car ride	поездка (ж)	[pɔéstka]
adventure	приключение (с)	[priklʲutʃénie]
picnic	пикник (м)	[pikník]

game (chess, etc.)	игра (ж)	[igrá]
player	игрок (м)	[igrók]
game (one ~ of chess)	партия (ж)	[pártija]

collector (e.g., philatelist)	коллекционер (м)	[kɔlektsionér]
to collect (stamps, etc.)	коллекционировать (нсв, пх)	[kɔlektsionírɔvatʲ]
collection	коллекция (ж)	[kɔléktsija]

crossword puzzle	кроссворд (м)	[krɔsvórd]
racetrack (horse racing venue)	ипподром (м)	[ipɔdróm]
disco (discotheque)	дискотека (ж)	[diskɔtéka]

| sauna | сауна (ж) | [sáuna] |
| lottery | лотерея (ж) | [lɔteréja] |

camping trip	поход (м)	[pɔhód]
camp	лагерь (м)	[lágerʲ]
tent (for camping)	палатка (ж)	[palátka]
compass	компас (м)	[kómpas]
camper	турист (м)	[turíst]

to watch (movie, etc.)	смотреть (нсв, нпх)	[smɔtrétʲ]
viewer	телезритель (м)	[telezrítelʲ]
TV show (TV program)	телепередача (ж)	[tele·peredátʃa]

137. Photography

| camera (photo) | фотоаппарат (м) | [foto·aparát] |
| photo, picture | фото, фотография (ж) | [fótɔ], [fotɔgráfija] |

photographer	фотограф (м)	[fotógraf]
photo studio	фотостудия (ж)	[foto·stúdija]
photo album	фотоальбом (м)	[foto·alʲbóm]
camera lens	объектив (м)	[ɔbjektíf]

telephoto lens	телеобъектив (м)	[tele·ɔbjektíf]
filter	фильтр (м)	[fílʲtr]
lens	линза (ж)	[línza]

optics (high-quality ~)	оптика (ж)	[óptika]
diaphragm (aperture)	диафрагма (ж)	[diafrágma]
exposure time (shutter speed)	выдержка (ж)	[vĩderʃka]

| viewfinder | видоискатель (м) | [vidɔ·iskátelʲ] |

digital camera	цифровая камера (ж)	[tsifrɔvája kámera]
tripod	штатив (м)	[ʃtatíf]
flash	вспышка (ж)	[fspĩʃka]

| to photograph (vt) | фотографировать (нсв, пх) | [fotɔɡrafírɔvatʲ] |

| to take pictures | снимать (нсв, пх) | [snimátʲ] |
| to have one's picture taken | фотографироваться (нсв, возв) | [fotɔɡrafírɔvatsa] |

focus	фокус (м)	[fókus]
to focus	наводить на резкость	[navɔdítʲ na réskɔstʲ]
sharp, in focus (adj)	резкий	[réskij]
sharpness	резкость (ж)	[réskɔstʲ]

| contrast | контраст (м) | [kɔntrást] |
| contrast (as adj) | контрастный | [kɔntrásnij] |

picture (photo)	снимок (м)	[snímɔk]
negative (n)	негатив (м)	[negatíf]
film (a roll of ~)	фотоплёнка (ж)	[fotɔ·plɵnka]
frame (still)	кадр (м)	[kádr]
to print (photos)	печатать (нсв, пх)	[petʃátatʲ]

138. Beach. Swimming

beach	пляж (м)	[plʲáʃ]
sand	песок (м)	[pesók]
deserted (beach)	пустынный	[pustĩnnij]

suntan	загар (м)	[zaɡár]
to get a tan	загорать (нсв, нпх)	[zaɡɔrátʲ]
tan (adj)	загорелый	[zaɡɔrélij]
sunscreen	крем (м) для загара	[krém dlʲa zaɡára]

bikini	бикини (с)	[bikíni]
bathing suit	купальник (м)	[kupálʲnik]
swim trunks	плавки (мн)	[pláfki]
swimming pool	бассейн (м)	[basæjn]
to swim (vi)	плавать (нсв, нпх)	[plávatʲ]

shower	**душ** (м)	[dúʃ]
to change (one's clothes)	**переодеваться** (нсв, возв)	[pereɔdevátsa]
towel	**полотенце** (с)	[pɔlɔténtse]
boat	**лодка** (ж)	[lótka]
motorboat	**катер** (м)	[káter]
water ski	**водные лыжи** (мн)	[vódnie lˠʒi]
paddle boat	**водный велосипед** (м)	[vódnij velɔsipéd]
surfing	**серфинг** (м)	[sǿrfiŋg]
surfer	**серфингист** (м)	[serfingíst]
scuba set	**акваланг** (м)	[akvaláŋg]
flippers (swim fins)	**ласты** (ж мн)	[lásti]
mask (diving ~)	**маска** (ж)	[máska]
diver	**ныряльщик** (м)	[nirʲálʲʃik]
to dive (vi)	**нырять** (нсв, нпх)	[nirʲátʲ]
underwater (adv)	**под водой**	[pɔd vɔdój]
beach umbrella	**зонт** (м)	[zónt]
sunbed (lounger)	**шезлонг** (м)	[ʃɛzlóŋg]
sunglasses	**очки** (мн)	[ɔtʃkí]
air mattress	**плавательный матрац** (м)	[plávatelʲnij matrás]
to play (amuse oneself)	**играть** (нсв, нпх)	[igrátʲ]
to go for a swim	**купаться** (нсв, возв)	[kupátsa]
beach ball	**мяч** (м)	[mʲátʃ]
to inflate (vt)	**надувать** (нсв, пх)	[naduvátʲ]
inflatable, air (adj)	**надувной**	[naduvnój]
wave	**волна** (ж)	[vɔlná]
buoy (line of ~s)	**буй** (м)	[búj]
to drown (ab. person)	**тонуть** (нсв, нпх)	[tɔnútʲ]
to save, to rescue	**спасать** (нсв, пх)	[spasátʲ]
life vest	**спасательный жилет** (м)	[spasátelʲnij ʒilét]
to observe, to watch	**наблюдать** (нсв, нпх)	[nablʲudátʲ]
lifeguard	**спасатель** (м)	[spasátelʲ]

TECHNICAL EQUIPMENT. TRANSPORTATION

Technical equipment

139. Computer

computer	компьютер (м)	[kɔmpjútɛr]
notebook, laptop	ноутбук (м)	[nɔutbúk]
to turn on	включить (св, пх)	[fklʲutʃítʲ]
to turn off	выключить (св, пх)	[vīklʲutʃitʲ]
keyboard	клавиатура (ж)	[klaviatúra]
key	клавиша (ж)	[kláviʃa]
mouse	мышь (ж)	[mīʃ]
mouse pad	коврик (м)	[kóvrik]
button	кнопка (ж)	[knópka]
cursor	курсор (м)	[kursór]
monitor	монитор (м)	[mɔnitór]
screen	экран (м)	[ɛkrán]
hard disk	жёсткий диск (м)	[ʒóstkij dísk]
hard disk capacity	объём (м) жёсткого диска	[ɔbjóm ʒóstkɔvɔ díska]
memory	память (ж)	[pámɪtʲ]
random access memory	оперативная память (ж)	[ɔperatívnaja pámɪtʲ]
file	файл (м)	[fájl]
folder	папка (ж)	[pápka]
to open (vt)	открыть (св, пх)	[ɔtkrītʲ]
to close (vt)	закрыть (св, пх)	[zakrītʲ]
to save (vt)	сохранить (св, пх)	[sɔhranítʲ]
to delete (vt)	удалить (св, пх)	[udalítʲ]
to copy (vt)	скопировать (св, пх)	[skɔpírɔvatʲ]
to sort (vt)	сортировать (нсв, пх)	[sɔrtirɔvátʲ]
to transfer (copy)	переписать (св, пх)	[perepisátʲ]
program	программа (ж)	[prɔgráma]
software	программное обеспечение (с)	[prɔgrámnɔe ɔbespetʃénie]
programmer	программист (м)	[prɔgramíst]
to program (vt)	программировать (нсв, пх)	[prɔgramírɔvatʲ]

hacker	хакер (м)	[háker]
password	пароль (м)	[paról^j]
virus	вирус (м)	[vírus]
to find, to detect	обнаружить (св, пх)	[ɔbnarúʒit^j]

byte	байт (м)	[bájt]
megabyte	мегабайт (м)	[megabájt]

data	данные (мн)	[dánnie]
database	база (ж) данных	[báza dánnih]

cable (USB, etc.)	кабель (м)	[kábel^j]
to disconnect (vt)	отсоединить (св, пх)	[ɔtsɔedinít^j]
to connect (sth to sth)	подсоединить (св, пх)	[pɔtsɔedinít^j]

140. Internet. E-mail

Internet	интернет (м)	[intɛrnǽt]
browser	браузер (м)	[bráuzer]
search engine	поисковый ресурс (м)	[pɔiskóvij resúrs]
provider	провайдер (м)	[prɔvájder]

webmaster	веб-мастер (м)	[vɛb-máster]
website	веб-сайт (м)	[vɛb-sájt]
webpage	веб-страница (ж)	[vɛb-stranítsa]

address (e-mail ~)	адрес (м)	[ádres]
address book	адресная книга (ж)	[ádresnaja kníga]

mailbox	почтовый ящик (м)	[pɔtʃtóvij jáʃik]
mail	почта (ж)	[pótʃta]
full (adj)	переполненный	[perepólnenij]

message	сообщение (с)	[sɔɔpʃénie]
incoming messages	входящие сообщения (с мн)	[fhɔd^jáʃie sɔɔpʃénija]
outgoing messages	исходящие сообщения (с мн)	[isxɔd^jáʃie sɔɔpʃénija]

sender	отправитель (м)	[ɔtpravítel^j]
to send (vt)	отправить (св, пх)	[ɔtprávit^j]
sending (of mail)	отправка (ж)	[ɔtpráfka]

receiver	получатель (м)	[pɔlutʃátel^j]
to receive (vt)	получить (св, пх)	[pɔlutʃít^j]

correspondence	переписка (ж)	[perepíska]
to correspond (vi)	переписываться (нсв, возв)	[perepísivatsa]

file	файл (м)	[fájl]

to download (vt)	скачать (св, пх)	[skatʃátʲ]
to create (vt)	создать (св, пх)	[sɔzdátʲ]
to delete (vt)	удалить (св, пх)	[udalítʲ]
deleted (adj)	удалённый	[udalǿnnij]

connection (ADSL, etc.)	связь (ж)	[svʲásʲ]
speed	скорость (ж)	[skórɔstʲ]
modem	модем (м)	[mɔdǽm]
access	доступ (м)	[dóstup]
port (e.g., input ~)	порт (м)	[pórt]

| connection (make a ~) | подключение (с) | [pɔtklʲutʃénie] |
| to connect to ... (vi) | подключиться (св, возв) | [pɔtklʲutʃítsa] |

| to select (vt) | выбрать (св, пх) | [vɨ̄bratʲ] |
| to search (for ...) | искать ... (нсв, пх) | [iskátʲ ...] |

Transportation

airplane	самолёт (м)	[samɔlǿt]
air ticket	авиабилет (м)	[aviabilét]
airline	авиакомпания (ж)	[avia·kɔmpánija]
airport	аэропорт (м)	[aɛrɔpórt]
supersonic (adj)	сверхзвуковой	[sverh·zvukɔvój]
captain	командир (м) корабля	[kɔmandír kɔrablʲá]
crew	экипаж (м)	[ɛkipáʃ]
pilot	пилот (м)	[pilót]
flight attendant (fem.)	стюардесса (ж)	[stʲuardǽsa]
navigator	штурман (м)	[ʃtúrman]
wings	крылья (с мн)	[krílja]
tail	хвост (м)	[hvóst]
cockpit	кабина (ж)	[kabína]
engine	двигатель (м)	[dvígatelʲ]
undercarriage (landing gear)	шасси (с)	[ʃassí]
turbine	турбина (ж)	[turbína]
propeller	пропеллер (м)	[prɔpéller]
black box	чёрный ящик (м)	[ʧórnij jáʃik]
yoke (control column)	штурвал (м)	[ʃturvál]
fuel	горючее (с)	[gɔrʲúʧee]
safety card	инструкция по безопасности	[instrúkʦija pɔ bezɔpásnɔsti]
oxygen mask	кислородная маска (ж)	[kislɔródnaja máska]
uniform	униформа (ж)	[unifórma]
life vest	спасательный жилет (м)	[spasátelʲnij ʒilét]
parachute	парашют (м)	[paraʃút]
takeoff	взлёт (м)	[vzlǿt]
to take off (vi)	взлетать (нсв, нпх)	[vzletátʲ]
runway	взлётная полоса (ж)	[vzlǿtnaja pɔlasá]
visibility	видимость (ж)	[vídimɔstʲ]
flight (act of flying)	полёт (м)	[pɔlǿt]
altitude	высота (ж)	[visɔtá]
air pocket	воздушная яма (ж)	[vɔzdúʃnaja jáma]
seat	место (с)	[méstɔ]
headphones	наушники (м мн)	[naúʃniki]

folding tray (tray table)	откидной столик (м)	[ɔtkidnój stólik]
airplane window	иллюминатор (м)	[iljuminátɔr]
aisle	проход (м)	[prɔhód]

142. Train

train	поезд (м)	[póezd]
commuter train	электричка (ж)	[ɛlektríʧka]
express train	скорый поезд (м)	[skórij póezd]
diesel locomotive	тепловоз (м)	[teplɔvós]
steam locomotive	паровоз (м)	[parɔvós]

| passenger car | вагон (м) | [vagón] |
| dining car | вагон-ресторан (м) | [vagón-restɔrán] |

rails	рельсы (мн)	[réljsi]
railroad	железная дорога (ж)	[ʒeléznaja dɔróga]
railway tie	шпала (ж)	[ʃpála]

platform (railway ~)	платформа (ж)	[platfórma]
track (~ 1, 2, etc.)	путь (м)	[pútj]
semaphore	семафор (м)	[semafór]
station	станция (ж)	[stántsija]

engineer (train driver)	машинист (м)	[maʃiníst]
porter (of luggage)	носильщик (м)	[nɔsíljʃik]
car attendant	проводник (м)	[prɔvɔdník]
passenger	пассажир (м)	[pasaʒír]
conductor (ticket inspector)	контролёр (м)	[kɔntrɔlǿr]

| corridor (in train) | коридор (м) | [kɔridór] |
| emergency brake | стоп-кран (м) | [stɔp-krán] |

compartment	купе (с)	[kupǽ]
berth	полка (ж)	[pólka]
upper berth	верхняя полка (ж)	[vérhnjaja pólka]
lower berth	нижняя полка (ж)	[níʒnjaja pólka]
bed linen, bedding	постельное бельё (с)	[pɔstéljnɔe beljǿ]

ticket	билет (м)	[bilét]
schedule	расписание (с)	[raspisánie]
information display	табло (с)	[tabló]

to leave, to depart	отходить (нсв, нпх)	[ɔtxɔdítj]
departure (of train)	отправление (с)	[ɔtpravlénie]
to arrive (ab. train)	прибывать (нсв, нпх)	[pribivátj]
arrival	прибытие (с)	[pribĭtie]
to arrive by train	приехать поездом	[priéhatj póezdɔm]
to get on the train	сесть на поезд	[séstj na póezd]

to get off the train	сойти с поезда	[sɔjtí s póezda]
train wreck	крушение (c)	[kruʃǽnie]
to derail (vi)	сойти с рельс	[sɔjtí s rélʲs]

steam locomotive	паровоз (м)	[parɔvós]
stoker, fireman	кочегар (м)	[kɔtʃegár]
firebox	топка (ж)	[tópka]
coal	уголь (м)	[úgɔlʲ]

143. Ship

| ship | корабль (м) | [kɔráblʲ] |
| vessel | судно (c) | [súdnɔ] |

steamship	пароход (м)	[parɔhód]
riverboat	теплоход (м)	[teplɔhód]
cruise ship	лайнер (м)	[lájner]
cruiser	крейсер (м)	[kréjser]

yacht	яхта (ж)	[jáhta]
tugboat	буксир (м)	[buksír]
barge	баржа (ж)	[barʒá]
ferry	паром (м)	[paróm]

| sailing ship | парусник (м) | [párusnik] |
| brigantine | бригантина (ж) | [brigantína] |

| ice breaker | ледокол (м) | [ledɔkól] |
| submarine | подводная лодка (ж) | [pɔdvódnaja lótka] |

boat (flat-bottomed ~)	лодка (ж)	[lótka]
dinghy (lifeboat)	шлюпка (ж)	[ʃlʲúpka]
lifeboat	спасательная шлюпка (ж)	[spasátelʲnaja ʃlʲúpka]
motorboat	катер (м)	[káter]

captain	капитан (м)	[kapitán]
seaman	матрос (м)	[matrós]
sailor	моряк (м)	[mɔrʲák]
crew	экипаж (м)	[ɛkipáʃ]

boatswain	боцман (м)	[bótsman]
ship's boy	юнга (м)	[júnga]
cook	кок (м)	[kók]
ship's doctor	судовой врач (м)	[sudɔvój vrátʃ]

deck	палуба (ж)	[páluba]
mast	мачта (ж)	[mátʃta]
sail	парус (м)	[párus]
hold	трюм (м)	[trʲúm]

bow (prow)	нос (м)	[nós]
stern	корма (ж)	[kɔrmá]
oar	весло (с)	[vesló]
screw propeller	винт (м)	[vínt]

cabin	каюта (ж)	[kajúta]
wardroom	кают-компания (ж)	[kajút-kɔmpánija]
engine room	машинное отделение (с)	[maʃínnɔe ɔtdelénie]
bridge	капитанский мостик (м)	[kapitánskij móstik]
radio room	радиорубка (ж)	[radio·rúpka]
wave (radio)	волна (ж)	[vɔlná]
logbook	судовой журнал (м)	[sudɔvój ʒurnál]

spyglass	подзорная труба (ж)	[pɔdzórnaja trubá]
bell	колокол (м)	[kólɔkɔl]
flag	флаг (м)	[flág]

| hawser (mooring ~) | канат (м) | [kanát] |
| knot (bowline, etc.) | узел (м) | [úzel] |

| deckrails | поручень (м) | [pórutʃenʲ] |
| gangway | трап (м) | [tráp] |

| anchor | якорь (м) | [jákɔrʲ] |
| to weigh anchor | поднять якорь | [pɔdnʲátʲ jákɔrʲ] |

| to drop anchor | бросить якорь | [brósitʲ jákɔrʲ] |
| anchor chain | якорная цепь (ж) | [jákɔrnaja tsæpʲ] |

| port (harbor) | порт (м) | [pórt] |
| quay, wharf | причал (м) | [pritʃál] |

| to berth (moor) | причаливать (нсв, нпх) | [pritʃálivatʲ] |
| to cast off | отчаливать (нсв, нпх) | [ɔttʃálivatʲ] |

| trip, voyage | путешествие (с) | [puteʃǽstvie] |
| cruise (sea trip) | круиз (м) | [kruís] |

| course (route) | курс (м) | [kúrs] |
| route (itinerary) | маршрут (м) | [marʃrút] |

fairway (safe water channel)	фарватер (м)	[farvátɛr]
shallows	мель (ж)	[mélʲ]
to run aground	сесть на мель	[séstʲ na mélʲ]

storm	буря (ж)	[búrʲa]
signal	сигнал (м)	[signál]
to sink (vi)	тонуть (нсв, нпх)	[tɔnútʲ]
Man overboard!	Человек за бортом!	[tʃelɔvék za bórtɔm]
SOS (distress signal)	SOS (м)	[sós]
ring buoy	спасательный круг (м)	[spasátelʲnij krúg]

144. Airport

airport	аэропорт (м)	[aɛrɔpórt]
airplane	самолёт (м)	[samɔlə́t]
airline	авиакомпания (ж)	[avia·kɔmpánija]
air traffic controller	авиадиспетчер (м)	[avia·dispétʃer]
departure	вылет (м)	[vɨ̃let]
arrival	прилёт (м)	[prilə́t]
to arrive (by plane)	прилететь (св, нпх)	[priletétʲ]
departure time	время (с) вылета	[vrémʲa vɨ̃leta]
arrival time	время (с) прилёта	[vrémʲa prilə́ta]
to be delayed	задерживаться (нсв, возв)	[zadérʒivatsa]
flight delay	задержка (ж) вылета	[zadérʃka vɨ̃leta]
information board	информационное табло (с)	[informatsiónnɔe tabló]
information	информация (ж)	[informátsija]
to announce (vt)	объявлять (нсв, пх)	[ɔbjɪvlʲátʲ]
flight (e.g., next ~)	рейс (м)	[réjs]
customs	таможня (ж)	[tamóʒnʲa]
customs officer	таможенник (м)	[tamóʒenik]
customs declaration	декларация (ж)	[deklarátsija]
to fill out (vt)	заполнить (св, пх)	[zapólnitʲ]
to fill out the declaration	заполнить декларацию	[zapólnitʲ deklarátsiju]
passport control	паспортный контроль (м)	[pásportnij kɔntrólʲ]
luggage	багаж (м)	[bagáʃ]
hand luggage	ручная кладь (ж)	[rutʃnája klátʲ]
luggage cart	тележка (ж) для багажа	[teléʃka dlʲa bagaʒá]
landing	посадка (ж)	[pɔsátka]
landing strip	посадочная полоса (ж)	[pɔsádotʃnaja pɔlɔsá]
to land (vi)	садиться (нсв, возв)	[sadítsa]
airstair (passenger stair)	трап (м)	[tráp]
check-in	регистрация (ж)	[registrátsija]
check-in counter	стойка (ж) регистрации	[stójka registrátsii]
to check-in (vi)	зарегистрироваться (св, возв)	[zaregistrírovatsa]
boarding pass	посадочный талон (м)	[pɔsádotʃnij talón]
departure gate	выход (м)	[vɨ̃hɔd]
transit	транзит (м)	[tranzít]
to wait (vt)	ждать (нсв, пх)	[ʒdátʲ]
departure lounge	зал (м) ожидания	[zál ɔʒidánija]

| to see off | провожать (нсв, пх) | [prɔvɔʒátʲ] |
| to say goodbye | прощаться (нсв, возв) | [prɔʃátsa] |

145. Bicycle. Motorcycle

bicycle	велосипед (м)	[velɔsipéd]
scooter	мотороллер (м)	[mɔtɔróler]
motorcycle, bike	мотоцикл (м)	[mɔtɔtsíkl]

to go by bicycle	ехать на велосипеде	[éhatʲ na velɔsipéde]
handlebars	руль (м)	[rúlʲ]
pedal	педаль (ж)	[pedálʲ]
brakes	тормоза (м мн)	[tɔrmɔzá]
bicycle seat (saddle)	седло (с)	[sedló]

pump	насос (м)	[nasós]
luggage rack	багажник (м)	[bagáʒnik]
front lamp	фонарь (м)	[fɔnárʲ]
helmet	шлем (м)	[ʃlém]

wheel	колесо (с)	[kɔlesó]
fender	крыло (с)	[kriló]
rim	обод (м)	[óbɔd]
spoke	спица (ж)	[spítsa]

Cars

automobile, car	автомобиль (м)	[aftɔmɔbílʲ]
sports car	спортивный автомобиль (м)	[spɔrtívnij aftɔmɔbílʲ]
limousine	лимузин (м)	[limuzín]
off-road vehicle	внедорожник (м)	[vnedɔróʒnik]
convertible (n)	кабриолет (м)	[kabriɔlét]
minibus	микроавтобус (м)	[mikrɔ·aftóbus]
ambulance	скорая помощь (ж)	[skóraja pómɔʃ]
snowplow	снегоуборочная машина (ж)	[snegɔ·ubórɔtʃnaja maʃína]
truck	грузовик (м)	[gruzɔvík]
tanker truck	бензовоз (м)	[benzɔvós]
van (small truck)	фургон (м)	[furgón]
road tractor (trailer truck)	тягач (м)	[tɪgátʃ]
trailer	прицеп (м)	[pritsǽp]
comfortable (adj)	комфортабельный	[kɔmfɔrtábelʲnij]
used (adj)	подержанный	[pɔdérʒenij]

hood	капот (м)	[kapót]
fender	крыло (с)	[krɨló]
roof	крыша (ж)	[krɨ̃ʃa]
windshield	ветровое стекло (с)	[vetrɔvóe stekló]
rear-view mirror	зеркало (с) заднего вида	[zérkalɔ zádnevɔ vída]
windshield washer	омыватель (м)	[ɔmivátelʲ]
windshield wipers	дворники (мн)	[dvórniki]
side window	боковое стекло (с)	[bɔkɔvóe stekló]
window lift (power window)	стеклоподъёмник (м)	[steklɔ·pɔdjómnik]
antenna	антенна (ж)	[antǽna]
sunroof	люк (м)	[lʲúk]
bumper	бампер (м)	[bámper]
trunk	багажник (м)	[bagáʒnik]

roof luggage rack	багажник (м)	[bagáʒnik]
door	дверца (ж)	[dvértsa]
door handle	ручка (ж)	[rútʃka]
door lock	замок (м)	[zámɔk]

license plate	номер (м)	[nómer]
muffler	глушитель (м)	[gluʃítelʲ]
gas tank	бензобак (м)	[benzɔbák]
tailpipe	выхлопная труба (ж)	[vihlɔpnája trubá]

gas, accelerator	газ (м)	[gás]
pedal	педаль (ж)	[pedálʲ]
gas pedal	педаль (ж) газа	[pedálʲ gáza]

brake	тормоз (м)	[tórmɔs]
brake pedal	педаль (ж) тормоза	[pedálʲ tórmɔza]
to brake (use the brake)	тормозить (нсв, нпх)	[tɔrmɔzítʲ]
parking brake	стояночный тормоз (м)	[stɔjánɔtʃnij tórmɔs]

clutch	сцепление (с)	[stsɛplénie]
clutch pedal	педаль (ж) сцепления	[pedálʲ stsɛplénija]
clutch disc	диск (м) сцепления	[dísk stsɛplénija]
shock absorber	амортизатор (м)	[amɔrtizátɔr]

wheel	колесо (с)	[kɔlesó]
spare tire	запасное колесо (с)	[zapasnóe kɔlesó]
hubcap	колпак (м)	[kɔlpák]

driving wheels	ведущие колёса (с мн)	[vedúʃie kɔlɵsa]
front-wheel drive (as adj)	переднеприводный	[perédne·prívɔdnij]
rear-wheel drive (as adj)	заднеприводный	[zádne·prívɔdnij]
all-wheel drive (as adj)	полноприводный	[pólnɔ·prívɔdnij]

gearbox	коробка (ж) передач	[kɔrópka peredátʃ]
automatic (adj)	автоматическая	[aftɔmatítʃeskaja]
mechanical (adj)	механическая	[mehanítʃeskaja]
gear shift	рычаг (м) коробки передач	[ritʃág kɔrópki peredátʃ]

| headlight | фара (ж) | [fára] |
| headlights | фары (ж мн) | [fári] |

low beam	ближний свет (м)	[blíʒnij svet]
high beam	дальний свет (м)	[dálʲnij svet]
brake light	стоп-сигнал (м)	[stóp-signál]

parking lights	габаритные огни (мн)	[gabarítnie ɔgní]
hazard lights	аварийные огни (мн)	[avaríjnie ɔgní]
fog lights	противотуманные фары (ж мн)	[prótivɔ·tumánnie fári]
turn signal	поворотник (м)	[pɔvɔrótnik]
back-up light	задний ход (м)	[zádnij hód]

148. Cars. Passenger compartment

car inside (interior)	салон (м)	[salón]
leather (as adj)	кожаный	[kóʒanij]
velour (as adj)	велюровый	[velʲúrɔvij]
upholstery	обивка (ж)	[ɔbífka]
instrument (gage)	прибор (м)	[pribór]
dashboard	приборный щиток (м)	[pribórnij ʃitók]
speedometer	спидометр (м)	[spidómetr]
needle (pointer)	стрелка (ж)	[strélka]
odometer	счётчик (м)	[ʃóttʃik]
indicator (sensor)	датчик (м)	[dáttʃik]
level	уровень (м)	[úrɔvenʲ]
warning light	лампочка (ж)	[lámpɔtʃka]
steering wheel	руль (м)	[rúlʲ]
horn	сигнал (м)	[signál]
button	кнопка (ж)	[knópka]
switch	переключатель (м)	[pereklʲutʃátelʲ]
seat	сиденье (с)	[sidénje]
backrest	спинка (ж)	[spínka]
headrest	подголовник (м)	[pɔdgɔlóvnik]
seat belt	ремень (м) безопасности	[reménʲ bezɔpásnɔsti]
to fasten the belt	пристегнуть ремень	[pristegnútʲ reménʲ]
adjustment (of seats)	регулировка (ж)	[regulirófka]
airbag	воздушная подушка (ж)	[vɔzdúʃnaja pɔdúʃka]
air-conditioner	кондиционер (м)	[kɔnditsiɔnér]
radio	радио (с)	[rádiɔ]
CD player	CD-проигрыватель (м)	[si·dí·prɔígrivatelʲ]
to turn on	включить (св, пх)	[fklʲutʃítʲ]
antenna	антенна (ж)	[antǽna]
glove box	бардачок (м)	[bardatʃók]
ashtray	пепельница (ж)	[pépelʲnitsa]

149. Cars. Engine

engine	двигатель (м)	[dvígatelʲ]
motor	мотор (м)	[mɔtór]
diesel (as adj)	дизельный	[dízelʲnij]
gasoline (as adj)	бензиновый	[benzínɔvij]
engine volume	объём (м) двигателя	[ɔbjóm dvígatelʲa]
power	мощность (ж)	[móʃnɔstʲ]

horsepower	лошадиная сила (ж)	[loʃidínaja síla]
piston	поршень (м)	[pórʃɛnʲ]
cylinder	цилиндр (м)	[tsilíndr]
valve	клапан (м)	[klápan]

injector	инжектор (м)	[inʒǽktor]
generator (alternator)	генератор (м)	[generátor]
carburetor	карбюратор (м)	[karbʲurátor]
motor oil	моторное масло (с)	[motórnoe máslo]

radiator	радиатор (м)	[radiátor]
coolant	охлаждающая жидкость (ж)	[ohlaʒdájuʃʲaja ʒīlkostʲ]
cooling fan	вентилятор (м)	[ventilʲátor]

battery (accumulator)	аккумулятор (м)	[akumulʲátor]
starter	стартер (м)	[stárter]
ignition	зажигание (с)	[zaʒigánie]
spark plug	свеча (ж) зажигания	[svetʃá zaʒigánija]

terminal (of battery)	клемма (ж)	[klémma]
positive terminal	плюс (м)	[plʲús]
negative terminal	минус (м)	[mínus]
fuse	предохранитель (м)	[predohranítelʲ]

air filter	воздушный фильтр (м)	[vozdúʃnij fílʲtr]
oil filter	масляный фильтр (м)	[máslɪnij fílʲtr]
fuel filter	топливный фильтр (м)	[tóplivnij fílʲtr]

150. Cars. Crash. Repair

car crash	авария (ж)	[avárija]
traffic accident	дорожное происшествие (с)	[doróʒnoe proiʃǽstvie]
to crash (into the wall, etc.)	врезаться (нсв, возв)	[vrézatsa]

to get smashed up	разбиться (св, возв)	[razbítsa]
damage	повреждение (с)	[povreʒdénie]
intact (unscathed)	целый	[tsǽlij]

breakdown	поломка (ж)	[polómka]
to break down (vi)	сломаться (св, возв)	[slomátsa]
towrope	буксировочный трос (м)	[buksiróvotʃnij trós]

puncture	прокол (м)	[prokól]
to be flat	спустить (св, нпх)	[spustítʲ]
to pump up	накачивать (нсв, пх)	[nakátʃivatʲ]
pressure	давление (с)	[davlénie]
to check (to examine)	проверить (св, пх)	[provéritʲ]
repair	ремонт (м)	[remónt]

auto repair shop	автосервис (м)	[aftɔ·sǽrvis]
spare part	запчасть (ж)	[zaptʃástʲ]
part	деталь (ж)	[detálʲ]

bolt (with nut)	болт (м)	[bólt]
screw (fastener)	винт (м)	[vínt]
nut	гайка (ж)	[gájka]
washer	шайба (ж)	[ʃájba]
bearing (e.g., ball ~)	подшипник (м)	[pɔdʃípnik]

tube	трубка (ж)	[trúpka]
gasket (head ~)	прокладка (ж)	[prɔklátka]
cable, wire	провод (м)	[próvɔd]

jack	домкрат (м)	[dɔmkrát]
wrench	гаечный ключ (м)	[gáetʃnij klʲútʃ]
hammer	молоток (м)	[mɔlɔtók]
pump	насос (м)	[nasós]
screwdriver	отвёртка (ж)	[ɔtvʲórtka]

fire extinguisher	огнетушитель (м)	[ɔgnetuʃítelʲ]
warning triangle	аварийный треугольник (м)	[avaríjnij treugólʲnik]

to stall (vi)	глохнуть (нсв, нпх)	[glóhnutʲ]
stall (n)	остановка (ж)	[ɔstanófka]
to be broken	быть сломанным	[bɨtʲ slómannim]

to overheat (vi)	перегреться (св, возв)	[peregrétsa]
to be clogged up	засориться (св, возв)	[zasorítsa]
to freeze up (pipes, etc.)	замёрзнуть (св, нпх)	[zamʲórznutʲ]
to burst (vi, ab. tube)	лопнуть (св, нпх)	[lópnutʲ]

pressure	давление (с)	[davlénie]
level	уровень (м)	[úrɔvenʲ]
slack (~ belt)	слабый	[slábij]

dent	вмятина (ж)	[vmʲátina]
knocking noise (engine)	стук (м)	[stúk]
crack	трещина (ж)	[tréʃina]
scratch	царапина (ж)	[tsarápina]

151. Cars. Road

road	дорога (ж)	[dɔróga]
highway	автомагистраль (ж)	[áftɔ·magistrálʲ]
freeway	шоссе (с)	[ʃɔssǽ]
direction (way)	направление (с)	[napravlénie]
distance	расстояние (с)	[rastɔjánie]
bridge	мост (м)	[móst]

parking lot	паркинг (м)	[párking]
square	площадь (ж)	[plóʃatʲ]
interchange	развязка (ж)	[razvʲáska]
tunnel	тоннель (м)	[tɔnǽlʲ]

gas station	автозаправка (ж)	[aftɔ·zapráfka]
parking lot	автостоянка (ж)	[aftɔ·stɔjánka]
gas pump (fuel dispenser)	колонка (ж)	[kɔlónka]
auto repair shop	гараж (м)	[garáʃ]
to get gas (to fill up)	заправить (св, пх)	[zaprávitʲ]
fuel	топливо (с)	[tóplivɔ]
jerrycan	канистра (ж)	[kanístra]

asphalt	асфальт (м)	[asfálʲt]
road markings	разметка (ж)	[razmétka]
curb	бордюр (м)	[bɔrdʲúr]
guardrail	ограждение (с)	[ɔgraʒdénie]
ditch	кювет (м)	[kʲuvét]
roadside (shoulder)	обочина (ж)	[ɔbótʃina]
lamppost	столб (м)	[stólb]

to drive (a car)	вести (нсв, пх)	[vestí]
to turn (e.g., ~ left)	поворачивать (нсв, нпх)	[pɔvɔrátʃivatʲ]
to make a U-turn	разворачиваться (нсв, возв)	[razvɔrátʃivatsa]
reverse (~ gear)	задний ход (м)	[zádnij hód]

to honk (vi)	сигналить (нсв, нпх)	[signálitʲ]
honk (sound)	звуковой сигнал (м)	[zvukɔvój signál]
to get stuck (in the mud, etc.)	застрять (св, нпх)	[zastrʲátʲ]
to spin the wheels	буксовать (нсв, нпх)	[buksɔvátʲ]
to cut, to turn off (vt)	глушить (нсв, пх)	[gluʃítʲ]

speed	скорость (ж)	[skórɔstʲ]
to exceed the speed limit	превысить скорость	[prevʲīsitʲ skórɔstʲ]
to give a ticket	штрафовать (нсв, пх)	[ʃtrafɔvátʲ]
traffic lights	светофор (м)	[svetɔfór]
driver's license	водительские права (мн)	[vɔdítelʲskie pravá]

grade crossing	переезд (м)	[pereézd]
intersection	перекрёсток (м)	[perekrǿstɔk]
crosswalk	пешеходный переход (м)	[peʃɛhódnij perehód]
bend, curve	поворот (м)	[pɔvɔrót]
pedestrian zone	пешеходная зона (ж)	[peʃɛhódnaja zóna]

PEOPLE. LIFE EVENTS

Life events

celebration, holiday	праздник (м)	[práznik]
national day	национальный праздник (м)	[naʦionálʲnij práznik]
public holiday	праздничный день (м)	[práznitʃnij dénʲ]
to commemorate (vt)	праздновать (нсв, пх)	[práznɔvatʲ]
event (happening)	событие (c)	[sɔbі̄tie]
event (organized activity)	мероприятие (c)	[merɔprijátie]
banquet (party)	банкет (м)	[bankét]
reception (formal party)	приём (м)	[prijóm]
feast	пир (м)	[pír]
anniversary	годовщина (ж)	[gɔdɔfʃʲína]
jubilee	юбилей (м)	[jubiléj]
to celebrate (vt)	отметить (св, пх)	[ɔtmétitʲ]
New Year	Новый год (м)	[nóvij gód]
Happy New Year!	С Новым Годом!	[s nóvim gódɔm]
Christmas	Рождество (c)	[rɔʒdestvó]
Merry Christmas!	Весёлого Рождества!	[vesʲólɔvɔ rɔʒdestvá]
Christmas tree	Новогодняя ёлка (ж)	[nɔvɔgódnʲaja jólka]
fireworks (fireworks show)	салют (м)	[salʲút]
wedding	свадьба (ж)	[svátʲba]
groom	жених (м)	[ʒeníh]
bride	невеста (ж)	[nevésta]
to invite (vt)	приглашать (нсв, пх)	[priglaʃátʲ]
invitation card	приглашение (c)	[priglaʃǽnie]
guest	гость (м)	[góstʲ]
to visit (~ your parents, etc.)	идти в гости	[itʲtí v gósti]
to meet the guests	встречать гостей	[fstretʃátʲ gɔstéj]
gift, present	подарок (м)	[pɔdárɔk]
to give (sth as present)	дарить (нсв, пх)	[darítʲ]
to receive gifts	получать подарки	[pɔlutʃátʲ pɔdárki]

bouquet (of flowers)	**букет** (м)	[bukét]
congratulations	**поздравление** (с)	[pɔzdravlénie]
to congratulate (vt)	**поздравлять** (нсв, пх)	[pɔzdravlʲátʲ]

greeting card	**поздравительная открытка** (ж)	[pɔzdravítelʲnaja ɔtkrĩtka]
to send a postcard	**отправить открытку**	[ɔtprávitʲ ɔtkrĩtku]
to get a postcard	**получить открытку**	[pɔluʧítʲ ɔtkrĩtku]

toast	**тост** (м)	[tóst]
to offer (a drink, etc.)	**угощать** (нсв, пх)	[ugɔʃátʲ]
champagne	**шампанское** (с)	[ʃampánskɔe]

to enjoy oneself	**веселиться** (нсв, возв)	[veselítsa]
merriment (gaiety)	**веселье** (с)	[vesélje]
joy (emotion)	**радость** (ж)	[rádɔstʲ]

| dance | **танец** (м) | [tánets] |
| to dance (vi, vt) | **танцевать** (нсв, н/пх) | [tantsɛvátʲ] |

| waltz | **вальс** (м) | [válʲs] |
| tango | **танго** (с) | [tángɔ] |

153. Funerals. Burial

cemetery	**кладбище** (с)	[kládbiʃe]
grave, tomb	**могила** (ж)	[mɔgíla]
cross	**крест** (м)	[krést]
gravestone	**надгробие** (с)	[nadgróbie]
fence	**ограда** (ж)	[ɔgráda]
chapel	**часовня** (ж)	[ʧasóvnʲa]

death	**смерть** (ж)	[smértʲ]
to die (vi)	**умереть** (св, нпх)	[umerétʲ]
the deceased	**покойник** (м)	[pɔkójnik]
mourning	**траур** (м)	[tráur]

to bury (vt)	**хоронить** (нсв, пх)	[hɔrɔnítʲ]
funeral home	**похоронное бюро** (с)	[pɔhɔrónnɔe bʲuró]
funeral	**похороны** (мн)	[póhɔrɔni]

wreath	**венок** (м)	[venók]
casket, coffin	**гроб** (м)	[grób]
hearse	**катафалк** (м)	[katafálk]
shroud	**саван** (м)	[sávan]

funeral procession	**траурная процессия** (ж)	[tráurnaja prɔtsǽsija]
funerary urn	**урна** (ж)	[úrna]
crematory	**крематорий** (м)	[krematórij]
obituary	**некролог** (м)	[nekrɔlóg]

| to cry (weep) | плакать (нсв, нпх) | [plákatʲ] |
| to sob (vi) | рыдать (нсв, нпх) | [ridátʲ] |

154. War. Soldiers

platoon	взвод (м)	[vzvód]
company	рота (ж)	[róta]
regiment	полк (м)	[pólk]
army	армия (ж)	[ármija]
division	дивизия (ж)	[divízija]

| section, squad | отряд (м) | [otrʲád] |
| host (army) | войско (с) | [vójskɔ] |

| soldier | солдат (м) | [sɔldát] |
| officer | офицер (м) | [ɔfitsǽr] |

private	рядовой (м)	[rɪdɔvój]
sergeant	сержант (м)	[serʒánt]
lieutenant	лейтенант (м)	[lejtenánt]
captain	капитан (м)	[kapitán]
major	майор (м)	[majór]
colonel	полковник (м)	[pɔlkóvnik]
general	генерал (м)	[generál]

sailor	моряк (м)	[mɔrʲák]
captain	капитан (м)	[kapitán]
boatswain	боцман (м)	[bótsman]

artilleryman	артиллерист (м)	[artileríst]
paratrooper	десантник (м)	[desántnik]
pilot	лётчик (м)	[lǿttʃik]
navigator	штурман (м)	[ʃtúrman]
mechanic	механик (м)	[mehánik]

pioneer (sapper)	сапёр (м)	[sapǿr]
parachutist	парашютист (м)	[paraʃutíst]
reconnaissance scout	разведчик (м)	[razvéttʃik]
sniper	снайпер (м)	[snájper]

patrol (group)	патруль (м)	[patrúlʲ]
to patrol (vt)	патрулировать (нсв, н/пх)	[patrulírovatʲ]
sentry, guard	часовой (м)	[tʃasɔvój]

warrior	воин (м)	[vóin]
patriot	патриот (м)	[patriót]
hero	герой (м)	[gerój]
heroine	героиня (ж)	[gerɔínʲa]
traitor	предатель (м)	[predátelʲ]
deserter	дезертир (м)	[dezertír]

to desert (vi)	дезертировать (нсв, нпх)	[dezertírɔvatʲ]
mercenary	наёмник (м)	[najómnik]
recruit	новобранец (м)	[nɔvɔbránets]
volunteer	доброволец (м)	[dɔbrɔvóles]
dead (n)	убитый (м)	[ubítij]
wounded (n)	раненый (м)	[ránenij]
prisoner of war	пленный (м)	[plénnij]

155. War. Military actions. Part 1

war	война (ж)	[vɔjná]
to be at war	воевать (нсв, нпх)	[vɔevátʲ]
civil war	гражданская война (ж)	[graʒdánskaja vɔjná]
treacherously (adv)	вероломно	[verɔlómnɔ]
declaration of war	объявление войны	[ɔbjɪvlénie vɔjnî]
to declare (~ war)	объявить (св, пх)	[ɔbjɪvítʲ]
aggression	агрессия (ж)	[agrǽsija]
to attack (invade)	нападать (нсв, нпх)	[napadátʲ]
to invade (vt)	захватывать (нсв, пх)	[zahvátivatʲ]
invader	захватчик (м)	[zahvátʧik]
conqueror	завоеватель (м)	[zavɔevátelʲ]
defense	оборона (ж)	[ɔbɔróna]
to defend (a country, etc.)	оборонять (нсв, пх)	[ɔbɔrɔnʲátʲ]
to defend (against ...)	обороняться (нсв, возв)	[ɔbɔrɔnʲátsa]
enemy	враг (м)	[vrág]
foe, adversary	противник (м)	[prɔtívnik]
enemy (as adj)	вражеский	[vráʒeskij]
strategy	стратегия (ж)	[stratǽgija]
tactics	тактика (ж)	[táktika]
order	приказ (м)	[prikás]
command (order)	команда (ж)	[kɔmánda]
to order (vt)	приказывать (нсв, пх)	[prikázivatʲ]
mission	задание (с)	[zadánie]
secret (adj)	секретный	[sekrétnij]
battle	сражение (с)	[sraʒǽnie]
combat	бой (м)	[bój]
attack	атака (ж)	[atáka]
charge (assault)	штурм (м)	[ʃtúrm]
to storm (vt)	штурмовать (нсв, пх)	[ʃturmɔvátʲ]
siege (to be under ~)	осада (ж)	[ɔsáda]
offensive (n)	наступление (с)	[nastuplénie]

to go on the offensive	**наступать** (нсв, нпх)	[nastupátʲ]
retreat	**отступление** (с)	[ɔtstuplénie]
to retreat (vi)	**отступать** (нсв, нпх)	[ɔtstupátʲ]
encirclement	**окружение** (с)	[ɔkruʒǽnie]
to encircle (vt)	**окружать** (нсв, пх)	[ɔkruʒátʲ]
bombing (by aircraft)	**бомбёжка** (ж)	[bɔmbɵ́ʒka]
to drop a bomb	**сбросить бомбу**	[zbrósitʲ bómbu]
to bomb (vt)	**бомбить** (нсв, пх)	[bɔmbítʲ]
explosion	**взрыв** (м)	[vzrîf]
shot	**выстрел** (м)	[vîstrel]
to fire (~ a shot)	**выстрелить** (св, нпх)	[vîstrelitʲ]
firing (burst of ~)	**стрельба** (ж)	[strelʲbá]
to aim (to point a weapon)	**целиться** (нсв, возв)	[tsǽlitsa]
to point (a gun)	**навести** (св, пх)	[navestí]
to hit (the target)	**попасть** (св, нпх)	[pɔpástʲ]
to sink (~ a ship)	**потопить** (св, пх)	[pɔtopítʲ]
hole (in a ship)	**пробоина** (ж)	[prɔbóina]
to founder, to sink (vi)	**идти ко дну** (нсв)	[itʲtí kɔ dnú]
front (war ~)	**фронт** (м)	[frónt]
evacuation	**эвакуация** (ж)	[ɛvakuátsija]
to evacuate (vt)	**эвакуировать** (н/св, пх)	[ɛvakuírɔvatʲ]
trench	**окоп** (м)	[ɔkóp]
barbwire	**колючая проволока** (ж)	[kɔlʲútʃaja próvɔlka]
barrier (anti tank ~)	**заграждение** (с)	[zagraʒdénie]
watchtower	**вышка** (ж)	[vîʃka]
military hospital	**госпиталь** (м)	[góspitalʲ]
to wound (vt)	**ранить** (н/св, пх)	[ránitʲ]
wound	**рана** (ж)	[rána]
wounded (n)	**раненый** (м)	[ránenij]
to be wounded	**получить ранение**	[pɔlutʃítʲ ranénie]
serious (wound)	**тяжёлый**	[tɪʒólɪj]

156. Weapons

weapons	**оружие** (с)	[ɔrúʒie]
firearms	**огнестрельное оружие** (с)	[ɔgnestrélʲnɔe ɔrúʒie]
cold weapons (knives, etc.)	**холодное оружие** (с)	[hɔlódnɔe ɔrúʒie]
chemical weapons	**химическое оружие** (с)	[himítʃeskɔe ɔrúʒie]
nuclear (adj)	**ядерный**	[jádernij]

nuclear weapons	ядерное оружие (с)	[jádernɔe ɔrúʒie]
bomb	бомба (ж)	[bómba]
atomic bomb	атомная бомба (ж)	[átɔmnaja bómba]
pistol (gun)	пистолет (м)	[pistɔlét]
rifle	ружьё (с)	[ruʒjǿ]
submachine gun	автомат (м)	[aftɔmát]
machine gun	пулемёт (м)	[pulemǿt]
muzzle	дуло (с)	[dúlɔ]
barrel	ствол (м)	[stvól]
caliber	калибр (м)	[kalíbr]
trigger	курок (м)	[kurók]
sight (aiming device)	прицел (м)	[pritsǽl]
magazine	магазин (м)	[magazín]
butt (shoulder stock)	приклад (м)	[priklád]
hand grenade	граната (ж)	[granáta]
explosive	взрывчатка (ж)	[vzriftʃátka]
bullet	пуля (ж)	[púlʲa]
cartridge	патрон (м)	[patrón]
charge	заряд (м)	[zarʲád]
ammunition	боеприпасы (мн)	[bɔepripási]
bomber (aircraft)	бомбардировщик (м)	[bɔmbardirófʃik]
fighter	истребитель (м)	[istrebítelʲ]
helicopter	вертолёт (м)	[vertɔlǿt]
anti-aircraft gun	зенитка (ж)	[zenítka]
tank	танк (м)	[tánk]
tank gun	пушка (ж)	[púʃka]
artillery	артиллерия (ж)	[artilérija]
to lay (a gun)	навести на ... (св)	[navestí na ...]
shell (projectile)	снаряд (м)	[snarʲád]
mortar bomb	мина (ж)	[mína]
mortar	миномёт (м)	[minɔmǿt]
splinter (shell fragment)	осколок (м)	[ɔskólɔk]
submarine	подводная лодка (ж)	[pɔdvódnaja lótka]
torpedo	торпеда (ж)	[tɔrpéda]
missile	ракета (ж)	[rakéta]
to load (gun)	заряжать (нсв, пх)	[zarɪʒátʲ]
to shoot (vi)	стрелять (нсв, нпх)	[strelʲátʲ]
to point at (the cannon)	целиться (нсв, возв)	[tsǽlitsa]
bayonet	штык (м)	[ʃtĩk]
rapier	шпага (ж)	[ʃpága]
saber (e.g., cavalry ~)	сабля (ж)	[sáblʲa]

spear (weapon)	копьё (c)	[kɔpjǿ]
bow	лук (м)	[lúk]
arrow	стрела (ж)	[strelá]
musket	мушкет (м)	[muʃkét]
crossbow	арбалет (м)	[arbalét]

157. Ancient people

primitive (prehistoric)	первобытный	[pervɔbı̃tnij]
prehistoric (adj)	доисторический	[dɔistorítʃeskij]
ancient (~ civilization)	древний	[drévnij]

Stone Age	Каменный Век (м)	[kámennij vek]
Bronze Age	Бронзовый Век (м)	[brónzɔvij vek]
Ice Age	ледниковый период (м)	[lednikóvij períud]

tribe	племя (c)	[plémʲa]
cannibal	людоед (м)	[lʲudɔéd]
hunter	охотник (м)	[ɔhótnik]
to hunt (vi, vt)	охотиться (нсв, возв)	[ɔhótitsa]
mammoth	мамонт (м)	[mámɔnt]

cave	пещера (ж)	[peʃéra]
fire	огонь (м)	[ɔgónʲ]
campfire	костёр (м)	[kɔstǿr]
cave painting	наскальный рисунок (м)	[naskálʲnij risúnɔk]
tool (e.g., stone ax)	орудие (c) труда	[ɔrúdie trudá]
spear	копьё (c)	[kɔpjǿ]
stone ax	каменный топор (м)	[kámennij tɔpór]
to be at war	воевать (нсв, нпх)	[vɔevátʲ]
to domesticate (vt)	приручать (нсв, пх)	[priruʧátʲ]

idol	идол (м)	[ídɔl]
to worship (vt)	поклоняться (нсв, возв)	[pɔklɔnʲátsa]
superstition	суеверие (c)	[suevérie]

evolution	эволюция (ж)	[ɛvɔlʲútsija]
development	развитие (c)	[razvítie]
disappearance (extinction)	исчезновение (c)	[isʃeznɔvénie]
to adapt oneself	приспосабливаться (нсв, возв)	[prispɔsáblivatsa]

archeology	археология (ж)	[arheɔlógija]
archeologist	археолог (м)	[arheólɔg]
archeological (adj)	археологический	[arheɔlɔgítʃeskij]

excavation site	раскопки (мн)	[raskópki]
excavations	раскопки (мн)	[raskópki]
find (object)	находка (ж)	[nahótka]
fragment	фрагмент (м)	[fragmént]

158. Middle Ages

people (ethnic group)	народ (м)	[naród]
peoples	народы (м мн)	[naródɨ]
tribe	племя (с)	[plémʲa]
tribes	племена (с мн)	[plemená]

barbarians	варвары (м мн)	[várvarɨ]
Gauls	галлы (м мн)	[gálɨ]
Goths	готы (м мн)	[gótɨ]
Slavs	славяне (мн)	[slavʲáne]
Vikings	викинги (м мн)	[víkingɨ]

| Romans | римляне (мн) | [rímlɪne] |
| Roman (adj) | римский | [rímskij] |

Byzantines	византийцы (м мн)	[vizantíjʦɨ]
Byzantium	Византия (ж)	[vizantíja]
Byzantine (adj)	византийский	[vizantíjskij]

emperor	император (м)	[imperátɔr]
leader, chief (tribal ~)	вождь (м)	[vóʃtʲ]
powerful (~ king)	могущественный	[mɔgúʃʲestvenɨj]
king	король (м)	[kɔrólʲ]
ruler (sovereign)	правитель (м)	[pravítelʲ]

knight	рыцарь (м)	[rɨ̃ʦarʲ]
feudal lord	феодал (м)	[feɔdál]
feudal (adj)	феодальный	[feɔdálʲnij]
vassal	вассал (м)	[vasál]

duke	герцог (м)	[gérʦɔg]
earl	граф (м)	[gráf]
baron	барон (м)	[barón]
bishop	епископ (м)	[epískɔp]

armor	доспехи (мн)	[dɔspéhi]
shield	щит (м)	[ʃít]
sword	меч (м)	[méʧ]
visor	забрало (с)	[zabrálɔ]
chainmail	кольчуга (ж)	[kɔlʲʧúga]

| Crusade | крестовый поход (м) | [krestóvij pɔhód] |
| crusader | крестоносец (м) | [krestɔnósets] |

territory	территория (ж)	[teritórija]
to attack (invade)	нападать (нсв, нпх)	[napadátʲ]
to conquer (vt)	завоевать (св, пх)	[zavɔevátʲ]
to occupy (invade)	захватить (св, пх)	[zahvatítʲ]
siege (to be under ~)	осада (ж)	[ɔsáda]
besieged (adj)	осаждённый	[ɔsaʒdǿnnij]

to besiege (vt)	осаждать (нсв, пх)	[ɔsaʒdátʲ]
inquisition	инквизиция (ж)	[inkvizítsija]
inquisitor	инквизитор (м)	[inkvizítɔr]
torture	пытка (ж)	[pĩtka]
cruel (adj)	жестокий	[ʒestókij]
heretic	еретик (м)	[eretík]
heresy	ересь (ж)	[éresʲ]
seafaring	мореплавание (с)	[mɔre·plávanie]
pirate	пират (м)	[pirát]
piracy	пиратство (с)	[pirátstvɔ]
boarding (attack)	абордаж (м)	[abɔrdáʃ]
loot, booty	добыча (ж)	[dɔbĩʧa]
treasures	сокровища (мн)	[sɔkróviʃa]
discovery	открытие (с)	[ɔtkrĩtie]
to discover (new land, etc.)	открыть (св, пх)	[ɔtkrĩtʲ]
expedition	экспедиция (ж)	[ɛkspedítsija]
musketeer	мушкетёр (м)	[muʃketɵr]
cardinal	кардинал (м)	[kardinál]
heraldry	геральдика (ж)	[gerálʲdika]
heraldic (adj)	геральдический	[geralʲdíʧeskij]

159. Leader. Chief. Authorities

king	король (м)	[kɔrólʲ]
queen	королева (ж)	[kɔrɔléva]
royal (adj)	королевский	[kɔrɔléfskij]
kingdom	королевство (с)	[kɔrɔléfstvɔ]
prince	принц (м)	[prínts]
princess	принцесса (ж)	[printsǽsa]
president	президент (м)	[prezidént]
vice-president	вице-президент (м)	[vítsɛ-prezidént]
senator	сенатор (м)	[senátɔr]
monarch	монарх (м)	[mɔnárh]
ruler (sovereign)	правитель (м)	[pravítelʲ]
dictator	диктатор (м)	[diktátɔr]
tyrant	тиран (м)	[tirán]
magnate	магнат (м)	[magnát]
director	директор (м)	[diréktɔr]
chief	шеф (м)	[ʃæf]
manager (director)	управляющий (м)	[upravlʲájuʃij]
boss	босс (м)	[bós]
owner	хозяин (м)	[hɔzʲáin]
head (~ of delegation)	глава (ж)	[glavá]

| authorities | власти (мн) | [vlásti] |
| superiors | начальство (с) | [natʃálʲstvɔ] |

governor	губернатор (м)	[gubernátɔr]
consul	консул (м)	[kónsul]
diplomat	дипломат (м)	[diplɔmát]
mayor	мэр (м)	[mǽr]
sheriff	шериф (м)	[ʃɛríf]

emperor	император (м)	[imperátɔr]
tsar, czar	царь (м)	[tsárʲ]
pharaoh	фараон (м)	[faraón]
khan	хан (м)	[hán]

160. Breaking the law. Criminals. Part 1

bandit	бандит (м)	[bandít]
crime	преступление (с)	[prestuplénie]
criminal (person)	преступник (м)	[prestúpnik]

thief	вор (м)	[vór]
stealing (larceny)	воровство (с)	[vɔrɔfstvó]
theft	кража (ж)	[kráʒa]

to kidnap (vt)	похитить (св, пх)	[pɔhítitʲ]
kidnapping	похищение (с)	[pɔhiʃénie]
kidnapper	похититель (м)	[pɔhitítelʲ]

| ransom | выкуп (м) | [vɨkup] |
| to demand ransom | требовать выкуп | [trébɔvatʲ vɨkup] |

| to rob (vt) | грабить (нсв, пх) | [grábitʲ] |
| robber | грабитель (м) | [grabítelʲ] |

to extort (vt)	вымогать (нсв, пх)	[vɨmɔgátʲ]
extortionist	вымогатель (м)	[vɨmɔgátelʲ]
extortion	вымогательство (с)	[vɨmɔgátelʲstvɔ]

to murder, to kill	убить (св, пх)	[ubítʲ]
murder	убийство (с)	[ubíjstvɔ]
murderer	убийца (ж)	[ubíjtsa]

gunshot	выстрел (м)	[vɨstrel]
to fire (~ a shot)	выстрелить (св, нпх)	[vɨstrelitʲ]
to shoot to death	застрелить (св, пх)	[zastrelítʲ]
to shoot (vi)	стрелять (нсв, нпх)	[strelʲátʲ]
shooting	стрельба (ж)	[strelʲbá]

| incident (fight, etc.) | происшествие (с) | [prɔiʃǽstvie] |
| fight, brawl | драка (ж) | [dráka] |

victim	жертва (ж)	[ʒǽrtva]
to damage (vt)	повредить (св, пх)	[pɔvredítʲ]
damage	ущерб (м)	[uʃérb]
dead body, corpse	труп (м)	[trúp]
grave (~ crime)	тяжкий	[tʲáʃkij]

to attack (vt)	напасть (св, нпх)	[napástʲ]
to beat (to hit)	бить (нсв, пх)	[bítʲ]
to beat up	избить (св, пх)	[izbítʲ]
to take (rob of sth)	отнять (св, пх)	[ɔtnʲátʲ]
to stab to death	зарезать (св, пх)	[zarézatʲ]
to maim (vt)	изувечить (св, пх)	[izuvétʃitʲ]
to wound (vt)	ранить (н/св, пх)	[ránitʲ]

blackmail	шантаж (м)	[ʃantáʃ]
to blackmail (vt)	шантажировать (нсв, пх)	[ʃantaʒírɔvatʲ]
blackmailer	шантажист (м)	[ʃantaʒíst]

protection racket	рэкет (м)	[rǽket]
racketeer	рэкетир (м)	[rɛketír]
gangster	гангстер (м)	[gángstɛr]
mafia, Mob	мафия (ж)	[máfija]

pickpocket	карманник (м)	[karmánnik]
burglar	взломщик (м)	[vzlómʃik]
smuggling	контрабанда (ж)	[kɔntrabánda]
smuggler	контрабандист (м)	[kɔntrabandíst]

forgery	подделка (ж)	[pɔddélka]
to forge (counterfeit)	подделывать (нсв, пх)	[pɔddélivatʲ]
fake (forged)	фальшивый	[falʲʃívij]

161. Breaking the law. Criminals. Part 2

rape	изнасилование (с)	[iznasílɔvanie]
to rape (vt)	изнасиловать (св, пх)	[iznasílɔvatʲ]
rapist	насильник (м)	[nasílʲnik]
maniac	маньяк (м)	[manják]

prostitute (fem.)	проститутка (ж)	[prɔstitútka]
prostitution	проституция (ж)	[prɔstitútsija]
pimp	сутенёр (м)	[sutenǿr]

drug addict	наркоман (м)	[narkɔmán]
drug dealer	торговец (м) наркотиками	[tɔrgóvets narkótikami]

to blow up (bomb)	взорвать (св, пх)	[vzɔrvátʲ]
explosion	взрыв (м)	[vzrîʃ]
to set fire	поджечь (св, пх)	[pɔdʒǽtʃʲ]

arsonist	поджигатель (м)	[podʒigátelʲ]
terrorism	терроризм (м)	[terɔrízm]
terrorist	террорист (м)	[terɔríst]
hostage	заложник (м)	[zalóʒnik]

to swindle (deceive)	обмануть (св, пх)	[ɔbmanútʲ]
swindle, deception	обман (м)	[ɔbmán]
swindler	мошенник (м)	[mɔʃǽnnik]

to bribe (vt)	подкупить (св, пх)	[pɔtkupítʲ]
bribery	подкуп (м)	[pótkup]
bribe	взятка (ж)	[vzʲátka]

poison	яд (м)	[jád]
to poison (vt)	отравить (св, пх)	[ɔtravítʲ]
to poison oneself	отравиться (св, возв)	[ɔtravítsa]

| suicide (act) | самоубийство (с) | [samɔubíjstvɔ] |
| suicide (person) | самоубийца (м, ж) | [samɔubíjtsa] |

to threaten (vt)	угрожать (нсв, пх)	[ugrɔʒátʲ]
threat	угроза (ж)	[ugróza]
to make an attempt	покушаться (нсв, возв)	[pɔkuʃátsa]
attempt (attack)	покушение (с)	[pɔkuʃǽnie]

| to steal (a car) | угнать (св, пх) | [ugnátʲ] |
| to hijack (a plane) | угнать (св, пх) | [ugnátʲ] |

| revenge | месть (ж) | [méstʲ] |
| to avenge (get revenge) | мстить (нсв, пх) | [mstítʲ] |

to torture (vt)	пытать (нсв, пх)	[pitátʲ]
torture	пытка (ж)	[pītka]
to torment (vt)	мучить (нсв, пх)	[mútʃitʲ]

pirate	пират (м)	[pirát]
hooligan	хулиган (м)	[huligán]
armed (adj)	вооружённый	[vɔɔruʒónnij]
violence	насилие (с)	[nasílie]
illegal (unlawful)	нелегальный	[nelegálʲnij]

| spying (espionage) | шпионаж (м) | [ʃpiɔnáʃ] |
| to spy (vi) | шпионить (нсв, нпх) | [ʃpiónitʲ] |

162. Police. Law. Part 1

justice	правосудие (с)	[pravɔsúdie]
court (see you in ~)	суд (м)	[súd]
judge	судья (ж)	[sudjá]
jurors	присяжные (мн)	[prisʲáʒnie]

| jury trial | суд (м) присяжных | [sút prisʲáʒnih] |
| to judge, to try (vt) | судить (нсв, пх) | [sudítʲ] |

lawyer, attorney	адвокат (м)	[advɔkát]
defendant	подсудимый (м)	[pɔtsudímij]
dock	скамья (ж) подсудимых	[skamjá pɔtsudímih]

| charge | обвинение (с) | [ɔbvinénie] |
| accused | обвиняемый (м) | [ɔbvinʲáemij] |

| sentence | приговор (м) | [prigɔvór] |
| to sentence (vt) | приговорить (св, пх) | [prigɔvɔrítʲ] |

guilty (culprit)	виновник (м)	[vinóvnik]
to punish (vt)	наказать (св, пх)	[nakazátʲ]
punishment	наказание (с)	[nakazánie]

fine (penalty)	штраф (м)	[ʃtráf]
life imprisonment	пожизненное заключение (с)	[pɔʒíznenɔe zaklʲutʃénie]
death penalty	смертная казнь (ж)	[smértnaja káznʲ]
electric chair	электрический стул (м)	[ɛlektrítʃeskij stúl]
gallows	виселица (ж)	[víselitsa]

| to execute (vt) | казнить (н/св, пх) | [kaznítʲ] |
| execution | казнь (ж) | [káznʲ] |

| prison, jail | тюрьма (ж) | [tʲurʲmá] |
| cell | камера (ж) | [kámera] |

escort (convoy)	конвой (м)	[kɔnvój]
prison guard	надзиратель (м)	[nadzirátelʲ]
prisoner	заключённый (м)	[zaklʲutʃónnij]

| handcuffs | наручники (мн) | [narútʃniki] |
| to handcuff (vt) | надеть наручники | [nadétʲ narútʃniki] |

prison break	побег (м)	[pɔbég]
to break out (vi)	убежать (св, нпх)	[ubeʒátʲ]
to disappear (vi)	исчезнуть (св, нпх)	[isʃéznutʲ]
to release (from prison)	освободить (св, пх)	[ɔsvɔbɔdítʲ]
amnesty	амнистия (ж)	[amnístija]

police	полиция (ж)	[pɔlítsija]
police officer	полицейский (м)	[pɔlitsǽjskij]
police station	полицейский участок (м)	[pɔlitsǽjskij utʃástok]
billy club	резиновая дубинка (ж)	[rezínɔvaja dubínka]
bullhorn	рупор (м)	[rúpɔr]

patrol car	патрульная машина (ж)	[patrúlʲnaja maʃína]
siren	сирена (ж)	[siréna]
to turn on the siren	включить сирену	[fklʲutʃítʲ sirénu]

siren call	вой (м) сирены	[vój siréni̯]
crime scene	место (с) преступления	[mésto prestuplénija]
witness	свидетель (м)	[svidételʲ]
freedom	свобода (ж)	[svobóda]
accomplice	сообщник (м)	[soópʃnik]
to flee (vi)	скрыться (св, возв)	[skrĭ̄tsa]
trace (to leave a ~)	след (м)	[sléd]

163. Police. Law. Part 2

search (investigation)	розыск (м)	[rózisk]
to look for ...	разыскивать ... (нсв, пх)	[razĭ̄skivatʲ ...]
suspicion	подозрение (с)	[podozrénie]
suspicious (e.g., ~ vehicle)	подозрительный	[podozrítelʲnij]
to stop (cause to halt)	остановить (св, пх)	[ostanovítʲ]
to detain (keep in custody)	задержать (св, пх)	[zaderʒátʲ]

case (lawsuit)	дело (с)	[délo]
investigation	следствие (с)	[slétstvie]
detective	детектив, сыщик (м)	[dɛtɛktíf], [sĭ̄ʃʲik]
investigator	следователь (м)	[slédovatelʲ]
hypothesis	версия (ж)	[vérsija]

motive	мотив (м)	[motíf]
interrogation	допрос (м)	[doprós]
to interrogate (vt)	допрашивать (нсв, пх)	[dopráʃivatʲ]
to question (~ neighbors, etc.)	опрашивать (нсв, пх)	[opráʃivatʲ]
check (identity ~)	проверка (ж)	[provérka]

round-up (raid)	облава (ж)	[obláva]
search (~ warrant)	обыск (м)	[óbisk]
chase (pursuit)	погоня (ж)	[pogónʲa]
to pursue, to chase	преследовать (нсв, пх)	[preslédovatʲ]
to track (a criminal)	следить (нсв, нпх)	[sledítʲ]

arrest	арест (м)	[arést]
to arrest (sb)	арестовать (св, пх)	[arestovátʲ]
to catch (thief, etc.)	поймать (св, пх)	[pojmátʲ]
capture	поимка (ж)	[poímka]

document	документ (м)	[dokumént]
proof (evidence)	доказательство (с)	[dokazátelʲstvo]
to prove (vt)	доказывать (нсв, пх)	[dokázivatʲ]
footprint	след (м)	[sléd]
fingerprints	отпечатки (м мн) пальцев	[otpetʃátki pálʲtsɛf]
piece of evidence	улика (ж)	[ulíka]

| alibi | алиби (с) | [álibi] |
| innocent (not guilty) | невиновный | [nevinóvnij] |

| injustice | несправедливость (ж) | [nespravedlívost'] |
| unjust, unfair (adj) | несправедливый | [nespravedlívij] |

criminal (adj)	криминальный	[kriminál'nij]
to confiscate (vt)	конфисковать (св, пх)	[konfiskovát']
drug (illegal substance)	наркотик (м)	[narkótik]
weapon, gun	оружие (c)	[orúʒie]
to disarm (vt)	обезоружить (св, пх)	[obezorúʒit']
to order (command)	приказывать (нсв, пх)	[prikázivat']
to disappear (vi)	исчезнуть (св, нпх)	[isʧéznut']

law	закон (м)	[zakón]
legal, lawful (adj)	законный	[zakónnij]
illegal, illicit (adj)	незаконный	[nezakónnij]

| responsibility (blame) | ответственность (ж) | [otvétstvenost'] |
| responsible (adj) | ответственный | [otvétstvenij] |

NATURE

The Earth. Part 1

space	космос (м)	[kósmɔs]
space (as adj)	космический	[kɔsmítʃeskij]
outer space	космическое пространство	[kɔsmítʃeskɔe prɔstránstvɔ]
world	мир (м)	[mír]
universe	вселенная (ж)	[fselénnaja]
galaxy	галактика (ж)	[galáktika]
star	звезда (ж)	[zvezdá]
constellation	созвездие (с)	[sɔzvézdie]
planet	планета (ж)	[planéta]
satellite	спутник (м)	[spútnik]
meteorite	метеорит (м)	[meteorít]
comet	комета (ж)	[kɔméta]
asteroid	астероид (м)	[astɛróid]
orbit	орбита (ж)	[ɔrbíta]
to revolve (~ around the Earth)	вращаться (нсв, возв)	[vraʃátsa]
atmosphere	атмосфера (ж)	[atmɔsféra]
the Sun	Солнце (с)	[sóntse]
solar system	Солнечная система (ж)	[sólnetʃnaja sistéma]
solar eclipse	солнечное затмение (с)	[sólnetʃnɔe zatménie]
the Earth	Земля (ж)	[zemlʲá]
the Moon	Луна (ж)	[luná]
Mars	Марс (м)	[márs]
Venus	Венера (ж)	[venéra]
Jupiter	Юпитер (м)	[jupíter]
Saturn	Сатурн (м)	[satúrn]
Mercury	Меркурий (м)	[merkúrij]
Uranus	Уран (м)	[urán]
Neptune	Нептун (м)	[neptún]
Pluto	Плутон (м)	[plutón]

Milky Way	Млечный Путь (м)	[mlétʃnij pútʲ]
Great Bear (Ursa Major)	Большая Медведица (ж)	[bolʲʃája medvéditsa]
North Star	Полярная Звезда (ж)	[polʲárnaja zvezdá]

Martian	марсианин (м)	[marsiánin]
extraterrestrial (n)	инопланетянин (м)	[inoplanetʲánin]
alien	пришелец (м)	[priʃǽlets]
flying saucer	летающая тарелка (ж)	[letájuʃʲaja tarélka]

spaceship	космический корабль (м)	[kosmítʃeskij koráblʲ]
space station	орбитальная станция (ж)	[orbitálʲnaja stántsija]
blast-off	старт (м)	[stárt]

engine	двигатель (м)	[dvígatelʲ]
nozzle	сопло (с)	[soplʲó]
fuel	топливо (с)	[tóplivo]

cockpit, flight deck	кабина (ж)	[kabína]
antenna	антенна (ж)	[antǽna]
porthole	иллюминатор (м)	[ilʲuminátor]
solar panel	солнечная батарея (ж)	[sólnetʃnaja bataréja]
spacesuit	скафандр (м)	[skafándr]

| weightlessness | невесомость (ж) | [nevesómostʲ] |
| oxygen | кислород (м) | [kisloród] |

| docking (in space) | стыковка (ж) | [stikófka] |
| to dock (vi, vt) | производить стыковку | [proizvodítʲ stikófku] |

observatory	обсерватория (ж)	[opservatórija]
telescope	телескоп (м)	[teleskóp]
to observe (vt)	наблюдать (нсв, нпх)	[nablʲudátʲ]
to explore (vt)	исследовать (н/св, пх)	[islédovatʲ]

165. The Earth

the Earth	Земля (ж)	[zemlʲá]
the globe (the Earth)	земной шар (м)	[zemnój ʃár]
planet	планета (ж)	[planéta]

atmosphere	атмосфера (ж)	[atmosféra]
geography	география (ж)	[geográfija]
nature	природа (ж)	[priróda]

globe (table ~)	глобус (м)	[glóbus]
map	карта (ж)	[kárta]
atlas	атлас (м)	[átlas]
Europe	Европа (ж)	[evrópa]

Asia	**Азия** (ж)	[ázija]
Africa	**Африка** (ж)	[áfrika]
Australia	**Австралия** (ж)	[afstrálija]

America	**Америка** (ж)	[amérika]
North America	**Северная Америка** (ж)	[sévernaja amérika]
South America	**Южная Америка** (ж)	[júʒnaja amérika]

| Antarctica | **Антарктида** (ж) | [antarktída] |
| the Arctic | **Арктика** (ж) | [árktika] |

166. Cardinal directions

north	**север** (м)	[séver]
to the north	**на север**	[na séver]
in the north	**на севере**	[na sévere]
northern (adj)	**северный**	[sévernij]

south	**юг** (м)	[júg]
to the south	**на юг**	[na júg]
in the south	**на юге**	[na júge]
southern (adj)	**южный**	[júʒnij]

west	**запад** (м)	[západ]
to the west	**на запад**	[na západ]
in the west	**на западе**	[na západe]
western (adj)	**западный**	[západnij]

east	**восток** (м)	[vɔstók]
to the east	**на восток**	[na vɔstók]
in the east	**на востоке**	[na vɔstóke]
eastern (adj)	**восточный**	[vɔstótʃnij]

167. Sea. Ocean

sea	**море** (с)	[móre]
ocean	**океан** (м)	[ɔkeán]
gulf (bay)	**залив** (м)	[zalíf]
straits	**пролив** (м)	[prɔlíf]

land (solid ground)	**земля** (ж), **суша** (ж)	[zemlʲá], [súʃa]
continent (mainland)	**материк** (м)	[materík]
island	**остров** (м)	[óstrɔf]
peninsula	**полуостров** (м)	[pɔlu·óstrɔf]
archipelago	**архипелаг** (м)	[arhipelág]

| bay, cove | **бухта** (ж) | [búhta] |
| harbor | **гавань** (ж) | [gávanʲ] |

| lagoon | лагуна (ж) | [lagúna] |
| cape | мыс (м) | [mīs] |

atoll	атолл (м)	[atól]
reef	риф (м)	[ríf]
coral	коралл (м)	[korál]
coral reef	коралловый риф (м)	[korálovij ríf]

deep (adj)	глубокий	[glubókij]
depth (deep water)	глубина (ж)	[glubiná]
abyss	бездна (ж)	[bézdna]
trench (e.g., Mariana ~)	впадина (ж)	[fpádina]

| current (Ocean ~) | течение (с) | [tetʃénie] |
| to surround (bathe) | омывать (нсв, пх) | [omivátʲ] |

| shore | побережье (с) | [poberéʒje] |
| coast | берег (м) | [béreg] |

flow (flood tide)	прилив (м)	[prilíf]
ebb (ebb tide)	отлив (м)	[otlíf]
shoal	отмель (ж)	[ótmelʲ]
bottom (~ of the sea)	дно (с)	[dnó]

wave	волна (ж)	[volná]
crest (~ of a wave)	гребень (м) волны	[grébenʲ volnī]
spume (sea foam)	пена (ж)	[péna]

storm (sea storm)	буря (ж)	[búrʲa]
hurricane	ураган (м)	[uragán]
tsunami	цунами (с)	[tsunámi]

| calm (dead ~) | штиль (м) | [ʃtílʲ] |
| quiet, calm (adj) | спокойный | [spokójnij] |

| pole | полюс (м) | [pólʲus] |
| polar (adj) | полярный | [polʲárnij] |

| latitude | широта (ж) | [ʃirotá] |
| longitude | долгота (ж) | [dolgotá] |

| parallel | параллель (ж) | [paralélʲ] |
| equator | экватор (м) | [ɛkvátor] |

sky	небо (с)	[nébo]
horizon	горизонт (м)	[gorizónt]
air	воздух (м)	[vózduh]

lighthouse	маяк (м)	[maják]
to dive (vi)	нырять (нсв, нпх)	[nirʲátʲ]
to sink (ab. boat)	затонуть (св, нпх)	[zatonútʲ]
treasures	сокровища (мн)	[sokróviʃa]

168. Mountains

mountain	гора (ж)	[gɔrá]
mountain range	горная цепь (ж)	[górnaja tsæpʲ]
mountain ridge	горный хребет (м)	[górnɨj hrebét]
summit, top	вершина (ж)	[verʃína]
peak	пик (м)	[pík]
foot (~ of the mountain)	подножие (с)	[pɔdnóʒie]
slope (mountainside)	склон (м)	[sklón]
volcano	вулкан (м)	[vulkán]
active volcano	действующий вулкан (м)	[déjstvujuʃʲij vulkán]
dormant volcano	потухший вулкан (м)	[pɔtúhʃij vulkán]
eruption	извержение (с)	[izverʒǽnie]
crater	кратер (м)	[krátɛr]
magma	магма (ж)	[mágma]
lava	лава (ж)	[láva]
molten (~ lava)	раскалённый	[raskalǿnnɨj]
canyon	каньон (м)	[kanjón]
gorge	ущелье (с)	[uʃʲélje]
crevice	расщелина (ж)	[raʃʲélina]
pass, col	перевал (м)	[perevál]
plateau	плато (с)	[plató]
cliff	скала (ж)	[skalá]
hill	холм (м)	[hólm]
glacier	ледник (м)	[ledník]
waterfall	водопад (м)	[vɔdɔpád]
geyser	гейзер (м)	[géjzer]
lake	озеро (с)	[ózerɔ]
plain	равнина (ж)	[ravnína]
landscape	пейзаж (м)	[pejzáʃ]
echo	эхо (с)	[ǽhɔ]
alpinist	альпинист (м)	[alʲpiníst]
rock climber	скалолаз (м)	[skalɔlás]
to conquer (in climbing)	покорять (нсв, пх)	[pɔkɔrʲátʲ]
climb (an easy ~)	восхождение (с)	[vɔsxɔʒdénie]

169. Rivers

river	река (ж)	[reká]
spring (natural source)	источник (м)	[istótʃnik]

riverbed (river channel)	русло (с)	[rúslɔ]
basin (river valley)	бассейн (м)	[basǽjn]
to flow into ...	впадать в ... (нсв)	[fpadátʲ f ...]

| tributary | приток (м) | [pritók] |
| bank (of river) | берег (м) | [béreg] |

current (stream)	течение (с)	[tetʃénie]
downstream (adv)	вниз по течению	[vnís pɔ tetʃéniju]
upstream (adv)	вверх по течению	[vvérh pɔ tetʃéniju]

inundation	наводнение (с)	[navɔdnénie]
flooding	половодье (с)	[pɔlɔvódje]
to overflow (vi)	разливаться (нсв, возв)	[razlivátsa]
to flood (vt)	затоплять (нсв, пх)	[zatɔplʲátʲ]

| shallow (shoal) | мель (ж) | [mélʲ] |
| rapids | порог (м) | [pɔróg] |

dam	плотина (ж)	[plɔtína]
canal	канал (м)	[kanál]
reservoir (artificial lake)	водохранилище (с)	[vódɔ·hraníliʃe]
sluice, lock	шлюз (м)	[ʃlʲús]

water body (pond, etc.)	водоём (м)	[vɔdɔjóm]
swamp (marshland)	болото (с)	[bɔlótɔ]
bog, marsh	трясина (ж)	[trɪsína]
whirlpool	водоворот (м)	[vɔdɔvɔrót]

stream (brook)	ручей (м)	[rutʃéj]
drinking (ab. water)	питьевой	[pitjevój]
fresh (~ water)	пресный	[présnɪj]

| ice | лёд (м) | [lʲód] |
| to freeze over (ab. river, etc.) | замёрзнуть (св, нпх) | [zamʲórznutʲ] |

170. Forest

| forest, wood | лес (м) | [lés] |
| forest (as adj) | лесной | [lesnój] |

thick forest	чаща (ж)	[tʃáʃa]
grove	роща (ж)	[róʃa]
forest clearing	поляна (ж)	[pɔlʲána]

thicket	заросли (мн)	[zárɔsli]
scrubland	кустарник (м)	[kustárnik]
footpath (troddenpath)	тропинка (ж)	[trɔpínka]
gully	овраг (м)	[ɔvrág]

tree	дерево (с)	[dérɛvɔ]
leaf	лист (м)	[líst]
leaves (foliage)	листва (ж)	[listvá]
fall of leaves	листопад (м)	[listɔpád]
to fall (ab. leaves)	опадать (нсв, нпх)	[ɔpadátʲ]
top (of the tree)	верхушка (ж)	[verhúʃka]
branch	ветка (ж)	[vétka]
bough	сук (м)	[súk]
bud (on shrub, tree)	почка (ж)	[pótʃka]
needle (of pine tree)	игла (ж)	[iglá]
pine cone	шишка (ж)	[ʃʃka]
tree hollow	дупло (с)	[dupló]
nest	гнездо (с)	[gnezdó]
burrow (animal hole)	нора (ж)	[nɔrá]
trunk	ствол (м)	[stvól]
root	корень (м)	[kórenʲ]
bark	кора (ж)	[kɔrá]
moss	мох (м)	[móh]
to uproot (remove trees or tree stumps)	корчевать (нсв, пх)	[kɔrtʃevátʲ]
to chop down	рубить (нсв, пх)	[rubítʲ]
to deforest (vt)	вырубать лес	[virubátʲ lʲés]
tree stump	пень (м)	[pénʲ]
campfire	костёр (м)	[kɔstǿr]
forest fire	пожар (м)	[pɔʒár]
to extinguish (vt)	тушить (нсв, пх)	[tuʃítʲ]
forest ranger	лесник (м)	[lesník]
protection	охрана (ж)	[ɔhrána]
to protect (~ nature)	охранять (нсв, пх)	[ɔhranʲátʲ]
poacher	браконьер (м)	[brakɔnjér]
steel trap	капкан (м)	[kapkán]
to gather, to pick (vt)	собирать (нсв, пх)	[sɔbirátʲ]
to lose one's way	заблудиться (св, возв)	[zabludítsa]

171. Natural resources

natural resources	природные ресурсы (м мн)	[priródnie resúrsi]
minerals	полезные ископаемые (с мн)	[pɔléznie iskɔpáemie]
deposits	залежи (мн)	[záleʒi]
field (e.g., oilfield)	месторождение (с)	[mestɔrɔʒdénie]

to mine (extract)	добывать (нсв, пх)	[dɔbivátʲ]
mining (extraction)	добыча (ж)	[dɔbïʧa]
ore	руда (ж)	[rudá]
mine (e.g., for coal)	рудник (м)	[rudník]
shaft (mine ~)	шахта (ж)	[ʃáhta]
miner	шахтёр (м)	[ʃahtǿr]

gas (natural ~)	газ (м)	[gás]
gas pipeline	газопровод (м)	[gazɔ·prɔvód]

oil (petroleum)	нефть (ж)	[néftʲ]
oil pipeline	нефтепровод (м)	[nefte·prɔvód]
oil well	нефтяная вышка (ж)	[neftɪnája vïʃka]
derrick (tower)	буровая вышка (ж)	[burɔvája vïʃka]
tanker	танкер (м)	[tánker]

sand	песок (м)	[pesók]
limestone	известняк (м)	[izvesnʲák]
gravel	гравий (м)	[grávij]
peat	торф (м)	[tórf]
clay	глина (ж)	[glína]
coal	уголь (м)	[úgɔlʲ]

iron (ore)	железо (с)	[ʒelézɔ]
gold	золото (с)	[zólɔtɔ]
silver	серебро (с)	[serebró]
nickel	никель (м)	[níkelʲ]
copper	медь (ж)	[métʲ]

zinc	цинк (м)	[ʦïnk]
manganese	марганец (м)	[márganeʦ]
mercury	ртуть (ж)	[rtútʲ]
lead	свинец (м)	[svinéʦ]

mineral	минерал (м)	[minerál]
crystal	кристалл (м)	[kristál]
marble	мрамор (м)	[mrámɔr]
uranium	уран (м)	[urán]

The Earth. Part 2

weather	погода (ж)	[pɔgóda]
weather forecast	прогноз (м) погоды	[prɔgnós pɔgódi]
temperature	температура (ж)	[temperatúra]
thermometer	термометр (м)	[termómetr]
barometer	барометр (м)	[barómetr]

humid (adj)	влажный	[vláʒnij]
humidity	влажность (ж)	[vláʒnostʲ]
heat (extreme ~)	жара (ж)	[ʒará]
hot (torrid)	жаркий	[ʒárkij]
it's hot	жарко	[ʒárkɔ]

| it's warm | тепло | [tepló] |
| warm (moderately hot) | тёплый | [tǿplij] |

| it's cold | холодно | [hólɔdnɔ] |
| cold (adj) | холодный | [hɔlódnij] |

sun	солнце (с)	[sóntse]
to shine (vi)	светить (нсв, нпх)	[svetítʲ]
sunny (day)	солнечный	[sólnetʃnij]
to come up (vi)	взойти (св, нпх)	[vzɔjtí]
to set (vi)	сесть (св, нпх)	[séstʲ]

cloud	облако (с)	[óblakɔ]
cloudy (adj)	облачный	[óblatʃnij]
rain cloud	туча (ж)	[tútʃa]
somber (gloomy)	пасмурный	[pásmurnij]

rain	дождь (м)	[dóʃtʲ], [dóʃ]
it's raining	идёт дождь	[idǿt dóʃtʲ]
rainy (~ day, weather)	дождливый	[dɔʒdlívij]
to drizzle (vi)	моросить (нсв, нпх)	[mɔrɔsítʲ]

pouring rain	проливной дождь (м)	[prɔlivnój dóʃtʲ]
downpour	ливень (м)	[lívenʲ]
heavy (e.g., ~ rain)	сильный	[sílʲnij]
puddle	лужа (ж)	[lúʒa]
to get wet (in rain)	промокнуть (св, нпх)	[prɔmóknutʲ]

| fog (mist) | туман (м) | [tumán] |
| foggy | туманный | [tumánnij] |

| snow | **снег** (м) | [snég] |
| it's snowing | **идёт снег** | [idɵt snég] |

173. Severe weather. Natural disasters

thunderstorm	**гроза** (ж)	[grɔzá]
lightning (~ strike)	**молния** (ж)	[mólnija]
to flash (vi)	**сверкать** (нсв, нпх)	[sverkátʲ]

thunder	**гром** (м)	[gróm]
to thunder (vi)	**греметь** (нсв, нпх)	[gremétʲ]
it's thundering	**гремит гром**	[gremít gróm]

| hail | **град** (м) | [grád] |
| it's hailing | **идёт град** | [idɵt grád] |

| to flood (vt) | **затопить** (св, пх) | [zatɔpítʲ] |
| flood, inundation | **наводнение** (с) | [navɔdnénie] |

earthquake	**землетрясение** (с)	[zemletrɪsénie]
tremor, shoke	**толчок** (м)	[tɔltʃók]
epicenter	**эпицентр** (м)	[ɛpitsǽntr]

| eruption | **извержение** (с) | [izverʒǽnie] |
| lava | **лава** (ж) | [láva] |

twister	**смерч** (м)	[smértʃ]
tornado	**торнадо** (м)	[tɔrnádɔ]
typhoon	**тайфун** (м)	[tajfún]

hurricane	**ураган** (м)	[uragán]
storm	**буря** (ж)	[búrʲa]
tsunami	**цунами** (с)	[tsunámi]

cyclone	**циклон** (м)	[tsiklón]
bad weather	**непогода** (ж)	[nepɔgóda]
fire (accident)	**пожар** (м)	[pɔʒár]
disaster	**катастрофа** (ж)	[katastrófa]
meteorite	**метеорит** (м)	[meteɔrít]

avalanche	**лавина** (ж)	[lavína]
snowslide	**обвал** (м)	[ɔbvál]
blizzard	**метель** (ж)	[metélʲ]
snowstorm	**вьюга** (ж)	[vjúga]

Fauna

predator	**хищник** (м)	[híʃnik]
tiger	**тигр** (м)	[tígr]
lion	**лев** (м)	[léf]
wolf	**волк** (м)	[vólk]
fox	**лиса** (ж)	[lisá]
jaguar	**ягуар** (м)	[jɪguár]
leopard	**леопард** (м)	[leɔpárd]
cheetah	**гепард** (м)	[gepárd]
black panther	**пантера** (ж)	[pantǽra]
puma	**пума** (ж)	[púma]
snow leopard	**снежный барс** (м)	[snéӡnij bárs]
lynx	**рысь** (ж)	[rïsʲ]
coyote	**койот** (м)	[kɔjót]
jackal	**шакал** (м)	[ʃakál]
hyena	**гиена** (ж)	[giéna]

animal	**животное** (с)	[ӡivótnɔe]
beast (animal)	**зверь** (м)	[zvérʲ]
squirrel	**белка** (ж)	[bélka]
hedgehog	**ёж** (м)	[jóʃ]
hare	**заяц** (м)	[záɪts]
rabbit	**кролик** (м)	[królik]
badger	**барсук** (м)	[barsúk]
raccoon	**енот** (м)	[enót]
hamster	**хомяк** (м)	[hɔmʲák]
marmot	**сурок** (м)	[surók]
mole	**крот** (м)	[krót]
mouse	**мышь** (ж)	[mïʃ]
rat	**крыса** (ж)	[krïsa]
bat	**летучая мышь** (ж)	[letúʧaja mïʃ]
ermine	**горностай** (м)	[gɔrnɔstáj]
sable	**соболь** (м)	[sóbɔlʲ]

marten	куница (ж)	[kunítsa]
weasel	ласка (ж)	[láska]
mink	норка (ж)	[nórka]

| beaver | бобр (м) | [bóbr] |
| otter | выдра (ж) | [vídra] |

horse	лошадь (ж)	[lóʃatʲ]
moose	лось (м)	[lósʲ]
deer	олень (м)	[ɔlénʲ]
camel	верблюд (м)	[verblʲúd]

bison	бизон (м)	[bizón]
wisent	зубр (м)	[zúbr]
buffalo	буйвол (м)	[bújvɔl]

zebra	зебра (ж)	[zébra]
antelope	антилопа (ж)	[antilópa]
roe deer	косуля (ж)	[kɔsúlʲa]
fallow deer	лань (ж)	[lánʲ]
chamois	серна (ж)	[sérna]
wild boar	кабан (м)	[kabán]

whale	кит (м)	[kít]
seal	тюлень (м)	[tʲulénʲ]
walrus	морж (м)	[mórʃ]
fur seal	котик (м)	[kótik]
dolphin	дельфин (м)	[delʲfín]

bear	медведь (м)	[medvétʲ]
polar bear	белый медведь (м)	[bélij medvétʲ]
panda	панда (ж)	[pánda]

monkey	обезьяна (ж)	[ɔbezjána]
chimpanzee	шимпанзе (с)	[ʃimpanzǽ]
orangutan	орангутанг (м)	[ɔrangutáng]
gorilla	горилла (ж)	[gɔríla]
macaque	макака (ж)	[makáka]
gibbon	гиббон (м)	[gibón]

elephant	слон (м)	[slón]
rhinoceros	носорог (м)	[nɔsɔróg]
giraffe	жираф (м)	[ʒiráf]
hippopotamus	бегемот (м)	[begemót]

| kangaroo | кенгуру (м) | [kengurú] |
| koala (bear) | коала (ж) | [kɔála] |

mongoose	мангуст (м)	[mangúst]
chinchilla	шиншилла (ж)	[ʃinʃíla]
skunk	скунс (м)	[skúns]
porcupine	дикобраз (м)	[dikɔbrás]

176. Domestic animals

cat	кошка (ж)	[kóʃka]
tomcat	кот (м)	[kót]
horse	лошадь (ж)	[lóʃatʲ]
stallion (male horse)	жеребец (м)	[ʒerebéts]
mare	кобыла (ж)	[kɔbɨla]
cow	корова (ж)	[kɔróva]
bull	бык (м)	[bɨk]
ox	вол (м)	[vól]
sheep (ewe)	овца (ж)	[ɔftsá]
ram	баран (м)	[barán]
goat	коза (ж)	[kɔzá]
billy goat, he-goat	козёл (м)	[kɔzǿl]
donkey	осёл (м)	[ɔsǿl]
mule	мул (м)	[múl]
pig, hog	свинья (ж)	[svinjá]
piglet	поросёнок (м)	[pɔrɔsǿnɔk]
rabbit	кролик (м)	[królik]
hen (chicken)	курица (ж)	[kúritsa]
rooster	петух (м)	[petúh]
duck	утка (ж)	[útka]
drake	селезень (м)	[sélezenʲ]
goose	гусь (м)	[gúsʲ]
tom turkey, gobbler	индюк (м)	[indʲúk]
turkey (hen)	индюшка (ж)	[indʲúʃka]
domestic animals	домашние животные (с мн)	[dɔmáʃnie ʒivótnie]
tame (e.g., ~ hamster)	ручной	[rutʃnój]
to tame (vt)	приручать (нсв, пх)	[prirutʃátʲ]
to breed (vt)	выращивать (нсв, пх)	[vɨráʃivatʲ]
farm	ферма (ж)	[férma]
poultry	домашняя птица (ж)	[dɔmáʃnʲaja ptítsa]
cattle	скот (м)	[skót]
herd (cattle)	стадо (с)	[stádɔ]
stable	конюшня (ж)	[kɔnʲúʃnʲa]
pigpen	свинарник (м)	[svinárnik]
cowshed	коровник (м)	[kɔróvnik]
rabbit hutch	крольчатник (м)	[krɔlʲtʃátnik]
hen house	курятник (м)	[kurʲátnik]

177. Dogs. Dog breeds

dog	собака (ж)	[sɔbáka]
sheepdog	овчарка (ж)	[ɔftʃárka]
German shepherd	немецкая овчарка (ж)	[nɛmétskaja ɔftʃárka]
poodle	пудель (м)	[púdelʲ]
dachshund	такса (ж)	[táksa]
bulldog	бульдог (м)	[bulʲdóg]
boxer	боксёр (м)	[bɔksǿr]
mastiff	мастиф (м)	[mastíf]
Rottweiler	ротвейлер (м)	[rɔtvéjler]
Doberman	доберман (м)	[dɔbermán]
basset	бассет (м)	[bássɛt]
bobtail	бобтейл (м)	[bɔptǽjl]
Dalmatian	далматинец (м)	[dalmatínets]
cocker spaniel	кокер-спаниель (м)	[kóker-spaniélʲ]
Newfoundland	ньюфаундленд (м)	[njufáundlend]
Saint Bernard	сенбернар (м)	[senbernár]
husky	хаски (м)	[háski]
Chow Chow	чау-чау (м)	[tʃáu-tʃáu]
spitz	шпиц (м)	[ʃpíts]
pug	мопс (м)	[móps]

178. Sounds made by animals

barking (n)	лай (м)	[láj]
to bark (vi)	лаять (нсв, нпх)	[lájʲtʲ]
to meow (vi)	мяукать (нсв, нпх)	[mʲúkatʲ]
to purr (vi)	мурлыкать (нсв, нпх)	[murlĩkatʲ]
to moo (vi)	мычать (нсв, нпх)	[mitʃátʲ]
to bellow (bull)	реветь (нсв, нпх)	[revétʲ]
to growl (vi)	рычать (нсв, нпх)	[ritʃátʲ]
howl (n)	вой (м)	[vój]
to howl (vi)	выть (нсв, нпх)	[vĩtʲ]
to whine (vi)	скулить (нсв, нпх)	[skulítʲ]
to bleat (sheep)	блеять (нсв, нпх)	[bléjatʲ]
to oink, to grunt (pig)	хрюкать (нсв, нпх)	[hrʲúkatʲ]
to squeal (vi)	визжать (нсв, нпх)	[viʒʒátʲ]
to croak (vi)	квакать (нсв, нпх)	[kvákatʲ]
to buzz (insect)	жужжать (нсв, нпх)	[ʒuʒʒátʲ]
to chirp (crickets, grasshopper)	стрекотать (нсв, нпх)	[strekɔtátʲ]

179. Birds

bird	птица (ж)	[ptítsa]
pigeon	голубь (м)	[gólupʲ]
sparrow	воробей (м)	[vɔrɔbéj]
tit (great tit)	синица (ж)	[sinítsa]
magpie	сорока (ж)	[sɔróka]

raven	ворон (м)	[vórɔn]
crow	ворона (ж)	[vɔróna]
jackdaw	галка (ж)	[gálka]
rook	грач (м)	[grátʃ]

duck	утка (ж)	[útka]
goose	гусь (м)	[gúsʲ]
pheasant	фазан (м)	[fazán]

eagle	орёл (м)	[ɔrǿl]
hawk	ястреб (м)	[jástreb]
falcon	сокол (м)	[sókɔl]
vulture	гриф (м)	[gríf]
condor (Andean ~)	кондор (м)	[kóndɔr]

swan	лебедь (м)	[lébetʲ]
crane	журавль (м)	[ʒurávlʲ]
stork	аист (м)	[áist]

parrot	попугай (м)	[pɔpugáj]
hummingbird	колибри (ж)	[kɔlíbri]
peacock	павлин (м)	[pavlín]

ostrich	страус (м)	[stráus]
heron	цапля (ж)	[tsáplʲa]
flamingo	фламинго (с)	[flamíngɔ]
pelican	пеликан (м)	[pelikán]

| nightingale | соловей (м) | [sɔlɔvéj] |
| swallow | ласточка (ж) | [lástɔtʃka] |

thrush	дрозд (м)	[drózd]
song thrush	певчий дрозд (м)	[péftʃij drózd]
blackbird	чёрный дрозд (м)	[tʃórnij drózd]

swift	стриж (м)	[stríʃ]
lark	жаворонок (м)	[ʒávɔrɔnɔk]
quail	перепел (м)	[pérepel]

woodpecker	дятел (м)	[dʲátel]
cuckoo	кукушка (ж)	[kukúʃka]
owl	сова (ж)	[sɔvá]
eagle owl	филин (м)	[fílin]

wood grouse	глухарь (м)	[gluhárʲ]
black grouse	тетерев (м)	[téteref]
partridge	куропатка (ж)	[kurɔpátka]

starling	скворец (м)	[skvɔréʦ]
canary	канарейка (ж)	[kanaréjka]
hazel grouse	рябчик (м)	[rʲápʧik]
chaffinch	зяблик (м)	[zʲáblik]
bullfinch	снегирь (м)	[snegírʲ]

seagull	чайка (ж)	[ʧájka]
albatross	альбатрос (м)	[alʲbatrós]
penguin	пингвин (м)	[pingvín]

180. Birds. Singing and sounds

| to sing (vi) | петь (нсв, н/пх) | [pétʲ] |
| to call (animal, bird) | кричать (нсв, нпх) | [kriʧátʲ] |

| to crow (rooster) | кукарекать (нсв, нпх) | [kukarékatʲ] |
| cock-a-doodle-doo | кукареку (с) | [kukarekú] |

to cluck (hen)	кудахтать (нсв, нпх)	[kudáhtatʲ]
to caw (crow call)	каркать (нсв, нпх)	[kárkatʲ]
to quack (duck call)	крякать (нсв, нпх)	[krʲákatʲ]
to cheep (vi)	пищать (нсв, нпх)	[piʃʲátʲ]
to chirp, to twitter	чирикать (нсв, нпх)	[ʧiríkatʲ]

181. Fish. Marine animals

bream	лещ (м)	[léʃ]
carp	карп (м)	[kárp]
perch	окунь (м)	[ókunʲ]
catfish	сом (м)	[sóm]
pike	щука (ж)	[ʃʲúka]

| salmon | лосось (м) | [lɔsósʲ] |
| sturgeon | осётр (м) | [ɔsøtr] |

herring	сельдь (ж)	[sélʲtʲ]
Atlantic salmon	сёмга (ж)	[sømga]
mackerel	скумбрия (ж)	[skúmbrija]
flatfish	камбала (ж)	[kámbala]

zander, pike perch	судак (м)	[sudák]
cod	треска (ж)	[treská]
tuna	тунец (м)	[tunéʦ]
trout	форель (ж)	[fɔrǽlʲ]

eel	угорь (м)	[úgorʲ]
electric ray	электрический скат (м)	[ɛlektrítʃeskij skát]
moray eel	мурена (ж)	[muréna]
piranha	пиранья (ж)	[piránja]

shark	акула (ж)	[akúla]
dolphin	дельфин (м)	[delʲfín]
whale	кит (м)	[kít]

crab	краб (м)	[kráb]
jellyfish	медуза (ж)	[medúza]
octopus	осьминог (м)	[osʲminóg]

starfish	морская звезда (ж)	[morskája zvezdá]
sea urchin	морской ёж (м)	[morskój jóʃ]
seahorse	морской конёк (м)	[morskój konǿk]

oyster	устрица (ж)	[ústritsa]
shrimp	креветка (ж)	[krevétka]
lobster	омар (м)	[omár]
spiny lobster	лангуст (м)	[langúst]

182. Amphibians. Reptiles

| snake | змея (ж) | [zmejá] |
| venomous (snake) | ядовитый | [jɪdɔvítɪj] |

| viper | гадюка (ж) | [gadʲúka] |
| cobra | кобра (ж) | [kóbra] |

| python | питон (м) | [pitón] |
| boa | удав (м) | [udáf] |

grass snake	уж (м)	[úʃ]
rattle snake	гремучая змея (ж)	[gremútʃaja zmejá]
anaconda	анаконда (ж)	[anakónda]

lizard	ящерица (ж)	[jáʃeritsa]
iguana	игуана (ж)	[iguána]
monitor lizard	варан (м)	[varán]
salamander	саламандра (ж)	[salamándra]

| chameleon | хамелеон (м) | [hameleón] |
| scorpion | скорпион (м) | [skorpión] |

| turtle | черепаха (ж) | [tʃerepáha] |
| frog | лягушка (ж) | [lɪgúʃka] |

| toad | жаба (ж) | [ʒába] |
| crocodile | крокодил (м) | [krokodíl] |

183. Insects

insect, bug	насекомое (с)	[nasekómɔe]
butterfly	бабочка (ж)	[bábɔʧka]
ant	муравей (м)	[muravéj]
fly	муха (ж)	[múha]
mosquito	комар (м)	[kɔmár]
beetle	жук (м)	[ʒúk]

wasp	оса (ж)	[ɔsá]
bee	пчела (ж)	[pʧelá]
bumblebee	шмель (м)	[ʃmélʲ]
gadfly (botfly)	овод (м)	[óvɔd]

| spider | паук (м) | [paúk] |
| spiderweb | паутина (ж) | [pautína] |

dragonfly	стрекоза (ж)	[strekɔzá]
grasshopper	кузнечик (м)	[kuznéʧik]
moth (night butterfly)	мотылёк (м)	[mɔtilǿk]

cockroach	таракан (м)	[tarakán]
tick	клещ (м)	[kléʃ]
flea	блоха (ж)	[blɔhá]
midge	мошка (ж)	[móʃka]

locust	саранча (ж)	[saranʧá]
snail	улитка (ж)	[ulítka]
cricket	сверчок (м)	[sverʧók]
lightning bug	светлячок (м)	[svetlʲiʧók]
ladybug	божья коровка (ж)	[bóʒja kɔrófka]
cockchafer	майский жук (м)	[májskij ʒúk]

leech	пиявка (ж)	[pijáfka]
caterpillar	гусеница (ж)	[gúsenitsa]
earthworm	червь (м)	[ʧérfʲ]
larva	личинка (ж)	[liʧínka]

184. Animals. Body parts

beak	клюв (м)	[klʲúf]
wings	крылья (с мн)	[krīlja]
foot (of bird)	лапа (ж)	[lápa]
feathers (plumage)	оперение (с)	[ɔperénie]
feather	перо (с)	[peró]
crest	хохолок (м)	[hɔhɔlók]

| gills | жабры (мн) | [ʒábri] |
| spawn | икра (ж) | [ikrá] |

larva	личинка (ж)	[liʧínka]
fin	плавник (м)	[plavník]
scales (of fish, reptile)	чешуя (ж)	[ʧeʃujá]

fang (canine)	клык (м)	[klᵻk]
paw (e.g., cat's ~)	лапа (ж)	[lápa]
muzzle (snout)	морда (ж)	[mórda]
maw (mouth)	пасть (ж)	[pástʲ]
tail	хвост (м)	[hvóst]
whiskers	усы (м мн)	[usᵻ]

| hoof | копыто (с) | [kɔpᵻtɔ] |
| horn | рог (м) | [róg] |

carapace	панцирь (м)	[pántsirʲ]
shell (of mollusk)	ракушка (ж)	[rakúʃka]
eggshell	скорлупа (ж)	[skɔrlupá]

| animal's hair (pelage) | шерсть (ж) | [ʃǽrstʲ] |
| pelt (hide) | шкура (ж) | [ʃkúra] |

185. Animals. Habitats

| habitat | среда (ж) обитания | [sredá ɔbitánija] |
| migration | миграция (ж) | [migrátsija] |

mountain	гора (ж)	[gɔrá]
reef	риф (м)	[ríf]
cliff	скала (ж)	[skalá]

forest	лес (м)	[lés]
jungle	джунгли (мн)	[dʒúngli]
savanna	саванна (ж)	[savána]
tundra	тундра (ж)	[túndra]

steppe	степь (ж)	[stépʲ]
desert	пустыня (ж)	[pustᵻnʲa]
oasis	оазис (м)	[ɔázis]

sea	море (с)	[móre]
lake	озеро (с)	[ózerɔ]
ocean	океан (м)	[ɔkeán]

swamp (marshland)	болото (с)	[bɔlótɔ]
freshwater (adj)	пресноводный	[presnɔvódnij]
pond	пруд (м)	[prúd]
river	река (ж)	[reká]

| den (bear's ~) | берлога (ж) | [berlóga] |
| nest | гнездо (с) | [gnezdó] |

tree hollow	**дупло** (с)	[dupló]
burrow (animal hole)	**нора** (ж)	[norá]
anthill	**муравейник** (м)	[muravéjnik]

Flora

186. Trees

tree	дерево (с)	[dérevɔ]
deciduous (adj)	лиственное	[lístvenɔe]
coniferous (adj)	хвойное	[hvójnɔe]
evergreen (adj)	вечнозелёное	[vetʃnɔ·zelǿnɔe]
apple tree	яблоня (ж)	[jáblɔnʲa]
pear tree	груша (ж)	[grúʃa]
sweet cherry tree	черешня (ж)	[tʃeréʃnʲa]
sour cherry tree	вишня (ж)	[víʃnʲa]
plum tree	слива (ж)	[slíva]
birch	берёза (ж)	[berǿza]
oak	дуб (м)	[dúb]
linden tree	липа (ж)	[lípa]
aspen	осина (ж)	[ɔsína]
maple	клён (м)	[klǿn]
spruce	ель (ж)	[élʲ]
pine	сосна (ж)	[sɔsná]
larch	лиственница (ж)	[lístvenitsa]
fir tree	пихта (ж)	[píhta]
cedar	кедр (м)	[kédr]
poplar	тополь (м)	[tópɔlʲ]
rowan	рябина (ж)	[rɪbína]
willow	ива (ж)	[íva]
alder	ольха (ж)	[ɔlʲhá]
beech	бук (м)	[búk]
elm	вяз (м)	[vʲás]
ash (tree)	ясень (м)	[jásenʲ]
chestnut	каштан (м)	[kaʃtán]
magnolia	магнолия (ж)	[magnólija]
palm tree	пальма (ж)	[pálʲma]
cypress	кипарис (м)	[kiparís]
mangrove	мангровое дерево (с)	[mángrɔvɔe dérevɔ]
baobab	баобаб (м)	[baɔbáb]
eucalyptus	эвкалипт (м)	[ɛfkalípt]
sequoia	секвойя (ж)	[sekvója]

187. Shrubs

| bush | куст (м) | [kúst] |
| shrub | кустарник (м) | [kustárnik] |

| grapevine | виноград (м) | [vinɔgrád] |
| vineyard | виноградник (м) | [vinɔgrádnik] |

raspberry bush	малина (ж)	[malína]
blackcurrant bush	чёрная смородина (ж)	[ʧórnaja smɔródina]
redcurrant bush	красная смородина (ж)	[krásnaja smɔródina]
gooseberry bush	крыжовник (м)	[kriʒóvnik]

acacia	акация (ж)	[akátsija]
barberry	барбарис (м)	[barbarís]
jasmine	жасмин (м)	[ʒasmín]

juniper	можжевельник (м)	[mɔʒevélʲnik]
rosebush	розовый куст (м)	[rózɔvij kúst]
dog rose	шиповник (м)	[ʃipóvnik]

188. Mushrooms

mushroom	гриб (м)	[gríb]
edible mushroom	съедобный гриб (м)	[sjedóbnij gríb]
poisonous mushroom	ядовитый гриб (м)	[jidɔvítij gríb]
cap (of mushroom)	шляпка (ж)	[ʃlʲápka]
stipe (of mushroom)	ножка (ж)	[nóʃka]

cep (Boletus edulis)	белый гриб (м)	[bélij gríb]
orange-cap boletus	подосиновик (м)	[pɔdɔsínɔvik]
birch bolete	подберёзовик (м)	[pɔdberɵzɔvik]
chanterelle	лисичка (ж)	[lisíʧka]
russula	сыроежка (ж)	[sirɔéʃka]

morel	сморчок (м)	[smɔrʧók]
fly agaric	мухомор (м)	[muhɔmór]
death cap	поганка (ж)	[pɔgánka]

189. Fruits. Berries

apple	яблоко (с)	[jáblɔkɔ]
pear	груша (ж)	[grúʃa]
plum	слива (ж)	[slíva]

| strawberry (garden ~) | клубника (ж) | [klubníka] |
| sour cherry | вишня (ж) | [víʃnʲa] |

| sweet cherry | черешня (ж) | [ʧeréʃnʲa] |
| grape | виноград (м) | [vinɔgrád] |

raspberry	малина (ж)	[malína]
blackcurrant	чёрная смородина (ж)	[ʧórnaja smɔródina]
redcurrant	красная смородина (ж)	[krásnaja smɔródina]
gooseberry	крыжовник (м)	[kriʒóvnik]
cranberry	клюква (ж)	[klʲúkva]

orange	апельсин (м)	[apelʲsín]
mandarin	мандарин (м)	[mandarín]
pineapple	ананас (м)	[ananás]
banana	банан (м)	[banán]
date	финик (м)	[fínik]

lemon	лимон (м)	[limón]
apricot	абрикос (м)	[abrikós]
peach	персик (м)	[pérsik]
kiwi	киви (м)	[kívi]
grapefruit	грейпфрут (м)	[gréjpfrut]

berry	ягода (ж)	[jágɔda]
berries	ягоды (ж мн)	[jágɔdɨ]
cowberry	брусника (ж)	[brusníka]
wild strawberry	земляника (ж)	[zemlɨníka]
bilberry	черника (ж)	[ʧerníka]

190. Flowers. Plants

| flower | цветок (м) | [ʦvetók] |
| bouquet (of flowers) | букет (м) | [bukét] |

rose (flower)	роза (ж)	[róza]
tulip	тюльпан (м)	[tʲulʲpán]
carnation	гвоздика (ж)	[gvɔzdíka]
gladiolus	гладиолус (м)	[gladiólus]

cornflower	василёк (м)	[vasilǿk]
harebell	колокольчик (м)	[kɔlɔkólʲʧik]
dandelion	одуванчик (м)	[ɔduvánʧik]
camomile	ромашка (ж)	[rɔmáʃka]

aloe	алоэ (с)	[alóɛ]
cactus	кактус (м)	[káktus]
rubber plant, ficus	фикус (м)	[fíkus]

lily	лилия (ж)	[lílija]
geranium	герань (ж)	[geránʲ]
hyacinth	гиацинт (м)	[giaʦ̆ínt]
mimosa	мимоза (ж)	[mimóza]

| narcissus | нарцисс (м) | [nartsîs] |
| nasturtium | настурция (ж) | [nastúrtsija] |

orchid	орхидея (ж)	[ɔrhidéja]
peony	пион (м)	[pión]
violet	фиалка (ж)	[fiálka]

pansy	анютины глазки (мн)	[anʲútini gláski]
forget-me-not	незабудка (ж)	[nezabútka]
daisy	маргаритка (ж)	[margarítka]

poppy	мак (м)	[mák]
hemp	конопля (ж)	[kɔnɔplʲá]
mint	мята (ж)	[mʲáta]

| lily of the valley | ландыш (м) | [lándiʃ] |
| snowdrop | подснежник (м) | [potsnéʒnik] |

nettle	крапива (ж)	[krapíva]
sorrel	щавель (м)	[ʃavélʲ]
water lily	кувшинка (ж)	[kufʃînka]
fern	папоротник (м)	[pápɔrtnik]
lichen	лишайник (м)	[liʃájnik]

conservatory (greenhouse)	оранжерея (ж)	[ɔranʒeréja]
lawn	газон (м)	[gazón]
flowerbed	клумба (ж)	[klúmba]

plant	растение (с)	[rasténie]
grass	трава (ж)	[travá]
blade of grass	травинка (ж)	[travínka]

leaf	лист (м)	[líst]
petal	лепесток (м)	[lepestók]
stem	стебель (м)	[stébelʲ]
tuber	клубень (м)	[klúbenʲ]
young plant (shoot)	росток (м)	[rɔstók]
thorn	шип (м)	[ʃîp]

to blossom (vi)	цвести (нсв, нпх)	[tsvestí]
to fade, to wither	вянуть (нсв, нпх)	[vʲánutʲ]
smell (odor)	запах (м)	[zápah]
to cut (flowers)	срезать (св, пх)	[srézatʲ]
to pick (a flower)	сорвать (св, пх)	[sɔrvátʲ]

191. Cereals, grains

| grain | зерно (с) | [zernó] |
| cereal crops | зерновые растения (с мн) | [zernɔvîe rasténija] |

ear (of barley, etc.)	колос (м)	[kólɔs]
wheat	пшеница (ж)	[pʃɛnítsa]
rye	рожь (ж)	[róʃ]
oats	овёс (м)	[ɔvǿs]
millet	просо (с)	[prósɔ]
barley	ячмень (м)	[jɪtʃménʲ]
corn	кукуруза (ж)	[kukurúza]
rice	рис (м)	[rís]
buckwheat	гречиха (ж)	[gretʃíha]
pea plant	горох (м)	[gɔróh]
kidney bean	фасоль (ж)	[fasólʲ]
soy	соя (ж)	[sója]
lentil	чечевица (ж)	[tʃetʃevítsa]
beans (pulse crops)	бобы (мн)	[bɔbî]

REGIONAL GEOGRAPHY

Countries. Nationalities

politics	политика (ж)	[polítika]
political (adj)	политический	[politíʧeskij]
politician	политик (м)	[polítik]
state (country)	государство (с)	[gɔsudárstvɔ]
citizen	гражданин (м)	[graʒdanín]
citizenship	гражданство (с)	[graʒdánstvɔ]
national emblem	национальный герб (м)	[naʦiɔnálʲnij gérb]
national anthem	государственный гимн (м)	[gɔsudárstvenij gímn]
government	правительство (с)	[pravítelʲstvɔ]
head of state	руководитель (м) страны	[rukɔvɔdítelʲ straní]
parliament	парламент (м)	[parláment]
party	партия (ж)	[pártija]
capitalism	капитализм (м)	[kapitalízm]
capitalist (adj)	капиталистический	[kapitalistíʧeskij]
socialism	социализм (м)	[sɔʦializm]
socialist (adj)	социалистический	[sɔʦialistíʧeskij]
communism	коммунизм (м)	[kɔmunízm]
communist (adj)	коммунистический	[kɔmunistíʧeskij]
communist (n)	коммунист (м)	[kɔmuníst]
democracy	демократия (ж)	[demɔkrátija]
democrat	демократ (м)	[demɔkrát]
democratic (adj)	демократический	[demɔkratíʧeskij]
Democratic party	демократическая партия (ж)	[demɔkratíʧeskaja pártija]
liberal (n)	либерал (м)	[liberál]
liberal (adj)	либеральный	[liberálʲnij]
conservative (n)	консерватор (м)	[kɔnservátɔr]
conservative (adj)	консервативный	[kɔnservatívnij]

republic (n)	республика (ж)	[respúblika]
republican (n)	республиканец (м)	[respublikánets]
Republican party	республиканская партия (ж)	[respublikánskaja pártija]

elections	выборы (мн)	[vĩbori]
to elect (vt)	выбирать (нсв, пх)	[vibirátʲ]
elector, voter	избиратель (м)	[izbirátelʲ]
election campaign	избирательная кампания (ж)	[izbirátelʲnaja kampánija]

voting (n)	голосование (с)	[gɔlɔsɔvánie]
to vote (vi)	голосовать (нсв, нпх)	[gɔlɔsɔvátʲ]
suffrage, right to vote	право (с) голоса	[právɔ gólɔsa]

candidate	кандидат (м)	[kandidát]
to be a candidate	баллотироваться (нсв, возв)	[balɔtírɔvatsa]
campaign	кампания (ж)	[kampánija]

| opposition (as adj) | оппозиционный | [ɔpɔzitsiónnij] |
| opposition (n) | оппозиция (ж) | [ɔpɔzítsija] |

visit	визит (м)	[vizít]
official visit	официальный визит (м)	[ɔfitsiálʲnij vizít]
international (adj)	международный	[meʒdunaródnij]

| negotiations | переговоры (мн) | [peregɔvóri] |
| to negotiate (vi) | вести переговоры | [vestí peregɔvóri] |

193. Politics. Government. Part 2

society	общество (с)	[ópʃestvɔ]
constitution	конституция (ж)	[kɔnstitútsija]
power (political control)	власть (ж)	[vlástʲ]
corruption	коррупция (ж)	[kɔrúptsija]

| law (justice) | закон (м) | [zakón] |
| legal (legitimate) | законный | [zakónnij] |

| justice (fairness) | справедливость (ж) | [spravedlívɔstʲ] |
| just (fair) | справедливый | [spravedlívij] |

committee	комитет (м)	[kɔmitét]
bill (draft law)	законопроект (м)	[zakónɔ·prɔǽkt]
budget	бюджет (м)	[bʲudʒǽt]
policy	политика (ж)	[pɔlítika]
reform	реформа (ж)	[refórma]
radical (adj)	радикальный	[radikálʲnij]
power (strength, force)	сила (ж)	[síla]

powerful (adj)	сильный	[síl'nij]
supporter	сторонник (м)	[storónnik]
influence	влияние (c)	[vlijánie]

regime (e.g., military ~)	режим (м)	[reʒím]
conflict	конфликт (м)	[konflíkt]
conspiracy (plot)	заговор (м)	[zágovor]
provocation	провокация (ж)	[provokátsija]

to overthrow (regime, etc.)	свергнуть (св, пх)	[svérgnut']
overthrow (of government)	свержение (c)	[sverʒǽnie]
revolution	революция (ж)	[revol'útsija]

| coup d'état | переворот (м) | [perevorót] |
| military coup | военный переворот (м) | [voénnij perevorót] |

crisis	кризис (м)	[krízis]
economic recession	экономический спад (м)	[ɛkonomítʃeskij spád]
demonstrator (protester)	демонстрант (м)	[demonstránt]
demonstration	демонстрация (ж)	[demonstrátsija]
martial law	военное положение (c)	[voénnoe poloʒǽnie]
military base	военная база (ж)	[voénnaja báza]

| stability | стабильность (ж) | [stabíl'nost'] |
| stable (adj) | стабильный | [stabíl'nij] |

| exploitation | эксплуатация (ж) | [ɛkspluatátsija] |
| to exploit (workers) | эксплуатировать (нсв, пх) | [ɛkspluatírovat'] |

racism	расизм (м)	[rasízm]
racist	расист (м)	[rasíst]
fascism	фашизм (м)	[faʃízm]
fascist	фашист (м)	[faʃíst]

194. Countries. Miscellaneous

foreigner	иностранец (м)	[inostránets]
foreign (adj)	иностранный	[inostránnij]
abroad (in a foreign country)	за границей	[za granítsɛj]

emigrant	эмигрант (м)	[ɛmigránt]
emigration	эмиграция (ж)	[ɛmigrátsija]
to emigrate (vi)	эмигрировать (н/св, нпх)	[ɛmigrírovat']

the West	Запад (м)	[západ]
the East	Восток (м)	[vostók]
the Far East	Дальний Восток (м)	[dál'nij vostók]
civilization	цивилизация (ж)	[tsivilizátsija]
humanity (mankind)	человечество (c)	[tʃelovétʃestvo]

the world (earth)	мир (м)	[mír]
peace	мир (м)	[mír]
worldwide (adj)	мировой	[mirɔvój]

homeland	родина (ж)	[ródina]
people (population)	народ (м)	[naród]
population	население (с)	[naselénie]
people (a lot of ~)	люди (м мн)	[lʲúdi]
nation (people)	нация (ж)	[nátsija]
generation	поколение (с)	[pɔkɔlénie]

territory (area)	территория (ж)	[teritórija]
region	регион (м)	[región]
state (part of a country)	штат (м)	[ʃtát]

tradition	традиция (ж)	[tradítsija]
custom (tradition)	обычай (м)	[ɔbɨ̈ʧaj]
ecology	экология (ж)	[ɛkɔlógija]

Indian (Native American)	индеец (м)	[indéets]
Gypsy (masc.)	цыган (м)	[tsigán]
Gypsy (fem.)	цыганка (ж)	[tsigánka]
Gypsy (adj)	цыганский	[tsigánskij]

empire	империя (ж)	[impérija]
colony	колония (ж)	[kɔlónija]
slavery	рабство (с)	[rábstvɔ]
invasion	нашествие (с)	[naʃǽstvie]
famine	голод (м)	[gólɔd]

195. Major religious groups. Confessions

| religion | религия (ж) | [relígija] |
| religious (adj) | религиозный | [religióznij] |

faith, belief	верование (с)	[vérɔvanie]
to believe (in God)	верить (нсв, пх)	[véritʲ]
believer	верующий (м)	[vérujuʃʲij]

| atheism | атеизм (м) | [atɛízm] |
| atheist | атеист (м) | [atɛíst] |

Christianity	христианство (с)	[hristiánstvɔ]
Christian (n)	христианин (м)	[hristianín]
Christian (adj)	христианский	[hristiánskij]

Catholicism	Католицизм (м)	[katɔlitsízm]
Catholic (n)	католик (м)	[katólik]
Catholic (adj)	католический	[katɔlíʧeskij]
Protestantism	Протестантство (с)	[prɔtestántstvɔ]

Protestant Church	Протестантская церковь (ж)	[protestánskaja ʦærkofʲ]
Protestant (n)	протестант (м)	[protestánt]
Orthodoxy	Православие (c)	[pravoslávie]
Orthodox Church	Православная церковь (ж)	[pravoslávnaja ʦærkofʲ]
Orthodox (n)	православный (м)	[pravoslávnij]
Presbyterianism	Пресвитерианство (c)	[presviteriánstvo]
Presbyterian Church	Пресвитерианская церковь (ж)	[presviteriánskaja ʦærkofʲ]
Presbyterian (n)	пресвитерианин (м)	[presviteriánin]
Lutheranism	Лютеранская церковь (ж)	[lʲuteránskaja ʦærkofʲ]
Lutheran (n)	лютеранин (м)	[lʲuteránin]
Baptist Church	Баптизм (м)	[baptízm]
Baptist (n)	баптист (м)	[baptíst]
Anglican Church	Англиканская церковь (ж)	[anglikánskaja ʦærkofʲ]
Anglican (n)	англиканин (м)	[anglikánin]
Mormonism	Мормонство (c)	[mormónstvo]
Mormon (n)	мормон (м)	[mormón]
Judaism	Иудаизм (м)	[iudaízm]
Jew (n)	иудей (м)	[iudéj]
Buddhism	Буддизм (м)	[budízm]
Buddhist (n)	буддист (м)	[budíst]
Hinduism	Индуизм (м)	[induízm]
Hindu (n)	индуист (м)	[induíst]
Islam	Ислам (м)	[islám]
Muslim (n)	мусульманин (м)	[musulʲmánin]
Muslim (adj)	мусульманский	[musulʲmánskij]
Shiah Islam	Шиизм (м)	[ʃiízm]
Shiite (n)	шиит (м)	[ʃiít]
Sunni Islam	Суннизм (м)	[sunízm]
Sunnite (n)	суннит (м)	[sunít]

196. Religions. Priests

| priest | священник (м) | [sviʃʲénik] |
| the Pope | Папа Римский (м) | [pápa rímskij] |

monk, friar	**монах** (м)	[mɔnáh]
nun	**монахиня** (ж)	[mɔnáhinʲa]
pastor	**пастор** (м)	[pástɔr]
abbot	**аббат** (м)	[abát]
vicar (parish priest)	**викарий** (м)	[vikárij]
bishop	**епископ** (м)	[epískɔp]
cardinal	**кардинал** (м)	[kardinál]
preacher	**проповедник** (м)	[prɔpɔvédnik]
preaching	**проповедь** (ж)	[própɔvetʲ]
parishioners	**прихожане** (мн)	[prihɔʒáne]
believer	**верующий** (м)	[vérujuʃij]
atheist	**атеист** (м)	[atɛíst]

197. Faith. Christianity. Islam

Adam	**Адам** (м)	[adám]
Eve	**Ева** (ж)	[éva]
God	**Бог** (м)	[bóh]
the Lord	**Господь** (м)	[gɔspótʲ]
the Almighty	**Всемогущий** (м)	[fsemɔgúʃij]
sin	**грех** (м)	[gréh]
to sin (vi)	**грешить** (нсв, нпх)	[greʃítʲ]
sinner (masc.)	**грешник** (м)	[gréʃnik]
sinner (fem.)	**грешница** (ж)	[gréʃnitsa]
hell	**ад** (м)	[ád]
paradise	**рай** (м)	[ráj]
Jesus	**Иисус** (м)	[iisús]
Jesus Christ	**Иисус Христос** (м)	[iisús hristós]
the Holy Spirit	**Святой Дух** (м)	[svɪtój dúh]
the Savior	**Спаситель** (м)	[spasítelʲ]
the Virgin Mary	**Богородица** (ж)	[bɔgɔróditsa]
the Devil	**Дьявол** (м)	[djávɔl]
devil's (adj)	**дьявольский**	[djávɔlʲskij]
Satan	**Сатана** (ж)	[sataná]
satanic (adj)	**сатанинский**	[satanínskij]
angel	**ангел** (м)	[ángel]
guardian angel	**ангел-хранитель** (м)	[ángel-hranítelʲ]
angelic (adj)	**ангельский**	[ángelʲskij]
apostle	**апостол** (м)	[apóstɔl]
archangel	**архангел** (м)	[arhángel]

the Antichrist	антихрист (м)	[antíhrist]
Church	Церковь (ж)	[tsǽrkɔfʲ]
Bible	библия (ж)	[bíblija]
biblical (adj)	библейский	[bibléjskij]

Old Testament	Ветхий Завет (м)	[vétxij zavét]
New Testament	Новый Завет (м)	[nóvij zavét]
Gospel	Евангелие (с)	[evángelie]
Holy Scripture	Священное Писание (с)	[svɪʃʲénɔe pisánie]
Heaven	Царство (с) Небесное	[tsárstvɔ nebésnɔe]

Commandment	заповедь (ж)	[zápɔvetʲ]
prophet	пророк (м)	[prɔrók]
prophecy	пророчество (с)	[prɔrótʃestvɔ]

Allah	Аллах (м)	[aláh]
Mohammed	Мухаммед (м)	[muhámmed]
the Koran	Коран (м)	[kɔrán]

mosque	мечеть (ж)	[metʃétʲ]
mullah	мулла (ж)	[mulá]
prayer	молитва (ж)	[mɔlítva]
to pray (vi, vt)	молиться (нсв, возв)	[mɔlítsa]

pilgrimage	паломничество (с)	[palómnitʃestvɔ]
pilgrim	паломник (м)	[palómnik]
Mecca	Мекка (ж)	[mékka]

church	церковь (ж)	[tsǽrkɔfʲ]
temple	храм (м)	[hrám]
cathedral	собор (м)	[sɔbór]
Gothic (adj)	готический	[gɔtítʃeskij]
synagogue	синагога (ж)	[sinagóga]
mosque	мечеть (ж)	[metʃétʲ]

chapel	часовня (ж)	[tʃasóvnʲa]
abbey	аббатство (с)	[abátstvɔ]
convent	монастырь (м)	[mɔnastírʲ]
monastery	монастырь (м)	[mɔnastírʲ]

bell (church ~s)	колокол (м)	[kólɔkɔl]
bell tower	колокольня (ж)	[kɔlɔkólʲnʲa]
to ring (ab. bells)	звонить (нсв, нпх)	[zvɔnítʲ]

cross	крест (м)	[krést]
cupola (roof)	купол (м)	[kúpɔl]
icon	икона (ж)	[ikóna]

soul	душа (ж)	[duʃá]
fate (destiny)	судьба (ж)	[sutʲbá]
evil (n)	зло (с)	[zló]
good (n)	добро (с)	[dɔbró]

vampire	вампир (м)	[vampír]
witch (evil ~)	ведьма (ж)	[védʲma]
demon	демон (м)	[démɔn]
spirit	дух (м)	[dúh]

| redemption (giving us ~) | искупление (с) | [iskuplénie] |
| to redeem (vt) | искупить (св, пх) | [iskupítʲ] |

church service, mass	служба (ж)	[slúʒba]
to say mass	служить (нсв, нпх)	[sluʒítʲ]
confession	исповедь (ж)	[íspovetʲ]
to confess (vi)	исповедоваться (н/св, возв)	[ispɔvédɔvatsa]

saint (n)	святой (м)	[svɪtój]
sacred (holy)	священный	[svɪʃénij]
holy water	святая вода (ж)	[svɪtája vɔdá]

ritual (n)	ритуал (м)	[rituál]
ritual (adj)	ритуальный	[rituálʲnij]
sacrifice	жертвоприношение (с)	[ʒértvɔ·prinɔʃǽnie]

superstition	суеверие (с)	[suevérie]
superstitious (adj)	суеверный	[suevérnij]
afterlife	загробная жизнь (ж)	[zagróbnaja ʒĩznʲ]
eternal life	вечная жизнь (ж)	[vétʃnaja ʒĩznʲ]

MISCELLANEOUS

198. Various useful words

background (green ~)	фон (м)	[fón]
balance (of situation)	баланс (м)	[baláns]
barrier (obstacle)	преграда (ж)	[pregráda]
base (basis)	база (ж)	[báza]
beginning	начало (с)	[natʃálɔ]
category	категория (ж)	[kategórija]
cause (reason)	причина (ж)	[pritʃína]
choice	выбор (м)	[vībɔr]
coincidence	совпадение (с)	[sɔfpadénie]
comfortable (~ chair)	удобный	[udóbnij]
comparison	сравнение (с)	[sravnénie]
compensation	компенсация (ж)	[kɔmpensátsija]
degree (extent, amount)	степень (ж)	[stépenʲ]
development	развитие (с)	[razvítie]
difference	различие (с)	[razlítʃie]
effect (e.g., of drugs)	эффект (м)	[ɛfékt]
effort (exertion)	усилие (с)	[usílie]
element	элемент (м)	[ɛlemént]
end (finish)	окончание (с)	[ɔkɔntʃánie]
example (illustration)	пример (м)	[primér]
fact	факт (м)	[fákt]
frequent (adj)	частый	[tʃástij]
growth (development)	рост (м)	[róst]
help	помощь (ж)	[pómɔʃ]
ideal	идеал (м)	[ideál]
kind (sort, type)	вид (м)	[víd]
labyrinth	лабиринт (м)	[labirínt]
mistake, error	ошибка (ж)	[ɔʃípka]
moment	момент (м)	[mɔmént]
object (thing)	объект (м)	[ɔbjékt]
obstacle	препятствие (с)	[prepʲátstvie]
original (original copy)	оригинал (м)	[ɔriginál]
part (~ of sth)	часть (ж)	[tʃástʲ]
particle, small part	частица (ж)	[tʃastítsa]
pause (break)	пауза (ж)	[páuza]

position	позиция (ж)	[pɔzítsija]
principle	принцип (м)	[príntsip]
problem	проблема (ж)	[prɔbléma]
process	процесс (м)	[prɔtsǽs]
progress	прогресс (м)	[prɔgrǽs]
property (quality)	свойство (с)	[svójstvɔ]
reaction	реакция (ж)	[reáktsija]
risk	риск (м)	[rísk]
secret	тайна (ж)	[tájna]
series	серия (ж)	[sérija]
shape (outer form)	форма (ж)	[fórma]
situation	ситуация (ж)	[situátsija]
solution	решение (с)	[reʃǽnie]
standard (adj)	стандартный	[standártnij]
standard (level of quality)	стандарт (м)	[standárt]
stop (pause)	остановка (ж)	[ɔstanófka]
style	стиль (м)	[stílʲ]
system	система (ж)	[sistéma]
table (chart)	таблица (ж)	[tablítsa]
tempo, rate	темп (м)	[tǽmp]
term (word, expression)	термин (м)	[términ]
thing (object, item)	вещь (ж)	[véʃ]
truth (e.g., moment of ~)	истина (ж)	[ístina]
turn (please wait your ~)	очередь (ж)	[ótʃeretʲ]
type (sort, kind)	тип (м)	[típ]
urgent (adj)	срочный	[srótʃnij]
urgently (adv)	срочно	[srótʃnɔ]
utility (usefulness)	польза (ж)	[pólʲza]
variant (alternative)	вариант (м)	[variánt]
way (means, method)	способ (м)	[spósɔb]
zone	зона (ж)	[zóna]